T0318904

African Roads to Prosperity

African Dynamics

VOLUME 14

The titles published in this series are listed at *brill.com/ad*

African Roads to Prosperity

*People en Route to Socio-Cultural and
Economic Transformations*

Edited by

Akinyinka Akinyoade
Jan-Bart Gewald

BRILL

LEIDEN | BOSTON

Cover illustration: 'Tamale Aboabu Lorry Park', photograph by Edward Nanbigne

Library of Congress Cataloging-in-Publication Data

African roads to prosperity : people en route to socio-cultural and economic transformations / edited by
Akinyinka Akinyoade, Jan-Bart Gewald.
     pages cm -- (African dynamics ; v. 14)
  ISBN 978-90-04-30171-9 (paperback : alk. paper) -- ISBN 978-90-04-30605-9 (e-book) 1. Africans--
Migrations--Economic aspects. 2. Immigrants--Economic conditions. 3. Immigrants--Social conditions.
4. Africa--Emigration and immigration--Economic aspects. I. Akinyoade, Akinyinka, editor, author.
II. Gewald, Jan-Bart, editor, author. III. Series: African dynamics ; v. 14.

JV8790.A66 2015
304.806--dc23

                                     2015035473

This publication has been typeset in the multilingual 'Brill' typeface. With over 5,100 characters covering
Latin, IPA, Greek, and Cyrillic, this typeface is especially suitable for use in the humanities.
For more information, please see www.brill.com/brill-typeface.

ISSN 1568-1777
ISBN 978-90-04-30171-9 (paperback)
ISBN 978-90-04-30605-9 (e-book)

Contents

Notes on Contributors

Akinyinka Akinyoade
is a senior researcher at the African Studies Centre (ASC) in Leiden. His primary research interest is in population studies, and he has worked extensively on issues related to health and development, fertility dynamics and family planning in West Africa, migration, and human trafficking and forced labour (Nigeria and Italy). At the ASC, he is the convener of its collaborative research group Agro-Food Clusters in Africa (AFCA), which explores food and nutrition security with special reference to the interplay between Africa's population growth and the continent's ability to feed itself. He co-edited one of the ASC flagship publications, *Digging Deeper: Inside Africa's Agricultural, Food and Nutrition Dynamics*. He also played a major role in the ASC's recent Tracking Development project, which compared the development trajectories of various African and Southeast Asian countries.
aakinyoade@ascleiden.nl

Amisah Zenabu Bakuri
has a BA (Hons) in History from Kwame Nkrumah University of Science and Technology in Kumasi, Ghana and a Research Masters in Modern History and International Relations from the University of Groningen in the Netherlands, where she is a research assistant at the Department of History and Political Science. Her interests include economic and social history, development studies, international relations, and African studies.
amisah.bakuri@gmail.com

Walter van Beek
is an anthropologist who has done extensive fieldwork in Cameroon and Mali over four decades. At present he is a senior researcher at the African Studies Centre and holds the chair of Anthropology of Religion at Tilburg University. His research in Cameroon was mainly in the north and centred on the Kapsiki/Higi, who straddle the border between Nigeria and Cameroon, in the Mandara Mountains. His main themes are religion and ecology, with a special interest in artisanal groups. He recently published *The Dancing Dead: Ritual and Religion Among the Kapsiki/Higi of North Cameroon and Northeastern Nigeria* (Oxford UP, 2012) and, on an artisanal group of blacksmiths, *The Forge and the Funeral: The Smith in Kapsiki/Higi Culture* (Michigan State UP, 2015).
vanbeek@ascleiden.nl

Marleen Dekker

is a development economist and human geographer. Her PhD research was on the impact of land reform on participation in social networks and risk-coping strategies in Zimbabwe. Her current work explores the role of social networks in accessing markets and (local) socio-economic development, with a strong focus on access to formal and informal insurance networks, including community-based health insurance. Her research is interdisciplinary in nature, combining methods and insights from economics, human geography, and sociology (notably social network analysis). A new research project is a collaborative venture with VU University Amsterdam, the University of East Anglia, and the University of Nottingham. The project uses an economic experiment to explore collaboration between spouses in monogamous and polygamous households in rural Nigeria. Since May 2014, Marleen has also coordinated the Secretariat of INCLUDE, the Knowledge Platform on Inclusive Development, which aims to promote evidence-based policy making in seven partner countries from the Netherlands Ministry of Foreign Affairs.

mdekker@ascleiden.nl

Ton Dietz

has been Director of the African Studies Centre since 1 May 2010 and is also Professor of the Study of African Development at Leiden University. He gave his inaugural address, entitled 'Silverlining Africa', on 14 January 2011. Prof. Dietz was appointed Professor of Human Geography at the University of Amsterdam in 1995. From 2002 until 2007 he was a (part-time) Professor of Social Sciences at Utrecht University and the Scientific Director of the Research School for Resource Studies for Development (CERES). He was the Scientific Director of the Amsterdam Research Institute for Metropolitan and International Development Studies (AMIDSt) in 2008 and 2009. His interests include human geography, political environmental geography, geography and developing countries, political geography of Africa, poverty analysis, rural development, food security and agrohubs, pastoralism, land and water conflict, dry-land development, impact of climate change, political ecology of forest areas, development aid, participatory assessment of development and change, participatory evaluation of development assistance, civil society, NGOs, Africa and the multi-polar world, and geopolitics.

dietzaj@ascleiden.nl

Rijk van Dijk

is an anthropologist and an expert on Pentecostalism, globalization and trans-nationalism, migration, youth, and healing. He has done extensive research on the rise of Pentecostal movements in the urban areas of Malawi, Ghana, and Botswana. He has co-edited a number of books, including *The Quest for Fruition Through Ngoma* (Oxford, James Currey 2000) with Ria Reis and Marja Spierenburg, and *Situating Globality: African Agency in the Appropriation of Global Culture* (Leiden, Brill 2004) with Wim van Binsbergen. His current research deals with religious, in particular Pentecostal, engagement with the domains of sexuality and HIV/AIDS in Botswana. Recently he published the co-edited volume *Religion and AIDS Treatment in Africa* (Ashgate, 2014) with Hansjoerg Dilger, Marian Burchardt and Thera Rasing. He is a senior researcher at the African Studies Centre in Leiden and holds the chair in the study of Religion and Sexuality in Africa at the AISSR, University of Amsterdam. He is also the chair of the International Research Network on Religion and AIDS in Africa and the editor-in-chief of the journal *African Diaspora: A Journal of Transnational Africa in a Global World.*

dijkr@ascleiden.nl

Isaie Dougnon

is Professor of Anthropology in the Department of Sociology and Anthropology at the University of Bamako (Mali). From 1998 to 2003, he worked on labour migration from Dogon Country to Office du Niger (Mali) and to Ghana, resulting in his first book, *Travail de Blanc, travail de Noir: La migration des paysans dogons vers l'Office du Niger et au Ghana 1910–1980* (Paris: Khartala). With a Humboldt fellowship (2012–2014) he is currently finishing his second book on life cycle, careers, and rites in the Malian public service. Thanks to a Fulbright fellowship, he has also developed a new book project on politics and higher education in Mali from independence to the present.

isaie.dougnon@googlemail.com

Jan-Bart Gewald

is Professor of Southern African History at Leiden University and a senior researcher at the African Studies Centre in Leiden. His research has ranged from the ramifications of genocide in Namibia, through to the socio-cultural parameters of trans-desert trade in Africa. In addition, he has conducted research on pan-Africanism in Ghana, spirit possession in the Republic of Niger, Dutch development cooperation, and social history in Eritrea. He has a particular interest in archaeology and has participated in archaeological research in southern Africa. He is currently particularly interested in eastern Ghana in the 1920s and 1930s, and colonial Zambia in the 1950s.

j.b.gewald@ascleiden.nl

Meike de Goede

is a lecturer in African History and Anthropology at Leiden University. She lived in Kinshasa, Democratic Republic of Congo, where she worked in the development sector and conducted research on Congolese history, democratization, peace-building, and the security sector. Her current research focuses on ICT 4 Development and Power in Ghana, and on history, meaning, and peace-building in the DRC.

m.j.de.goede@hum.leidenuniv.nl

Edward Nanbigne

is a research fellow in African literature and drama and is presently head of the Language, Literature and Drama Section of the Institute of African Studies, University of Ghana. He teaches students both at the undergraduate and graduate levels. He holds PhD and MPhil degrees in African Studies as well as a Bachelor of Arts (Art) degree from the University of Ghana, Legon. He also obtained a Diploma in English from the Advanced Teacher Training College (now University of Education, Winneba). Dr Nanbigne is a member of the publications committee and an editorial board member of the *Contemporary Journal of African Studies* (previously known as *Research Review of the Institute of African Studies*). His research interests are in discourse, literature, and oral literature in African societies, especially among the Dagaaba. In a collaborative research project, he has recorded folktales throughout Ghana, a project that seeks to create an archive of Ghanaian folktales. He is also involved in other collaborative research on Dagomba, chiefly praise poetry, Dagomba musketeers, innovative transportation systems, and narratives of slavery.

nanbigne@gmail.com

Samuel Aniegye Ntewusu

is a social historian. He holds a PhD in History from the University of Leiden and an MPhil in African Studies from the University of Ghana. Since August 2011 he has worked as a research fellow at the Institute of African Studies, University of Ghana. His research covers a variety of areas, including colonialism, transport, mining, slavery, and chieftaincy.

ntewusu@yahoo.com

Benjamin Kofi Nyarko

received a Bachelor of Arts (Social Sciences) and a Diploma of Education in 1994 and a Master of Philosophy in Geography in 2000 from the University of Cape Coast in Ghana; a postgraduate diploma from ITC Eschede in the Netherlands in 1997; and a PhD in Geography from the Center For Development

Research, University of Bonn, Germany in 2007. He is a senior lecturer at the Department of Geography and Regional Planning at the University of Cape Coast and lectures in climate change, earth sciences, water resources survey, and geospatial techniques. He is interested in interdisciplinary research and has supervised graduate theses in these areas. He is a member of the Ghana Geographical Association, American Geophysical Union (AGU), Association of American Geographers (AAG), and Society of Wetland Scientists.

bnyarko@ucc.edu.gh

Taiwo Olabisi Oluwatoyin

received her primary degree in English Language Education at the University of Ilorin Nigeria, a Certificate in Gender Studies at the University of Amsterdam, and a Master's Degree in Development Studies, with a specialization in Women and Gender Studies, at the Erasmus University, Rotterdam. She is currently CEO of the Women's Capabilities Enhancements and Empowerment Organization (WCEEO), a non-governmental organization based in Abuja, Nigeria. Her areas of interest are gender and migration, human trafficking, women's empowerment, gender equality, social protection, gender justice, child protection, and social exclusion/inclusion.

tgurlbisi@gmail.com

Augustine Tanle

has a PhD in Migration Studies and is Associate Professor at the Department of Population and Health, University of Cape Coast, Ghana. His research interests are migration and refugee studies, reproductive health, population, environment and development, and social research methods. Most of his publications are on migration and refugee studies. He supervises and assesses MPhil and PhD theses in and outside his university. He is one of the reviewers of the *Ghana Journal of Geography* and also an *ad hoc* reviewer for several academic journals. He is currently head of the Department of Population and Health at the University of Cape Coast.

augtanle@yahoo.com

Shehu Tijjani Yusuf

received his doctorate in African History from the University of Leiden. He teaches history at Bayero University, Kano, Nigeria. His main research interests include the social and economic history of Nigeria and the history of science and technology in Africa, with a focus on the history of railways in Nigeria in the nineteenth and twentieth centuries. His publications have appeared in academic journals and co-edited books.

stijjani@gmail.com

PART 1

Introduction

∴

African Roads to Prosperity: People En Route to Socio-Cultural and Economic Transformations

Akinyinka Akinyoade and Jan-Bart Gewald

This volume is the result of a joint collaborative research project undertaken at the African Studies Centre with colleagues in Africa that was entitled 'Roads to Prosperity and Their Social Zones of Transit'. The project sought to gain an understanding of the emergence and transformation of certain places in Africa that became marked as spaces of transit for people in search of better socio-economic prospects. When people travelled long distances from locations to reach destinations that were expected to place them on the road to prosperity, many became stuck halfway—either on their way out or on their way back. The thousands of would-be African migrants to Europe trapped and stranded on the North African shores of the Mediterranean, the Yoruba settlements of Ivory Coast and Ghana, and the communities of *Nyassas* throughout southern Africa are cases in point.

The movement of people has been the norm in Africa. No matter what their economic base—be they hunter-gatherers, pastoralists, or agriculturalists—environmental conditions determined that people had to move to live.[1] This movement of people came to be exacerbated in the process of massive labour migration engendered by colonial rule from at least the 1870s onward. Throughout Africa, places along railway tracks or along major roads quickly turned into locales of transit. There exists a wide-ranging literature on the history, development, and significance of this labour migration process in terms of the effects at the places of origin and at the places of destination. Much less literature exists on the history and present-day significance of zones of transit. These zones of transit have a social life of their own, not only in the way they connect origin and destination for travellers, but also in the way in which they produce social realities that determine the social–economic and political relations that are shaped in these locations. Passers-by have had a lasting impact on these

---

1 Seasonal change as well as environmental degradation dictated the continual movement of people in the continent. This ceased only with the introduction of new inputs, be they crops, guano and artificial fertilizer, or pumps and mechanization—all of which allowed for intensification of the exploitation of already existing agricultural resources, as well as the exploitation of hitherto closed agricultural resources.

© KONINKLIJKE BRILL NV, LEIDEN, 2015 | DOI 10.1163/9789004306059_002

relations, as some inter-married with the locals, decided to settle, to make a living, to start a business, and to raise their children there. In a sense, they began creating an intra-regional diaspora whereby ties with 'home' developed in particular ways and whereby 'integration' became at the same time a contested process. Intra-regional diasporas that create extensive ties across time and space—within the context of a particular regional dynamic, such as in the case of labour migration in southern Africa—have so far been little studied. This is not to deny there have been numerous and extensive studies dealing with the impact of migration in the zones of origin and destination.[2]

The collaborative research project 'Roads to Prosperity and Their Social Zones of Transit' sought to understand more of the histories and present-day realities of the zones of transit, both from the sending and receiving perspectives—that is, from the perspective of 'home' as well as from the perspective of the transit location itself. Initially, the collaborative research project sought to focus on southern and West Africa. In the southern African context, sending locations for the mines and industries of South Africa were western Zambia, Swaziland, and Malawi, particularly in the period 1900–1994, with transit zones being Botswana and Zimbabwe.[3] In West Africa, a major sending zone was southwestern Nigeria, with thousands of migrants stranded on their journey to the European Union and America in Ghana and Côte d'Ivoire. However, occurring side by side with the much studied South–North migration is the less fanciful and less studied South–South migration. Over the decades, South–South migration has been giving rise to new routes and transit zones, plus new identities for travellers in their search for greener pastures. Ibo traders from Nigeria are anecdotally known to spend time and resources in Ghana, an essential first part of the chain that connects them to countries in southern Africa, then onward to China or Portugal and Brazil, and eventually back to Nigeria. In sub-regional contexts, configurations of immigrants are changing, yielding amoebic patterns of urbanization, with attendant socio-economic and political impacts on receiving countries. Côte d'Ivoire is an

---

2 For example, on the continued importance of migrant labour in contemporary South Africa, see Aurelia Segatti & Loren B. Landau (eds) *Contemporary Migration in South Africa: A Regional Development Issue* (Washington: World Bank, 2011). For a brief introduction to the conflicts that have arisen from this continued migration, see J. Crush, D. MacDonald, V. Williams, K. Lefko-Everett, D. Dorey, R. Taylor & R. la Sablonnière, *The Perfect Storm: The Reality of Xenophobia in Contemporary South Africa.* SAMP Migration Policy Series 50, 2008, Southern African Migration Programme, Queen's University, Kingston, Canada, and IDASA (Institute for Democracy in South Africa), Cape Town, South Africa.

3 This is not to claim in any way that this was a one-way stream of people, or that countries such as Zimbabwe or Swaziland were not destinations in and of themselves.

example of the rising influence of immigrants in national democratic culture, and particularly in electoral experience that brought the country to violence and an economic standstill.[4]

For the purposes of the collaborative research project, two workshops were held in Leiden. An introductory workshop was held in early 2013, which bore the title 'Conceptual Developments in the Study of Transient Spaces in Trajectories to Prosperity'. This workshop aimed to generate a multidisciplinary yet shared conceptual framework in the study of transience in people's trajectories to prosperity. The workshop sought to address the question of how transience could best be analysed, both in terms of how people involved in the process of labour migration, as well as in other forms of mobility in the pursuit of well-being, perceive *spaces* of transit as well as *times* of transit. As 'being in transit' must be analysed in terms of space and time, the workshop participants attempted to develop a common conceptual language that would assist in analysis of the economic, political, cultural, and historical processes that gave rise to particular manifestations of transience. The workshop explored concepts drawn particularly from the social sciences, such as liminality, generational cohorts, upward social mobility, social capital, life course, journey, and pathways, and was fortunate to be able to receive the expert input of Professor Baz Lecocq, Humboldt University, Berlin.

The second workshop, which also served as a writer's workshop and was entitled 'A Comparative Analysis of the Economic, Cultural and Historical Formations of Transience in Africa's Experience of the Pursuit of Prosperity', was held in Leiden in late 2014. This workshop attempted to bring together in a comparative analysis the results of the research that had taken place within the collaborative research project. Case studies were presented of the various cultural, social, economic, and historical aspects that are formative in African societies' experiences of how people negotiated the spaces and times of being in transit on the road to prosperity. The workshop analysed the various outcomes of the process of mobility and the experience of spaces and times of transit across gender, generational, and class differences. The experiences of flow and fixity were explored by pointing at differences in the way people were able to complete the full trajectory of a perceived road to prosperity. The case studies presented at the workshop indicated the variety of roads to prosperity,

---

4   Nicolas Cook, 'Côte d'Ivoire Post-Election Crisis', CRS Congressional Report for Congress Prepared for Members and Committees of Congress, Congressional Research Service, 28 January 2011, http://fpc.state.gov/documents/organization/156548.pdf; also, Jennifer Cooke, 'The Election Crisis in Côte d'Ivoire', Center for Strategic and International Studies CSIS, 2010, http://csis.org/publication/election-crisis-ivory-coast.

where many appeared to have become stuck halfway, may have lost contact with the sending or the receiving communities, may have entered into new relationships halfway through their journey, or may have adopted an entirely different identity.

All in all, the complexity of the material presented at the final workshop indicated very clearly that there was no single road to prosperity; and if anything could be definitely stated, it was that roads to prosperity were always conditional and dependent upon perceived goals, which varied and changed continually. Nonetheless, our collaborative research indicates that there are important continuities of connection over time. In the present, people continue to migrate and move along routes that were pioneered nearly one hundred years ago. Zones of sending and receiving continue to operate, yet the precise configuration of this connectivity has changed (in terms of composition of migrants and local populations, of socio-economic dynamics, and of political realities). In this volume, transience is explored both in terms of being in transit in a geographical location and in terms of being in transit in the course of life. Through historical and empirical study, these case studies shed light on these transformations of transit zones and on their perception at the sending and receiving side.

In addition to this current introductory chapter, the following two chapters, written by Amisah Bakuri and Ton Dietz, serve as the introductory chapters to this volume. Amisah Bakuri's first chapter, 'Roads to prosperity: Social zones of transit', is in essence a position paper drafted on behalf of the collaborative research group in conjunction with Machteld Oosterkamp of the African Studies Centre Library and Documentation Centre, and it covers an overview of part of the available literature dealing with transit migration. As Bakuri notes, her contribution seeks to:

> address the question of what transit migration is and how transit migration can be conceptualized and analysed together with other related concepts, in order to better understand how people involved in the process of labour migration and other forms of mobility in the pursuit of well-being perceive of spaces of transit as well as of times of transit.

To do so, she has provided an overview of part of the literature available dealing with migration in Africa, as well as introductory comments relating to this material.

The third introductory chapter, written by Ton Dietz and entitled 'Roads to prosperity: Reflections about a concept', provides an overview of the literature available and notes that this edited volume 'goes beyond the direct connections between "roads" and "prosperity" and tries to approach the concept of roads to prosperity...in a broader, social science sense'. Dietz suggests that a promising approach to obtain deeper insights into transition processes in transit places along new 'roads to prosperity' would be what he terms *geographical liminality*, a geographical–anthropological approach which acknowledges temporality: 'A concept that could become useful is "liminal places/cities", using an anthropological concept indicating an in-between phase in peoples' lives, and using that as a geographical concept'. He concludes with a word of warning:

> We should study not only the migrants and the routes they take, but certainly also the support structures along those routes. And 'support' should not be interpreted as a romantic term—of people who are willing to help. Geographical liminality often comes with a lot of exploitation, abuse, and violence....

In this volume, the contributions have been grouped together into three broad sections, all of which could, broadly speaking, fall within the concept of geographical liminality as defined by Dietz. All authors are well aware of the importance of time and space in a physical sense: that is, for example, place A or B in or during this or that period of time. The four chapters included within the section 'Zones of transit' fall firmly within this category. But there are also four chapters that investigate the importance of time and space not only in a strictly physical place but also in a more incorporeal sense. In other words, how do people transfer within a 'zone of transit' from one specific societal position to another. For example, how do people move up or down the social ladder within a zone of transit. Where the chapters have focused specifically upon the social mobility of people within a zone of transit, we have chosen to group these chapters together within the section 'Zones of transference'. However, there are of course always exceptions to the distinctions which we have set to impose, and this is particularly clear in those contributions which have sought to focus upon place and space as well as what their impact is upon inter-social relations. We have chosen to place the last four chapters of this volume in a section which we refer to as 'Zones of transit and transference'.

Zones of Transit

The first chapter in this section is Jan-Bart Gewald's systematic assessment of the development of Wenela, Katima Mulilo as a zone of transit in Barotseland, a holding zone for migrants on the extreme frontier of the South African empire. From the early 1900s, thousands of young men were recorded to have made the long journey southwards from southern Angola and southern Bulozi to the mines of the South African Witwatersrand, in search of employment and reward in anticipation of a better life at home. Although most men eventually returned home to 'walk majestically', there were those who never returned home. Many of these died, or they chose to remain in the urban areas of South Africa. However, there were also those who very nearly made it home but then chose instead to remain in Katima Mulilo. This paper indicates that personal choices coupled to historical developments in southern Africa, in particular the Angolan civil war and the wars of liberation for South Africa and Namibia, effectively prevented a number of migrants from returning home. Instead, they became part of a new urban centre that developed on the furthest reaches of the South African empire.

The second chapter in this section is situated in West Africa, where Shehu Tijjani Yusuf examines the role of the Nigerian railways in the development and emergence of commercial centres which served as spaces of transit for migrants of southern origin in northern Nigeria (circa 1908–1970s). As was noted, the migrants concentrated at those centres with greatest economic opportunities. The study showcases why the southern migrants came to the north, what they were doing, why they returned home, and why some of them decided to stay behind. It argues that the employment opportunities and trade which marked the advent of the railways were the magnet that attracted southerners to the north. Many of the migrants worked in the government service and the imperialist trading firms, while many went into commercial activities. After long years of sojourning in the north, many of them went back home, though some decided to stay behind in spite of the odds and the challenges. The study shows that many of those who remained weighed the opportunity cost in favour of familial connections, attachment to place, and economic prosperity. To them, migration is a permanent and not a temporary objective. The completion of the railway from Lagos to Kano, and its subsequent expansion during the first and the second decades of the twentieth century, provided outlets for migrants from the south and beyond to search for greener pastures in the north.

Also centred on West Africa is Isaie Dougnon's chapter on migration and competition around commercial spaces, with special emphasis on Songhay migrants at the Kumasi Central Market, Ghana (1930–1948). Drawing from insights garnered from contemporary Mali, Dougnon notes:

[f]or more than 50 years, researchers working on migration in Africa have placed the accent on migrants in search of wage labour with white or

black employers and the process of their proletarization and their temporary or permanent urbanization.

Dougnon suggests that 'the categories of migrants that work for themselves have been widely ignored by researchers in the social sciences'. Drawing on the Archives of Kumasi in Ghana, Dougnon was able to bring to the fore detailed information on Songhay migrants who had come from what is today Mali and had established themselves as independent traders and merchants in the market of Kumasi. In his work he plots the rise and fall of these migrants in what was once the largest market in West Africa.

The last chapter in this section is Marleen Dekker's study on the settlement of Malawians, Zambians, South Africans, and Mozambicans in Zimbabwe's Resettlement Areas. This interesting chapter explores the experiences of the aforementioned migrants in resettlement areas and questions whether or not resettlement allowed the migrants to leave behind their experiences at the zone of transition associated with labour migration. The experiences of these migrants have been documented mainly in the context of their work on farms and mines, arguably zones of transition where the residential status of the migrant was dependent on the type of contract under which he or she was employed. The resettlement experiences of migrants with a foreign background are compared with the experiences of those who were born in Zimbabwe, based on life histories collected in the early 1990s, survey data collected in 2000, and in-depth interviews in December 2013–January 2014 with settlers with a 'foreign' background.

Zones of Transference

The second section, aptly labelled 'Zones of transference', also comprises four chapters. The first chapter in this series is an outcome of research conducted by Rijk van Dijk, who contextually analysed social spaces identified as zones of transference, which are social spaces that form a zone of transit in terms of upward social mobility. The leading question of this chapter, entitled 'A romantic zone of transference? Botswana, Ghanaian migrants and marital social mobility', examines how a zone of transit may interlink with or may be disconnected from a point of transference. Some of these zones of transference that may help to transfer people from one social class into another are well known and studied—such as the school. However, other zones of transference have remained much more implicit or inchoate. Whereas the concept of 'nonspaces' intends to indicate the geographical locations in which migrants can be perceived to be in transit in their mobility from their places of origin to the places of destination (or vice versa)—including such spaces as airport lounges, hotel lobbies, border posts, and bus terminals—such 'in-between' spaces of transit have rarely been explored in terms of social mobility. Studying the migration of Ghanaians to Botswana, which has been taking place since the 1970s, therefore becomes topical. Because of the opportunities of upward social mobility that Botswana as a country of destination appeared to provide, some Ghanaians began to perceive of marriage to local partners as a particular form of such transference. A number of 'mixed-marriage' couples were interviewed to highlight how and why this form of transnational marriage became a kind of romantic point of transference. As research shows, in some cases, Ghanaian men married local women who were usually much more highly educated than they were. Several Botswana women also favoured such foreigners, and it became clear how the institution of marriage came to function as a status marker of distinction over the last two decades in Botswana.

The second contribution in this section is by Walter van Beek, who studied the blacksmiths of Kapsiki/Higi society located in north Cameroon and northeast Nigeria. The chapter focuses on an examination of the opportunities of the margins on the way to prosperity of artisans, referred to as 'smiths' (*rerhɛ*), since not all blacksmiths forge iron. The *rerhɛ* group bear all the hallmarks of a small 'caste'. They are feared to some extent as strange and dirty people with peculiar food and drink customs, are endogamous, and are despised by the majority of non-smiths (*melu*), who constitute about 95% of the population. Beek's research was hinged on unravelling the options for economic betterment of the *rerhɛ*. Specifically, what does their curious social station imply for their chances for prosperity? Does their caste-like status hamper their way on the road to prosperity, and what are the specific dynamics of 'smith-modernity'? It was discovered on one hand that without the *rerhɛ*, Kapsiki society cannot survive: the smith's compound remains the port of call for any iron tool or brass jewellery, medicinal services, divination, and whenever one needs music at a festival. On the other hand, being a *rerhɛ* is a serious obstacle to the kind of contacts and networks a commercial entrepreneur has to rely on, particularly in the regional context where the Kapsiki area has become important in trade with Nigeria. For any smith, this is well out of the reach of his control. On their road to prosperity, the Kapsiki *rerhɛ* experience both the advantages and disadvantages of their special position, as the new division of labour offers them opportunities-with-blockages. Essentially, they remain craftsmen in a wider world, acceptable to the 'others' as long as they retain something of their 'in-between-ness' and as long as they behave as behoves their lower social status. Their social position is difficult to escape, yielding lifelong experience both as birthright and birth-doom.

The third chapter in 'Zones of transference', contributed by Augustine Tanle and Benjamin Nyarko, is on migrants' assessment of prospects in migration in the case of conservancy labourers located in the University of Cape Coast in Ghana. The collaborators note that unequal socio-economic development in Ghana has led to the emergence of two main economic zones: the northern and the southern zones. A by-product of this inequality is a north–south migration pattern, mainly from rural areas of the northern parts (comprising the Northern, Upper West, and Upper East Regions) to urban centres in the southern parts (covering the remaining seven regions) of the country. Though the current migration stream is voluntary, the pattern is considered to be a legacy of the colonial policy of forced labour recruitment of men from the then Northern Territories to the mining and construction industries in the southern parts of Ghana. The chapter focuses on the experiences of conservancy labourers who work in the various halls of students' residence at the University of Cape Coast. These labourers are mostly in-migrants who hail from the aforementioned three northern regions of the country. Their motives for migration and their views on prospects associated with migration are assessed. The findings indicate that inadequate job opportunities and the possibility of being employed at the University of Cape Coast constituted the push and pull factors at the origin and destination, respectively. Although this category of northern migrants falls within the lowest income bracket of workers on the university campus, in their eyes their socio-economic status has improved, particularly when compared with their status before migrating. Some household or family members at the places of origin also benefit from the improvement in socio-economic status of migrants, through remittances and funding of education of close relations and/or their children. This gesture, which supports children's education in deprived communities at the places of origin, could contribute to poverty reduction in the three poorest regions acknowledged by the Ghana Statistical Service.

Rounding up this section is the chapter in which Oluwatoyin Taiwo and Akinyinka Akinyoade critically examine the long-held assertion that Nigerian women working in the unregulated parts of the Dutch sex market are coerced into migration and are trafficked victims for commercial sexual exploitation. Primary information was obtained and triangulated from semi-structured interviews of a sample of 'victims of trafficking', Dutch state security agents, and non-governmental organization (NGO) officials providing social services for some of the 'rescued' women. Against the backdrop of their frustration at not having earned enough income to make substantial remittances to Nigeria, despite years of working in the Dutch sex industry, an intricate picture of having being coerced into travelling to Europe is painted by some of the rescued women. Such women consciously label themselves as victims of trafficking in order to access Dutch state welfare services and to cover the socio-economic gaps they have experienced. While acknowledging that some women may indeed have been coerced into the journey abroad, a pattern of lies is increasingly being recognized by state agents. This is causing distrust and gradually placing all victims of trafficking into more vulnerable positions.

Zones of Transit and Transference

The last but not the least important section in this volume draws contributions from West and Southwest Africa. Firstly, Samuel Ntewusu and Edward Nanbigne examine the evolution and use of tricycles in Wa and Tamale in northern Ghana. Their chapter focuses on the historical processes that influenced the introduction of the tricycles popularly referred to as *nyaaba lorry* ('lorry of embarrassment') in Wa and *so be nya dagna* ('no injuries') in Tamale. From the colonial period up to national independence, transport policy had been in favour of 'roads for cars' for the fast movement of people and goods, and this has remained the case to the present day. Minimal provision has been made in road construction for other forms of transport in Ghanaian towns and cities. The cumulative effect of over-concentration on motor cars and the consequent negative factors associated with this, both in terms of inadequate roads and higher fares, has been the evolution of another form of transport: the tricycle or 'Motor King', which thrived and continues to thrive on the disadvantages that road construction and use brought about in the towns and cities. The chapter argues that roads not only provide windows of opportunity for motor vehicles but also create different income earning sources and capacities for operators of tricycles and traders in both Wa and Tamale.

The setting of the second chapter in this section is also in Ghana, where Akinyinka Akinyoade provides insights into the lives of Nigerians in transit at Jerusalem House, located in the Odorkor suburb of Accra. The study focuses on the transient nature of the life of the Nigerian immigrant in Ghana. Transience is explored both in terms of geographical location and in terms of the course of life. In recent times, the profile of immigrants from Nigeria is gradually changing from Yoruba to Ibo. Through in-depth interviews, the research sheds light on the experiences and transformations of Ibo migrant traders at their zone of transit in Jerusalem House. This house is of special social, economic, and governance importance for the average trader-immigrant. These traders use ingenious means to integrate, and they receive a lasting imprint based on their experiences moulded in this location. In the larger picture, the traders are passers-by who see Ghana as a transit point in the increasingly important South–South migration. Particularly in Jerusalem House, a different perspective of 'home' and 'family' is used by these Nigerian immigrants.

The penultimate chapter is Amisah Bakuri's work on Ghanaian migrants in the Netherlands who used Germany as a transit zone in the course of their journey to greener pastures. This study explores the experiences of some *burgers* in the Netherlands who came through Germany. Of particular concern is an answer to the question of why migrants stay 'in transit' and their experiences in transit. The interviews conducted shed light on how interviewees perceived Germany as a place of transit and how Germany became a place of transit over time. Other questions answered include why some Ghanaians that left for Germany continued the move to the Netherlands and the connections they maintain with their home country. The research arose out of a curiosity to understand the term *burger*, a term used in Ghana in reference to any individual who has travelled outside Ghana. *Burger* is argued to be derived from the name of the German city Hamburg; in this case, *burger* becomes a fond appellation for the Ghanaian who has gone to Hamburg, regardless of whether the migrant in question actually settled in Hamburg or elsewhere. It could also have come from the Ghanaians who eventually settled in the Netherlands, where the Dutch word *burger* means citizen—some of these Ghanaian migrants acquired citizenship status in these European states. The most frequent motives for migration among Ghanaian migrants are great expectations of prestige and individual socio-economic improvement. Remittances and goods that migrants send home give a clear message to others to follow suit: if you want to be more prosperous, go abroad. The frequency of remittances (and occasional visits back home) enhances ones *burger* status. In spite of the strong bond these migrants maintain with people in Ghana through visits and remittances, the opportunity to return to stay permanently in Ghana is not equal for all migrants. This is influenced not only by financial, political, and social circumstances but also by the legal ability of the *burger* to re-enter Europe.

The final chapter is Mieke de Goede's stimulating research on the Congo. Her chapter, 'Kinshasa: A city of refugees', offers reflections based on personal observations and exchanges with Congolese people immediately after the post-war elections in 2006 and the years following, when the initial democratic opening quickly turned sour. The research examines how people feel abandoned and not helped at all despite the billions of dollars of development aid that have been poured into the country over the past decades. It also raises the question of the extent to which the rest of the world is fundamentally entangled in this collective Congolese trauma, epitomized by the fact that a decade and a half of intense peacekeeping, humanitarian assistance, and development aid have left the population more demoralized and desperate than before. The chapter is a respectful assessment of the stories of people following the euphoria of the peace agreement and the promises it held for real change in people's everyday lives, a euphoria which now appears long gone. The disillusionment captured in this research is based on personal life stories and the concerns of individuals who now feel trapped in a situation they cannot change. Some have developed escapisms through which they can flee mentally and deny reality, either through witchcraft, or religion, or music and dance. Others are striving to physically leave the country, because they have lost all hope that a better future for themselves and their children is possible in the Congo. Escaping this victimhood and regaining control over one's life requires leaving the Congo and accessing the powerful outside world. But entanglement with the outside world also has another element—the outside is simultaneously a space of oppression and of liberation. The wealthy Congolese elite, who have most access to the Western world and have considerable control over their own lives, are also the ones that speak very loudly of Western neo-colonial practices. The chapter suggests that perhaps people's response to what is in fact a sense of hopelessness is essentially a critique not only of Congolese governance, but also of the development sector.

CHAPTER 2

Roads to Prosperity: Social Zones of Transit

Amisah Zenabu Bakuri

Introduction

Migration is a global phenomenon that crosses space and time. It is an age-old human means to improve life and can be defined as the movement of people from one place in the world to another for the purpose of taking up permanent or semi-permanent residence. What makes migration a subject worth researching for the collaborative research group 'Roads to Prosperity' is its linkage with several other topics, such as those related to culture, society, politics, globalization, economic polarization, and nation-states that sometimes problematize the free movement of people (often leading to transit). This complexity, we argue, presents a challenge to migration research, particularly to researchers attempting to understand the different patterns and processes of migration.

Gathering evidence from a variety of countries and employing an array of methodological tools individually, researchers in the collaborative research group 'Roads to Prosperity' set out to examine the emergent and evolving processes and patterns of transit migration in Africa. The researchers aimed to shed some light, through historical and empirical study, on the formation and transformations of transit zones and on the perception of these at the sending and receiving sides. We aimed at generating a multidisciplinary yet shared conceptual framework in the study of transit migrants in their trajectories to prosperity. This paper will therefore address the question of what transit migration is and how transit migration can be conceptualized and analysed together with other related concepts. The aim is to better understand how people involved in the process of labour migration and other forms of mobility in the pursuit of well-being perceive of spaces of transit as well as of times of transit.

'Being in transit' must be analysed in terms of space and time, and a common conceptual knowledge needs to be developed in view of the economic, political, social, cultural, and historical processes that give rise to particular manifestations of transience. We therefore explore concepts related to transit migration, such as liminality, generational cohorts, upward social mobility, and social capital.

The purpose of this paper is to approach the subject from a conceptual perspective. We provide a general picture rather than the specifics of each

© KONINKLIJKE BRILL NV, LEIDEN, 2015 | DOI 10.1163/9789004306059_003

country, while the latter are addressed by each of the researchers in the collaborative research group. This paper examines the definitions of some concepts of migration to assess contradictions arising from these definitions and to critically reflect on the physical and social aspects of migration in Africa.

Migration: A Terminological Approach

To better understand transit migration, we first focus on some migration terminologies. Migration has several terminologies that allow for many possible trajectories, time spans, and directions of research. Migration can be temporary or long term, voluntary or forced. It occurs in stages or in cycles, and it can be unidirectional or varied. In simple terms, however, human migration is often defined as the movement of people from one political or administrative unit to another for the purpose of taking up permanent or semi-permanent residence.[1] It has been noted that people either choose to move (voluntary migration) or they are forced to move (involuntary migration).

Migration in search of better opportunities occurs on a variety of scales: inter-continental, intra-continental, inter-regional, and from rural to urban areas. In our studies, we focus on both the voluntary and involuntary migration that arises in transit migration. Several types of migration have been identified by scholars in the field of migration, such as international migration—crossing the frontiers that separate one country from another (PISA 2003)—and internal migration—a move from one administrative area to another within the same country (Greenwood 1975; Davin 1998). Some scholars argue that internal and international migration are part of the same process and should be analysed together.

Some of the terms that enhance the understanding of the concept of migration include the following: emigration, leaving one country for another; immigration, moving into a new country; and population transfer, which can refer to a government forcing a large group of people out of a region, usually based on ethnicity or religion (Rosefielde 2009). This is also classified by some scholars as an 'involuntary' or 'forced migration'. Forced migration or 'reluctant' or 'imposed migration' is when individuals are not forced out of their country but leave because of unfavourable situations, which can be the result of warfare, political problems, or religious persecution (NGS 2005).

---

1   The United Nations defines an international migrant as a person who stays outside of their usual country of residence for at least one year.

There are also terms like 'step migration': a series of shorter, less extreme migrations from a person's place of origin to a final destination. A series of migrations within a defined group of people (family, ethnic group) is commonly known as 'chain migration'. A chain migration often begins with the migration of one member leading to several people joining this person at the new location. Chain migration results in migration fields, the clustering of people from a specific region into certain neighbourhoods or locations (MacDonald & MacDonald 1964). The voluntary movements of immigrants back to their place of origin can be referred to as 'return migration' (King 1978). This is also sometimes known as 'circular migration', while 'seasonal migration' is the process of moving for a period of time in response to labour or climatic conditions.

Another term often used in migration is 'mobility'. With respect to physical movement, the term mobility encompasses a broader range of people: migrants as well as tourists, business people, and armed forces. Mobility is not limited to the physical movement of people only but goes beyond physical movement to include social movement in the status of individuals. (Schapendonk 2010), however, notes that the mobility processes of migrants have been understudied.

Research so far on migration has discussed the agency and motives of migrants who, within their capabilities, negotiate available options and constraints in pursuit of their life goals. It also looks at both ends of human migration (origin and destination) and at the process of migration. Research focuses on migration from a macro-regional perspective or at a meso- or micro-level, investigating areas such as the reasons and conditions under which people leave the specific social, legal, and economic settings of their place of departure, coupled with the impact of out-migration on families and societies; the dimensions and patterns of movement through space and time (circular, seasonal, or definite); the migrants' process of acceptance into or exclusion from their host societies, coupled with their impact on the host countries, regions, or localities; and the interconnections between the places of departure and arrival.

Some migration researchers also study migrants' agency in migration processes (e.g. motivations, networks, impact on structures such as family and state) within specific structural constraints. Other researchers have looked at migrant agency within structural constraints by including to a certain degree involuntary migrants such as enslaved or indentured workers and refugees. This research group focuses extensively on individual migrants and the reasons that lead to transit migration in the context of international migration.

Reasons for Migrating

People decide to move from one political or administrative region to another for various reasons. They consider the advantages and disadvantages of staying versus moving, as well as factors such as distance, travel costs, travel time, modes of transportation, terrain, and cultural and social barriers. In general, these reasons have been categorized under push–pull factors. Push factors are the reasons for emigrating (leaving a country) because of some difficulties— for instance, food shortage, economic difficulties, war, and environmental disasters. Pull factors are generally the reasons for immigrating (moving into a country) because of something desirable at the destination country. This can be a better climate; better food supply; better social, political, or religious freedom; and better job or education opportunities. Several types of push and pull factors may influence people in their movement, and these factors may exist simultaneously.

These and many other reasons have been given as motivations for people to migrate. In our bid to explain transit migration, we seek to discover from individual migrants why they migrate and whether the same reasons keep them in transit or not. In understanding these migrants and their motivations for migrating, we look at 'place utility'. Place utility is the desirability of a place based on its social, economic, or environmental situation, and is often used to compare the value of living in different locations (Lieber 1978). An individual migrant's idea of place utility may or may not reflect the actual conditions of that location. Does this lead to transit or not? This is one of the questions that need to be explored in the study of transit migrants. Another term used in migration is 'intervening opportunities', which helps in the understanding of individual (transit) migrants. Intervening opportunities are simply the local or nearby opportunities considered more attractive or slightly better than equal opportunities farther away, such that migrants tend to settle in a location closer to their point of origin if other factors are equal (Stouffer 1940).

Clearly, migration has several terminologies and migrants have several reasons for embarking on their journey. Our focus is mainly on transit migration, which will be explored extensively later in this paper. The various terminologies mentioned (which are not exhaustive) provide an overview of the terminologies associated with migration and also assist in understanding and researching transit migration and migrants. Several definitions and criticisms can be provided for these terms; however, we provide only a broad and general explanation owing to focus and space.

Overview of History of Migration within Africa

Throughout the history of mankind, people have migrated in search of better opportunities. While the decision to migrate is driven by many complex factors, most people decide to migrate in order to earn a better living, to live in a better environment, or to join family or friends elsewhere. Some migrants move involuntarily (e.g. refugees escaping persecution, people devastated by conflict or natural disasters, victims of trafficking), but those who willingly choose to migrate are largely driven by the desire for greater happiness, prosperity, and well-being (The World Migration Report, 2013).

Migration is a very important world issue. In 2002, for instance, the United Nations estimated that over 110 million people now reside outside the country of their birth (United Nations 2002). This clearly has major economic, social, cultural, and political implications for the migrant and for the sending and receiving countries.

According to the bilateral migration matrix data from the (World Bank 2010), it is estimated that in 2010 the number of people living in countries other than their birthplace was around 215 million, of whom 31 million are from Africa. Of the 31 million emigrants from Africa, about 2.3 million are recognized as being refugees displaced mainly by war or drought or some form of natural disaster (UNPD 2010).[2] It must be noted that official data on migration in Africa, and most especially that of Sub-Saharan Africa, may not provide an accurate number of people crossing borders, owing to infrequent and inconsistent recording of the movement of people across borders.

HDR (2009) and Shaw (2007) reported that a marked feature of the movement of people across the globe is that at least half takes place within the same continent, while the other half is transcontinental.[3] For Africa, the intra-Africa emigration rate is noted by (Shimeles 2010) to be about 52%. However, Shimeles observes that this figure is close to 65% for countries in Sub-Saharan Africa, representing the largest intra-continental movement of people in the world. In general, the complexities of intra-continental migration in Africa have been attributed to the history of state formation, where colonial borders failed to take into account linguistic and ethnic commonalities. In addition, this form of migration is said to reflect movement in search of job opportunities across neighbouring countries.

---

2   (Hatton & Williamson 2005) stated that many refugees in Africa are as a result of coups, civil war, insurgency, and government crisis. Nevertheless, recently, while most African countries have experienced relative peace and economic stability, there are still many emigrants from these countries to other Sub-Saharan African countries. Some perceive these countries as transit zones only.

3   See also HDR (2009) and (Shaw 2007) for relevant discussion on intra-African migration in Africa.

It is clear that in most cases cross-border migration dominates movement of people within the African continent, particularly among migrants from West Africa, where close to 90% of intra-African migration is believed to take place within the West African sub-region (Yaro n.d.; Shimeles 2010). Southern Africa has become a hotspot for most migrants from Africa. South Africa's economy is evidently the attraction for miners and other potential job seekers from neighbouring countries as well as from faraway countries in East Africa. The end of apartheid further increased emigration from other sub-regions. For instance, South Africa is a popular destination place for emigrants from Mozambique, Swaziland, Lesotho, Botswana, and Zimbabwe (Shimeles 2010). Evidently, the prospect of a better job or of upward social mobility plays a significant role in attracting these migrants. For East Africa and countries around the Horn, the pattern is that of the movement of refugees (*ibid.*). Sudan is the most common destination for migrants from Chad, Eritrea, and Ethiopia, while Kenya is a popular destination for migrants from Uganda and Tanzania. Interestingly, Tanzania itself is a destination most favoured by migrants from the Democratic Republic of Congo, Zambia, and Burundi. Some of these migrants, in heading for these locations, for various reasons may not reach their intended destinations and may settle in other destinations, with the intention of moving on when conditions are deemed favourable.

The prospect of a better life or of upward social mobility is undoubtedly an important factor behind people's decision to migrate, but it is not a sufficient reason to do so. Ability to migrate is also an important element, and this often introduces a threshold effect on the decision of individuals to stay or migrate (see Shaw (2007); HDR 2009), or even to go through an intervening country/countries. To a certain extent, migration may be impeded by, among other things, economic, social, cultural, and political factors.

(Shimeles 2010) observes that Africa, especially Sub-Saharan Africa, is one of the regions with a sizeable number of migrants leaving their countries of origin. There are variations, however, across time and countries. Migration in Africa is predominantly a South–South phenomenon and has shown little change in the last decade. West Africa's domination as a sub-region with the highest mobility rate since the early 1970s was noted by (Russell et al. 1990). They attribute this partly to better coordination of West African states due to historical ties and better integration as a result of the Economic Community of West African States (ECOWAS).

In summary, while the broad discussion presented above may provide some indication of the overall scale of intra-regional migration in Africa, it does not reveal much of the changing patterns of movement within Africa, including transit migration. Given the wide range of countries within the African continent, with their very different historical, political, economic, social, and geographical contexts, there are few reasons to expect that they will share too many parallels in their different migration trends simply by virtue of their being on the same continent.

In addition, with considerable intra-Africa migration of people (as noted above), it seems more feasible to describe changing patterns of migration such as the formation, rise, and transformations of zones of transit of specific countries or of hotspots of particular migrant groups that may have led to chain migration, where at least there are shared geographical boundaries—rather than trying to identify commonalities across Africa as a whole. Rather than attempting to cover the whole of Africa, the individual researchers therefore largely limited their discussion to specific countries. Despite these cautions about generalizations across the African continent, it is possible to identify some very broad migration patterns. We will focus particularly on transit migration.

Transit Migration: Some Difficulties of the Concept

'Transit migration is a synthetic concept that merges transit and migration' (Düvell et al. 2008). The concept is very dynamic and loaded scientifically, ideologically, and politically. Transit migration as a terminology has persisted in discussions of migration, but its nature, meaning, usefulness, and appropriateness have been unsettled and can be challenged (Cassarino & Fargues 2006; Düvell et al. 2008; Castagnone 2011). The changing aspirations and motives of migrants with time make it very difficult to explain transit migration.

The notion of transit migration emerged in policy discourse during the 1990s (Fait 2013) and different meanings have been given to it (Castagnone 2011). In this paper we argue that these are created meanings but unable to fully address or describe all the complex experiences, political contexts, and global realities of transit migration and transit migrants. We point out the difficulties in explaining the concept of transit migration as well as expose the limits of such explanations in the light of African migrants' experiences within Africa. Our empirical data shows that while the category of transit migration emerging out of the European securitization agenda can fit some of the experiences of Sub-Saharan African migrants, there are also distinctive African migrant experiences which cannot be easily included in this category. Furthermore, we aim to highlight the development of zones of transit using the experiences of migrants.

Historically, transit migration emerged as a concept in the beginning of the 1990s and referred mainly to migration from Eastern to Western Europe.

Because of the 'illegal' character of this migration, the concept is often used as an equivalent for irregular migration. It is mainly for this reason that the concept is highly politicized (Düvell 2006a), since it is primarily perceived as a European threat (Baldwin-Edwards 2006). It was said that 'masses of migrants' were at the eastern and the southern border zones of Europe waiting to enter Western Europe 'illegally'. However, the estimation of the number of people is debatable. Again, many of these transit migrants were noted to have aimed to enter Western Europe, while it was never definite, at least not *a priori*, whether they actually managed to do so.

Also, in traditional migration jargon, transit sometimes referred to transit visas or transit migration (Pitea 2010). Pitea notes that traditionally, transit migration was a short-term phenomenon, usually part of pre-defined routes that the migrant or traveller undertook without the intention of remaining in the country of transit. Migration is frequently not a straightforward process where people simply move from their origin to another desired or intended place. Instead, many migrants are in transit for a considerable length of time, sometimes for several years (Wahlbeck 2008).

In between origin and destination in migration, there exist situations with certain factors that act as obstacles and impede the movement of a person to the actual (intended) destination. Such obstacles can be the distance between the origin and destination, attachment to native place, travelling costs, maintenance of double establishments, social condemnation, migratory laws, and discouragement by the recipient countries, language, religion, and customs. In a broader sense, zones of transit in migration arise as a result of ethnic, religious, social, cultural, economic, diplomatic, political, and environmental factors. These factors can be positive for some migrants, negative for others, and neutral for yet others.

Global migration dynamics have evolved over time, with transit migration becoming more diversified and evolving into a complex phenomenon whereby migrants enter and reside (voluntarily or involuntarily) in a country for various amounts of time with the intention of obtaining access to a third country/ countries (Pitea 2010). Some migrants are prevented or hindered from continuing their migration journey and may end up 'stranded' in what was originally thought to be their transit country.

To understand the concept of transit and zones of transit in migration, we take a cue from (Vertovec 2003) and heed his call to consider disciplinary borrowing if it strengthens our theoretical and conceptual frameworks. We therefore look at zones of transit of migrants through the lenses of the closely related disciplines of anthropology, geography, politics, and sociology. This leads to the shared perspective that there is a degree of social constructivism at work in understanding transit migration and how zones of transit emerge, constructivism which at the very least involves a series of assumptions about the behaviour of a diverse range of individuals.[4] The phenomenon of transit migration is not an easy one to study; therefore, we use a number of different perspectives and case studies to describe this particular migration phase. Transit migration is clearly difficult to delimit. As (Düvell et al. 2008) noted, there is no single and commonly agreed definition of transit migration.

It is not possible to clearly distinguish between transit migration and non-transit migration, since one type of migration easily develops into the other type. Thus, it is argued here that transit migration has to be connected to the broader migration process and the influence and experiences of the migrants themselves. We argue along with (Papadopoulou-Kourkoula 2005) that transit migration is not a migrant category; rather, it is a migratory phase that cuts across various migrant categories. Irregular migrants, asylum seekers, refugees granted asylum, regularized migrants, students, and trafficked persons may all find themselves in the condition of transit at some point. In many cases, transit migration is conflated with 'irregular migration'. In this research, irregular migration and transit migration are not synonyms, although the two may over-lap in some instances.

Looking at this important aspect of migration patterns, our research describes not only how transit migration is created and sustained by individual decisions but also how these individual decisions are shaped by political deci-sions, cultural factors, and opportunity structures. The outcome of migration depends as much on social and political structures as on social networks and other individual factors.

Transit migration as a term used in this paper refers to certain forms of sup-posedly temporary migration and to migrants who move from their country of origin to another country (or countries), either because it was intended from the outset or in response to changing conditions, rising pressures, or new incentives, and with the hope of moving on to another country.

'Temporariness' embodied within the concept of transit is also conceptually very difficult to define (Castagnone 2011). How long or short a time should a migrant stay for the migration phase to be described as transit migration? Transits may in fact last for considerable lengths of time. The waiting periods are fluid and not fixed; they could be days, weeks, months, or even years.

More generally, the term transit migration also refers to both real and imag-ined long journeys and complex odysseys. Often they may be long in terms of distance and time, can continually change direction, and, at times, may be

---

4 These assumptions apply not only to individuals but also to institutions. This paper, however, focuses extensively on individuals who embark on migration and less on the institutions involved.

hazardous or beneficial to the migrant. Transit migration can also refer to types of migration that are not straight-line, one-off moves but involve various stages, including forced interruptions of journeys after a period of stay in a country other than the final destination. More abstractly, transit migration can refer to identity processes and related ambitions (or mere dreams) of people who wish to move to a more prosperous country or a better social status without ever making practical efforts.

Transit migrants often emerge from various sets of circumstances. Contrary to popular belief, not all migrants have specific plans before leaving their homeland; it is during the migrants' journey or even in the host country that the migration plans take real shape. Migrants can originate from the neighbouring regions of their destination country or from distant lands. In some cases, when migrants find that they cannot obtain a 'visa' to their dream destination, a certain proportion turn to transit. Those from distant countries experience long journeys that may involve crossing an intervening country or countries. The entering of a state in order to travel on to another is mainly conceptualized as transit migration (Baldwin-Edwards 2006; de Haas 2006; Düvell 2006b; Papadopoulou-Kourkoula 2009).

Transit migrants move in many different ways. Some may decide to follow traditional migration routes, some of which are considered ancient while others are believed to be as a result of contemporary development. Migrants often move within established migration systems; this, however, is not a rigid typology. Given the dynamic nature of migration patterns, a country can serve simultaneously as a zone of transit for some migrants and a final destination for others. Furthermore, the status of such countries can evolve. Likewise, notions of 'final destination' may change owing to migrants' journeys and/or migrants' settlement experiences. A country initially considered to be a place of temporary stay can end up becoming a country of permanent stay—and the reverse can also be true. The perceptions and intentions of migrants themselves are thus fluid (A European Network of Excellence on International Migration 2008).

For Sub-Saharan African migrants heading for socio-economic prosperity in other countries within and outside Africa, their migration process is highly dynamic (Adepoju 1994; Adepoju 2004). Perceived transit areas may turn into (in)voluntary destinations, since some migrants decide to settle in places as a second-best option, while others are forced to stay and 'wait' for considerable periods of time for their opportunity to make the next step of their journey on their road to prosperity.

Migration processes do not automatically end when someone has lived for some years in a specific place or when a desired destination is reached. For many transit migrants, migration consists of repeated moves and temporary settlements, and their plans and dreams as well as their available migration opportunities are rather variable than fixed. In this framework, a more dynamic understanding of migration is required. In our view, Sub-Saharan African migrants on their roads to prosperity should be understood in terms of mobility (and its restrictions) rather than in terms of a permanent or semi-permanent change of location.

In this paper, transit migration is understood as a situation that arises between origin and destination countries, often characterized by indefinite migrant stay (legal or illegal). Such situations can develop into further migration (Papadopoulou-Kourkoula 2009). The length of stay can be known only retrospectively. Regardless of the intentions of migrants, their journey and/or travel plans may change over time. A final destination can actually turn out to be only one step in a much longer journey; on the other hand, a short stopover could end up as a final destination.

To better understand migration patterns, there seems to be a growing academic interest in the migration process of individuals (i.e. the act of migrating). Traditionally, this act was more or less neglected in migration research. The main focus of researchers on migration was on the decision of individual migrants and the reasons for their embarking on their journey, as well as on the impact of migration on host and sending societies. This is somewhat different in the framework of transit migration, since some researchers have examined transit migration as a phase in the larger migration framework of African migrants (particularly Sub-Saharan Africa) with an in-depth approach. Hamood (2006) focused on the case of Sub-Saharan African migration through Libya; Collyer (2006) researched undocumented African migrants in Morocco; and Brachet (2005) researched trans-Saharan migration through Niger and Algeria. Therefore, a range of countries are perceived as zones of transit where migrants are either stuck or using the country as a stepping stone to get to their dream countries.

Migrants from Sub-Saharan Africa heading to Europe have been much studied. These studies provide valuable insights into migration methods and the experiences of migrants in zones of transit. However, the studies generally look at these migrants as transiting to Europe particularly (i.e. the North). These studies neglect transit migration within Sub-Saharan Africa, and their focus is also mainly on North Africa as a transit zone.

Empirical study on zones of transit needs to be analysed with respect to the migration process by using a broader, yet focused approach. Firstly, analysis employing a broader yet focused geographical perspective than the studies mentioned above will enhance conceptualizing zones of transit in Sub-Saharan Africa—for instance, based on fieldwork in several different countries: Nigeria, Zimbabwe, Botswana, and Zambia. Therefore, the analysis of the migration process does not end at the final destination but will include transit zones. These zones of transit do not necessarily lead migrants to Europe.

It is also important to analyse zones of transit by focusing on migration networks, migration facilitators, and the sharing of information among migrants. This will help gain insights into the dynamics of transit migration and migrants' (im)mobilities during their process of migration. Fieldwork has been conducted in these particular countries, since they have specific characteristics with respect to Sub-Saharan African migration.

Some countries are primarily viewed as important sending countries, some primarily as transit countries, and some are often considered as destination countries. However, in reality these categorizations cannot be clearly applied; all countries are, to some extent or simultaneously, sending, transit, and receiving countries.

Finally, it is important to note that it is impossible to outline the migration process of all Sub-Saharan African migrants. African migrants are very diverse. These migrants have different reasons for and aims in embarking on migration. They all have different personal characteristics and may come from different countries and regions of origin with different migration routes and migration means. The researchers in the collaborative research group therefore attempt only to provide insights into the migration process of some Sub-Saharan Africans travelling through West and southern Africa. We do not intend to outline the migration process of all African migrants in general.

This section of the paper looked at the approach to and the terminology of transit migration itself as a source of analysis, focusing on the use and difficulties of the concept rather than any potentially objective facts behind it. The complexities of the concept of transit migration reflect an exciting scholarly controversy in an area of research that is very much in flux. Given the different interpretations that can be applied to transit migration, we should be critical of the various political intentions behind the use of the concept, and the popularity of the term in political, policy, and academic circles points to a number of areas which warrant further scrutiny. There is therefore a need to highlight the complexity of these processes, and at the same time this complexity suggests a number of directions for further fruitful research.

Social Mobility

Up to this point, we have looked at transit in terms of the physical movement of people geographically, moving from one country to another and possibly getting stuck along the way to their intended destination. However, transit migration can also be seen in terms of social mobility. Social mobility is another concept that cannot easily be defined, but it is a very important concept when studying migration. In the words of historian C.R. (James 1963): 'it is not quality of goods and utility that matter, but movement; not where you are or what you have, but where you come from, where you are going, and the rate at which you are getting there'. Social mobility can be explained simply as movement of individuals, families, or groups through a system of social stratification or hierarchy based on social variables such as wealth, occupation, and education.

Studying social mobility raises some questions: How easily do individuals move up the social ladder to access jobs or education in line with their potential? Do people get stuck in reaching their social aspirations? Migration can be an important factor in upward mobility. Blau & Duncan (1967), Morrison (1977), and DaVanzo (1981) have all made the observation that migration promotes the socio-economic status of migrants as a result of individuals migrating to areas where opportunities for social mobility are better.

Upward social mobility is a change in a person's social status resulting in that person's rising to a higher position in their status hierarchy/system. On the other hand, downward mobility means a person's social status falls to a lower position in their status hierarchy/system (Gerber 2010). In social mobility, some individuals can find themselves stuck on their way to socio-economic prosperity. This is also directly linked to the discussion of transit migration above.

In studying transit migration and the experiences of transit migrants, it becomes necessary to look at transit in social status. People may aim to reach a higher social status, but obstacles can cause them to get stuck at one particular status. How do they make a life out of such situations? There seems to be a strong correlation between social mobility and transit migration on the one hand, and social capital on the other hand, in that when one is 'stuck' in transition the existence or nonexistence of social networks and social capital plays an important role.

Social Capital and Social Networks in Transit Migration

Social capital can be broadly defined as 'the values that people hold and the resources that they can access, which both result in and are the result of collective and socially negotiated ties and relationships' (Edwards et al. 2003: 2). One of the founding fathers of social capital theory, Robert (Putnam 2000), highlights the importance of social capital in terms of the relationship of individuals to others within societies, communities, and families. Networks of trust, values, and reciprocity are significant for making community relationships work and sustaining the connections of migrants in transit (Reynolds 2008).

The ability of the transit migrant to secure certain resources through membership in interpersonal networks and social institutions at the zone of transit, as observed by (Portes 1998), can be converted into information, referrals, or direct help.

An individual's connections and networks in a destination country increase the likelihood of his/her migration (Massey et al. 1993). It has been argued that social capital reduces costs of migration and helps in adaptation to the host society (Gurak & Caces 1992; Espinosa & Massey 1999; Palloni et al. 2001). Transit migrants (newcomers, in particular) with social networks benefit positively from these networks. Friends and relatives sort through jobs to reserve better ones for their network members (Nee & Sanders 2001; Aguilera & Massey 2003). In this way, migrants with few social networks are likely to miss opportunities that are available only through such networks. These networks can provide migrants with valuable information (Aguilera & Massey 2003) in transit or even on their journey. It should be pointed out that the advantage of social capital in migration and transit migration is determined by the nature of the ties which bind the individual to his/her social network members. In this sense, information about the opportunities that exist or difficulties that could emerge can best be generated through social ties. These ties are often reinforced by migrant associations in host societies.

Social capital is a particularly useful concept in exploring the issue of the formation, rise, and transformation of zones of transit and in exploring the relationship between intent, opportunity, and resources of transit migrants. (Franklin 2007) notes that social capital fosters unity, providing individuals with a sense of belonging and offering opportunities to them.

The social network is an important part of migrants' life, in terms of the destination of migrants and the dynamics or mobility pattern from internal to international destinations. In the process, social networks are established within transit zones, which then tend to determine the trajectory of mobility. The social networks are reflected in the development of trans-cultural linkages, such as links with 'veterans' and groups that facilitate the lives of migrants and that sometimes provide them with details of how life is in transit, its difficulties and prospects. Consequently, the decision and behaviour of an individual migrant in transit can be dependent on their prevailing social network.

Antwi Bosiakoh (2009) notes that a social network serves as social capital in the choice of destination and insertion of the migrant into their host communities. Morosanu (2010) observes that migrant networks are very important in the stages of migration (from initial departure through to arrival, transit, circulation, and return). The (opportunity) costs associated with the decision to migrate include those linked to transport and also to the time required to arrive safely and the adaptation period in the host country (in search of a job or accommodation or getting used to the climate), and decisions can be determined by the existence—or lack—of social networks.

These social networks of migrants are often insufficient to completely support their migration process; most transit migrants need assistance for specific phases of their journey, but these networks can play an important role. Moreover, some transit migrants form collectives '*en route*' to assist them and as a form of protection on their journey. In order to adjust to the host society, new migrants may rely on the experience of 'veterans' and on interaction with locals, and it usually takes time for a migrant to adapt to the strangeness of time and place (Cwerner 2001). Migrants' social networks provide both the means and the motivation for (dis)continued movement, even as destinations become more elusive.

The existence in the country of destination of a community of people with whom a migrant can identify and fit in easily certainly determines whether the migrant will stay or not. Most African countries share extensive commonalities along borders, sometimes cutting through four or five countries. It is well recognized that cross-border movements are facilitated by common linguistic and historical roots. For instance, Shimeles (2010) observed that a large number of emigrants from Somalia, Djibouti, Ethiopia, and Eritrea are found in the same region owing to strong ethnic, religious, and linguistic ties along the very extensive borders shared by these countries. Similarly, emigrants from Burundi and Rwanda can easily fit into the population in Uganda and Tanzania because of large ethnic groups residing in these countries that speak the same language and share historical ties.

In southern Africa, it is easy for migrants from Lesotho, Swaziland, Mozambique, and Botswana to blend into communities in South Africa, making mobility and settlement comparatively easy for aspiring migrants. Côte d'Ivoire is a melting pot for neighbouring countries, because most migrants are able to communicate with people in the surrounding countries and share similar religious and historical bonds (*ibid.*). However, in recent times, these melting points have borne the brunt of attacks from 'indigenes'. For example, in South Africa in 2008 and in 2013, foreigners (Somalis, Malawians, Zimbabweans, Chinese, and a host of others) experienced waves of anti-immigrant violence.[5] Also, in Côte d'Ivoire, it was reported that some immigrants from West Africa

---

5 *The New York Times,* 'Immigrants Fleeing Fury of South African Mobs'. 23 May 2008. http://www.nytimes.com/2008/05/23/world/africa/23safrica.html?_r=0. Accessed 22 December 2013.

were massacred.[6] Despite these incidences, migration continues to be a social norm that can, if successful, secure both wealth and, perhaps more importantly, prestige for the migrant through a journey that is often helped by social networks.

Life Course, Journey, and Pathways

To be able to better understand the life of the transit migrant, there is a need to look for universal, predictable events and pathways, and also at how historical time, social location, and culture affect individual migrants' experience of each life stage before and during transition. In this setting, 'generational cohorts' play an important role. Generational cohort in this context refers to a group of persons who were born at almost the same historical time and who may experience particular social changes within a given culture. They can have similar educational trajectories, family life trajectories, and work trajectories, but it must be noted that cohorts can also have different life trajectories because of the unique historical events each cohort may encounter.

The different patterns of social networks in which persons are placed produce differences in their life course experiences. Similarly, the different locations of the transit migrant produce very different life course trajectories. The intersection of multiple trajectories (for instance, family life, educational life, and work life) initiates new prospects for variety in the life course patterns of transit migrants; hence, researchers studying transit migration may have to observe carefully the life course and pathways of individual migrants.

Liminality in Migration

It is widely recognized that involvement in migration transforms migrants' identities, yet there is no sustained explanation of the conditions that make migration an identity-transforming experience. We draw on Victor (Turner 1969; Turner 1979) notion of liminality to specify how transit migration is linked with the concept of transformation, and we propose that transit migration is a liminal phenomenon. It separate participants from their previous society and

---

6 (Human Rights Watch 2011), 'Côte d'Ivoire: West African Immigrants Massacred'. http://www.hrw.org/news/2011/03/31/c-te-d-ivoire-west-african-immigrants-massacred. Accessed 22 December 2013.

gives them a chance to remould themselves into another society. For those involved, the total effect is a threshold effect, in that the experience becomes a dividing line in personal histories and can have immediate and long-term consequences.

Liminality is from the Latin word *limen*, meaning threshold. In Turner's anthropology of the ritual process, the liminal stage is the second phase of a three-stage process:

1. The separation stage: the ritual subject is separated from previous structural conditions. In the context of transit migration, the individual is separated from his/her 'home country'.
2. The liminal stage: the individual redefines his/her identity under conditions that have 'few or none of the attributes of the past or coming state' ((Turner 1969): 94).
3. The final stage: the subject settles back into the social structure.

We focus mainly on the second stage of Turner's concept of liminality, as it is directly linked with transit migration. This is because the transit migrant has left the home state and finds him-/herself in a zone of transit. Turner states that there is a transitional state between the two phases—separation and liminal—when individuals are 'betwixt and between': they do not belong to the society that they were previously a part of anymore, and they are not yet incorporated into the new society. Transit migration can also be accompanied by separation among migrants, as the migration process itself is often characterized by a transitional phase whereby one family member can leave all other members, or the rest of the family stays behind in the home country (Briody 1987).

The notion of 'home' remains part of the migrants' life in transition. (Massey 1992) discusses the dynamic constructedness of home and identity as concepts interrelated through migration. So, as Brah asks, 'where is home?'(1996: 192). Where can an individual call his or her home? Brah also asks an important question about the difference between 'feeling at home' and claiming a place as one's home.

According to Grillo (2007), the concept of 'betwixt and between' can represent both physical and symbolic liminality. There are some transit migrants who fall into this category. For instance, the failed asylum seekers who do not have 'papers' but still feel the receiving country is 'home' or the place they call home. In like manner, there are those who may not have social networks in their country of origin and are unable to feel 'at home' there, although they can legally claim citizenship. There are also those who are born in the receiving country but who refuse to accept it as home. Given these complexities, it is very difficult to locate the home country of a transit migrant.

Migration separates migrants from previous social structures and locates them in a liminal situation. The characteristics of this liminal situation, noted by Turner as freedom, egalitarianism, communion, and creativity, provide the conditions for personal change. We argue that not all of these characteristics may be experienced by the transit migrant; they may be empowered or disillusioned (Tarrow 1994). Seldom do transit migrants remain the same as a result of the liminal experience of their movement. Liminal experiences vary in depth because of the different experiences of transit migrants, and the consequent degree of the change will also vary with each migrant. Also, the length of stay in the transit country leads migrants to find different strategies and skills for establishing and maintaining themselves.

Conclusion

> Migration or more exactly mobility [...] technically, does not become 'permanent' until an individual reaches his or her death place, and even then [...] it still need not necessarily be permanent.
>
> SKELDON 1997

Transit migration is difficult to define simply and explain; hence, it must be viewed as a process rather than as the status of a migrant or the migration process. We have noted that the process of transit migration is somewhere between the migrants' origin and destination (intended or actual). 'Transit migrant' is an all-embracing category, encompassing irregular migrants, asylum seekers, refugees granted asylum, regularized migrants, students, labour migrants, and trafficked persons.

Transit migration is therefore an analytically problematic concept, given the heterogeneous experiences it embraces. It often refers to individuals' intentions, challenges, and opportunities, taking into account the dynamic and changing nature of migration processes. The problematic nature of the concept grows even larger when we look at a 'transit country' or 'zone of transit'. These zones of transit can be sending or receiving countries, depending on the migrant. We therefore noted that the intentions of migrants can change during their journey, as a result changing the status of the country they are in from being a final destination to being a place of transit, or vice versa.

It has been argued that to fully understand transit migration, concepts such as liminality, social capital, social networks, and upward social mobility are important. These concepts clarify the notion of transit migration and aid in understanding individual transit migrants. People on their roads to socio-economic prosperity can get stuck socially or physically owing to intervening obstacles. Some are helped or informed of opportunities and difficulties by their social networks and social capital.

It is also a complex matter to determine the home country of a migrant, the country where the migrant feels he/she belongs, unless the migrants' experiences, pathways, and life course are taken into consideration. What remains clear, however, is that there are migrants who travel through one or more countries and, voluntarily or not, stay in them for considerable lengths of time before reaching their final destination and/or returning to their country of origin. This fact alone calls for more in-depth research of migrant journeys and all the trajectories encompassed therein.

References

A European Network of Excellence on International Migration (2008), Integration and Social Cohesion. Transit, Migration and Politics: Trends and Constructions on the Fringes of Europe. Policy Brief No. 12.

Adepoju, A. (1994), The Demographic Profile: Sustained High Mortality and Fertility and Migration for Employment, in: A. Adepoju & C. Oppong (eds) *Gender, Work and Population in Sub-Saharan Africa*. Portsmouth, NH: Heinemann, pp. 17–34.

Adepoju, A. (2004), Migration in West Africa. A Paper Prepared for the Policy Analysis and Research Programme of the Global Commission on International Paper.

Aguilera, M.B. & D. Massey (2003), Social Capital and the Wages of Mexican Migrants. *New Hypotheses and Tests, Social Forces* 82(2): 671–701.

Antwi Bosiakoh, T. (2009), *The Role of Migrant Associations in Adjustment, Integration and Development: The Case of Nigerian Migrant Associations in Accra, Ghana*. Legon: Centre for Migration Studies, University of Ghana.

Baldwin-Edwards, M. (2006), Between a Rock and a Hard Place: North Africa as a Region of Emigration, Immigration and Transit Migration. *Review of African Political Economy* 33(108): 311–324.

Blau, P.M. & O.D. Duncan. (1967), *The American Occupational Structure*. New York: Wiley.

Brachet, J. (2005). Migrants, transporteurs et agents d'Etat: Rencontre sur l'axe agadez sebha. *Autreport* 36: 43–62.

Brah, A. (1996), *Cartographies of Diaspora: Contesting Identities*. London: Routledge.

Briody, E.K. (1987), Patterns of Household Immigration into South Texas. *International Migration Review* 21: 27–47.

Cassarino, J.P. & P. Fargues (2006), Policy Responses in MENA Countries of Transit for Migrants: An Analytical Framework for Policy Making, in: N. Sørensen, *Mediterranean Transit*. Denmark: Danish Institute for International Studies, pp. 101–107.

Castagnone, E. (2011), Transit Migration: A Piece of the Complex Mobility Puzzle. The Case of Senegalese Migration. *Cahiers de l'Urmis*. 13 October. Available at: http://urmis.revues.org/927. Accessed 16 August 2015.

Collyer, M. (2006), States of Insecurity: Consequences of Saharan Transit Migration. COMPAS Working Paper WP-06-31. University of Oxford. http://www.compas.ox.ac.uk/fileadmin/files/Publications/working_papers/WP_2006/WP0631_Collyer.pdf. Accessed 15 August 2013.

Cwerner, S.B. (2001), The Times of Migration. *Journal of Ethnic and Migration Studies,* 27(1): 7–36.

DaVanzo, J.S. (1981), Repeat Migration, Information Costs, and Location-Specific Capital. *Population and Environment* 4: 45–73.

Davin, D. (1998), *Internal Migration in Contemporary China*. Basingstoke: Macmillan Press.

Düvell, F. (2006a), *Crossing the Fringes of Europe: Transit Migration in the EU's Neighbourhood*. Working Paper No. 33, Oxford: Centre on Migration, Policy and Society. http://www.compas.ox.ac.uk/publications/Working%20papers/wp-06-33.shtml. Accessed 5 January 2014.

Düvell, F. (2006b), Questioning Conventional Migration Concepts: The Case of Transit Migration. Paper presented to workshop 'Gaps and Blind Spots of Migration Research' (25 June 2006). Budapest: Central European University.

Düvell, F., F. Pastore, H. de Haas, M. Collyer & I. Molodikova (2008), *Transit, Migration and Politics: Trends and Constructions on the Fringes of Europe*. Summary paper written for the EU Network on International Migration, Integration and Social Cohesion (IMISCOE) and COMPAS. https://www.google.co.uk/url?sa=t&rct=j&q=&esrc=s&source=web&cd=1&cad=rja&uact=8&ved=0CCMQFjAAahUKEwjH-ceR6q3HAhXG1hQKHS4UA54&url=https%3A%2F%2Fwww.compas.ox.ac.uk%2Ffileadmin%2Ffiles%2FPublications%2FReports%2FDuvell%2520transit%2520IMISCOE%2520report.pdf&ei=UKDQVceRFcatU66ojPAJ&usg=AFQjCNEqWLHNd5YYoir6Rr2q6Ow_cQG3sw&bvm=bv.99804247,d.d24. Accessed 20 January 2014.

Edwards, R., J. Franklin & J. Holland (2003), Families and Social Capital: Exploring the Issues. London: Social Capital ESRC Research Group Working Paper Series, No. 1. South Bank University.

Espinosa, K. & D.S. Massey (1999), Undocumented Migration and the Quantity and Quality of Social Capital, in: L. Pries, *Migration and Translational Social Spaces. Research in Ethnic Relations*. Hants: Ashgate Publishing, pp. 106–137.

Fait, N. (2013), African Migrations Towards Turkey: Beyond the Stepping Stone. *Ankara University SBF Journal* 68(1): 21–38.

Franklin, J. (2007), Social Capital: Between Harmony and Dissonance. Families and Social Capital ESRC Research Group, Working Paper 22. London: London South Bank University.

Gerber, L.M. (2010), *Sociology* (7th Canadian ed.). Toronto: Pearson Canada.

Greenwood, M.J. (1975), Research on Internal Migration in the United States: A Survey. *Journal of Economic Literature* 13 (2): 397–433.

Grillo, R. (2007), Betwixt and Between: Trajectories and Projects of Transmigration. *Journal of Ethnic and Migration Studies* 33(2): 199–217.

Gurak, D.T. & Fe Caces (1992), Networks Shaping Migration Systems, in: M.M. Kritz, L.L. Lean & H. Zlotnik, *International Migration Systems: A Global Approach*, Oxford: Clarendon Press, pp. 150–189.

Haas, H. de (2006), Trans-Saharan Migration to North Africa and the EU: Historical Roots and Current Trends. Migration Information Source. 1 November. http://www .migrationinformation.org/article/trans-saharan-migration-north-africa-and-eu -historical-roots-and-current-trends/. Accessed 12 November 2013.

Hamood, S. (2006), *African Transit Migration Through Libya to Europe: The Human Cost*. Cairo: FMRS, AUC.

Hatton, T. & J. Williamson (2005), *Global Migration and the World Economy: Two Centuries of Policy and Performance*. Massachusetts: MIT Press, Cambridge.

HDR (Human Development Report) (2009), Overcoming Barriers: Human Mobility and Development. New York: United Nations Development Programme.

Human Rights Watch (2011), 1 April. http://www.hrw.org/news/2011/03/31/c-te-d-ivoire -west-african-immigrants-massacred. Accessed December 2013.

James, C.L.R. (1963), *Beyond a Boundary*. London: Stanley Paul and Company.

King, R.L. (1978), Return Migration: A Neglected Aspect of Population Geography. *Area* 10(3): 175–182.

Lieber, S. (1978), Place Utility and Migration. *Geografiska Annaler. Series B, Human Geography* 60(1): 16–27.

MacDonald, J.S. & L.D. MacDonald (1964), Chain Migration, Ethnic Neighborhood Formation and Social Networks. *The Milbank Memorial Fund Quarterly* 42(1): 82–97.

Massey, D. (1992), Politics and Space/Time. *New Left Review* 196: 65–84.

Massey, D.S., J. Arango, G. Hugo, A. Kouaouci, A. Pellegrino & J.E. Taylor (1993), Theories of International Migration: A Review and Appraisal. *Population and Development Review*, 19(3): 431–466.

Massey, D.S., J. Arango, G. Hugo, A. Kouaouci, A. Pellegrino & J.E. Taylor (1998), *Worlds in Motion: Understanding International Migration at the End of the Millennium*. Oxford: Clarendon Press.

Morosanu, L. (2010), Mixed Migrant Ties: Social Networks and Social Capital in Migration Research. CARIM AS IV, Robert Schuman Centre for Advanced Studies, San Domenico di Fiesole (FI): European University Institute. http://cadmus.eui.eu/bitstream/handle/ 1814/14048/CARIM_ASN_2010_43.pdf. Accessed 20 December 2013.

Morrison, P.A. (1977), The Functions and Dynamics of the Migration Process, in: A.A. Brown & E. Neuberger, *In Internal Migration: A Comparative Perspective*. New York: Academic Press.

Nee, V. & J.M. Sanders (2001), Understanding the Diversity of Immigrant Incorporation: A Forms-of-Capital Model. *Ethnic and Racial Studies* 24(3): 386–411.

NGS (National Geographic Society) (2005), Human Migration Guide (6–8). *National Geographic Society.* http://www.nationalgeographic.com/xpeditions/lessons/09/g68/ migrationguidestudent.pdf Accessed 16 May 2014.

Palloni, A., D.S. Massey, M. Ceballos & K. Espinosa (2001), Social Capital and International Migration: A Test Using Information on Family Networks. *American Journal of Sociology* 106(5): 1262–1298.

Papadopoulou-Kourkoula, A. (2005), Exploring the Asylum-Migration Nexus: A Case Study of Transit Migrants in Europe. *Global Migration Perspectives* 23. Global Commission on International Migration.

Papadopoulou-Kourkoula, A. (2009), *Transit Migration: The Missing Link Between Emigration and Settlement*. Basingstoke: Palgrave Macmillan.

PISA (Programme for International Students Assessment) (2003), Where Immigrant Students Succeed: A Comparative Review of Performance and Engagement. Paris: OECD Publications.

Pitea, R. (2010), Transit Migration: Challenges in Egypt, Iraq, Jordan and Lebanon. Carim Research Reports 2010, 2.

Portes, A. (1998), Social Capital: Its Origins and Applications in Modern Sociology. *Annual Review of Sociology* 24: 1–24.

Putnam, R. (2000), *Bowling Alone: The Collapse and Revival of American Community*. New York: Simon & Schuster.

Reynolds, T. (2008), Ties That Bind: Families, Social Capital and Caribbean Second-Generation Return Migration. Working Paper 46, London South Bank University and University of Sussex.

Rosefielde, S. (2009), *Red Holocaust*. New York and London: Routledge.

Russell, S.S., K. Jacobsen & W.D. Stanley (1990), International Migration and Development in Sub-Saharan Africa. Washington DC: Discussion Paper Series 101, World Bank.

Schapendonk, J. (2010), Staying Put in Moving Sands: The Stepwise Migration Process of Sub-Saharan African Migrants Heading North, in: U. Engel & P. Nugent, *Respacing Africa*. Leiden: Brill.

Shaw, W. (2007), Migration in Africa: A Review of Economic Literature on International Migration in 10 Countries. Memo: World Bank.

Shimeles, A. (2010), *Migration Patterns, Trends and Policy Issues in Africa*. 2010: Working Papers Series No. 119. Tunis: African Development Bank.

Skeldon, R. (1997), *Migration and Development: A Global Perspective*. Harlow: Longman.

Stouffer, S.A. (1940), Intervening Opportunities: A Theory Relating Mobility and Distance. *American Sociological Review* 5(6): 845–867.

Tarrow, S. (1994), *Power in Movement: Social Movements, Collective Action and Politics*. Cambridge: Cambridge University Press.

The World Migration Report (2013), Migrant Well-Being and Development. http://www .google.nl/url?sa=t&rct=j&q=&esrc=s&source=web&cd=2&ved=0CDUQFjAB&url =http%3A%2F%2Fpublications.iom.int%2Fbookstore%2Ffree%2FWMR2013_EN .pdf&ei=zYu2UtOFNePMoQWHuID4Dw&usg=AFQjCNH6eiYGG5I2_pcqLKEt. Accessed 25 November 2013.

Turner, V. (1969), *The Ritual Process: Structure and Anti-Structure*. Chicago: Aldine.

Turner, V. (1979), Frame, Flow and Reflection: Ritual and Drama as Public Liminality. *Japanese Journal of Religious Studies* 6(4): 465–499.

UN (United Nations) (2002), *Replacement Migration: Is It a Solution to Declining and Ageing Populations?* New York: Technical report, United Nations Population Divisions, Department of Economics and Social Affairs.

UNPD (United Nations Population Division) (2010), World Population Prospects: The 2010 Revision New York: United Nations Department of Economic and Social Affairs.

Vertovec, S. (2003), Migration and Other Modes of Transnationalism: Towards Conceptual Cross-Fertilization. *International Migration Review* 37(3): 641–665.

Wahlbeck, Ö. (2008), Book Review of 'Transit Migration: The Missing Link Between Emigration and Settlement' by Aspasia Papadopoulou-Kourkoula, Palgrave Macmillan, 2008. *Migration Letters* 6(2): 205–206.

World Bank (2010), *Migration and Remittances Fact Book*. Development Prospects Group.

Yaro, J.A. (n.d.), *Migration in West Africa: Patterns, Issues and Challenges*. Centre for Migration Studies, University of Ghana, Legon. http://www.waifem-cbp.org/v2/ dloads/MIGRATION%20IN%20WEST%20AFRICA%20PATTERNS.pdf. Accessed 15 May 2014.

CHAPTER 3

Roads to Prosperity: Reflections about a Concept

Ton Dietz

As far as I could discover, 'roads to prosperity' was introduced as a concept by J. Vanke in a journal article published in 1988 (Vanke 1988) and also published as a kind of policy brief by a London-based transport think tank. It had a question mark in the title. It had nothing metaphorical; it was just about roads and prosperity. Vanke's thesis was this: investments in roads and other forms of physical infrastructure *do not* create massive economic benefits, as transport costs are only a minor part of production costs. In addition, he stated that there are many negative effects on local production and trade during and after road building: local depots have to close, local businesses are outcompeted, and the positive employment effects are often exaggerated. Despite this, the UK Government called its road building programme in 1989 'Roads for Prosperity'. Wikipedia-En had this to say:

> Roads for Prosperity (often incorrectly called Road to Prosperity) was a controversial white paper published by the Conservative UK Government in 1989 detailing the 'largest road building program for the UK since the Romans', produced in response to rapid increases in car ownership and use over the previous decade. It embraced what Margaret Thatcher had described as 'the great car economy' although implementation led to widespread road protests and many of the schemes contained within it were abandoned in 1996.[1]

As a counterpoint to the rather negative position of Vanke and the British protesters against road building in the 1990s, an American author (Fernald 1999) published a very influential article in the *American Economic Review* at the end of the 1990s, also called 'Roads to Prosperity'. According to Fernald, road construction (as an aggregate measure) had a very clear impact on the productivity of an area (as an aggregate measure) and hence on prosperity. But he could not really establish the causality, and also, after some years, the effects were not that clear any more. All his cases came from the US, however, during a period (the 1950s and 1960s) in which there was massive public-funded road building activity.

---

1   http://en.wikipedia.org/wiki/Roads_for_Prosperity. Accessed 19 July 2015.

© KONINKLIJKE BRILL NV, LEIDEN, 2015 | DOI 10.1163/9789004306059_004

In the 2000s, the concept 'roads to prosperity' also appeared in studies about Africa. The Tanzanian economist and current director of the Central Bank of Tanzania, one of the architects of economic reform in his country, Benno Ndulu, used the concept in a paper dealing with the importance of infrastructure development and regional integration, in an attempt to increase economic growth and counter what he called the disadvantages of geography and sovereignty fragmentation (Ndulu 2006). At the same time also, Seetanah Boopen, working in Mauritius, tried to convince scholars and planners about the importance of infrastructure development for economic growth, using many examples from Africa (Boopen 2006). This was followed by like-minded publications by Ayogu in 2007 and by Fleshman in 2009, reaching out to policymakers. So again, all these publications use the phrase 'roads to prosperity' in a rather straightforward, or even economic, sense. And all of them make a plea for more investments in road building as a requirement for Africa's economic take-off.

In the *African Dynamics* book of 2014, Lia van Weesenbeeck maps the evidence for Africa in 2005, and she concludes:

> The availability of high-quality roads is a major problem in Sub-Saharan Africa. ...there are only a limited number of primary roads and these are mainly concentrated in West Africa and South Africa, leaving the interior of the continent largely inaccessible.
>
> VAN WEESENBEECK 2014: 41–43

And in a footnote, she adds: 'The number of railroads and inland waterways in Sub-Saharan Africa is very limited, although efforts to restore and upgrade old railways have recently been made.'

However, there had already been earlier attempts to reconstruct the impact of road building on local economies in Africa. A student at the University of Amsterdam, Marjo Gallé (1989), wrote her master's thesis on a major road building project in northwest Kenya, connecting the city of Kitale (and hence the rest of the Kenyan economic heartland) with the remote areas in the northwest of the country (West Pokot and Turkana) and further to south Sudan and northeast Uganda. She reconstructed the impact of the road-building activities on the local economy and the immediate impact after the road had been built on the settlements near the new road. She looked for comparative studies about the impact of road building in developing countries and could find hardly any. With one major exception: a very oft-cited study by three arch-fathers of American modern economic development geography—Edward Taaffe, Richard Morrill, and Peter Gould—published in 1963. They looked at (current) Ghana and Nigeria in the period before independence. The study was often cited but rarely replicated, despite its opening sentence: 'In the economic growth of underdeveloped countries a critical factor has been the improvement of internal accessibility through the expansion of a transportation network' (Taaffe *et al.* 1963: 503).

In studies that use the phrase 'roads to prosperity', economic studies dominate, both in Africa and globally. The emphasis is often on so-called impulse responses and effects during and some years after road building. One of the recent studies in this tradition is Leduc and Wilson's 2012 study based on US cases of public spending on roads. This study also comes to conclusions that are not so surprising: road building '...temporarily boosts private sector productivity and local demand'. But long-term impact depends.... One would like to know more about what it depends on!

There are very few studies that go beyond economics and deal with the social and cultural effects of better and faster connections between places and people, and on what happens with social relationships and cultural identities in places that are in a process of becoming in-between stations, linking one type of area with another type of area, along the roads that are seen by migrants *en route* as 'roads to prosperity': places of poverty and relative deprivation leading to places of prospects and hope of a better life. In 2002 Fasha Ghannam wrote a book entitled *Remaking the Modern Space: Relocation and the Politics of Identity in a Global Cairo*, and this book has a chapter called 'Roads to Prosperity', mainly about 'getting connected', also in a social sense. This was an early exception. There are also a few recent studies on the social functioning of so-called transit places and cities in buffer zones, with some recent work on North Africa with its notorious Ceuta and Melilla Spanish enclaves in Northern Morocco (see for example, Baldwin-Edwards 2006; Collyer 2007). The concept of 'transit' places should also be treated with caution, however. In the UK it even became government policy (in 2003, although at first not very explicitly) to 'deport asylum seekers to transit processing centres' (Noll 2003).

This book goes beyond the direct connections between 'roads' and 'prosperity' and tries to approach the concept of roads to prosperity also in a broader, social science sense. An approach that is promising as a way to gain deeper insights into transition processes in transit places along new roads to prosperity is a geographical–anthropological approach, with sufficient historical depth. A concept that could become useful is 'liminal places/cities', using an anthropological concept indicating an in-between phase in peoples' lives and using that as a geographical concept. A stimulating recent contribution to this nascent approach is Jones and Moreno-Carranco (2008), who connect global spaces with everyday lives in these liminal cities. But at the same time these studies should not be place-bound. Dealing with migrants, they should focus on migration as a process and on mobility, connecting places along the route to people's migration and social trajectories. Many of these trajectories look alike, and this becomes evident when we do lifetime studies. The 'normal' routes that many people take in life are nowadays from rural to small urban places (for study, first jobs, marriage), sometimes on to relatively nearby large cities, and sometimes from there to the wider world, and sometimes back to areas of origin/birth later in life. All along these migration routes we find places of liminality, waiting places: between school and a first job, and between an undesired place and a desired destination, sometimes stranded in the undesired location for quite some time. Many of these places of liminality are planned to be liminal places—as buffer zones, halting places, and border towns without fast transit opportunities. And there is often a shady economy in and around these liminal places, where liminal people are offered shelter, 'paper work', temporary jobs, sex, and entertainment while *en route* (or stuck). The world's harbour places abound with these functions, and places and zones that play a role as anti-immigration fortresses also have some of these liminal characteristics.

And this brings us to the recent development in migration literature. For Africa it should be highlighted here that most migration movements are *not* international but internal movements. And much of international migration is *not* cross-continental but in the same macro-region. Africa should also not be depicted as an expulsion area. There has also been considerable into-Africa international migration (Indians, Lebanese, Europeans and, recently, Chinese): the 'desired places' were in Africa, not outside the continent, and migrants were non-Africans wanting to come to Africa—not the other way around! It is also interesting to see that old perceptions of migration as unidirectional movements are being questioned. Dick Foeken and Sam Owuor coined the very useful concept of multi-spatial livelihoods (based on Kenyan cases, e.g. see Foeken & Owuor 2001; Owuor 2006). And recent research by Valentina Mazzucato uses the concept of double engagements, based on Ghanaian cases (Mazzucato 2008). A geographical approach, however, should be added to the economic and socio-cultural approaches. Along pre-colonial, colonial, and post-colonial routes in Africa there are many networks of support, both for the means of transport (resting places for camels and horses, petrol stations) and for travellers (hotels, bars, brothels, temporary shelter and informal work places, paperwork intermediaries, religious and ethnic 'safe havens' with culturally rooted support structures or [e.g. near refugee camps] international support structures). These services are available not only in places that act as barriers or created liminal places (like the border towns near cumbersome or dangerous border crossings), but in fact in all resting and waiting places along the route. We should study not only the migrants and the routes they take, but certainly also the support structures along those routes. And 'support' should not be interpreted as a romantic term—of people who are willing to help. Geographical liminality often comes with a lot of exploitation, abuse, and violence, and next to that also benevolence, assistance, compassion, and acts of heroism.

Liminal places can and often do see a lot of fluctuations. At some points in history they attract many new people, based on images of safety, support, and inclusion. But these images can easily turn negative again, as places of severe danger, exploitation, and exclusion, and migrants may then seek other liminal places, where life is easier for them. Also, things may change along borders: places that at some points in time act as real barriers may at other points turn into connection hubs—or may lose their function completely, owing to shifting roads and routes and shifting borders and barriers. What at one point were or are transit places became or can become dead ends later.

References

Ayogu, M. (2007), *Infrastructure* and *Economic Development* in *Africa: A Review. Journal of African Economies* 16 (suppl. 1): 75–126.

Baldwin-Edwards, M. (2006), 'Between a Rock & a Hard Place': North Africa as a Region of Emigration, Immigration & Transit Migration. *Review of African Political Economy* 33(108): 311–324.

Boopen, S. (2006), Transport Infrastructure and Economic Growth: Evidence from Africa Using Dynamic Panel Estimates. *The Empirical Economic Letters* 5: 37–52.

Collyer, M. (2007), In-Between Places: Trans-Saharan Transit Migrants in Morocco and the Fragmented Journey to Europe. *Antipode* 39(4): 668–690.

Fernald, J.G. (1999), Roads to Prosperity? Assessing the Link Between Public Capital and Productivity. *The American Economic Review* 89(3): 619–638.

Fleshman, M. (2009), Laying Africa's Roads to Prosperity. Targeting the Infrastructure Gap. *Africa Renewal.* January 2009: 12.

Foeken, D. & S.O Owuor (2001), Multi-Spatial Livelihoods in Sub-Saharan Africa: Rural Farming by Urban Households: The Case of Nakuru, Town, Kenya, in: M. de Bruijn, R. van Dijk & D. Foeken (eds) *Mobile Africa: Changing Patterns of Movement in Africa and Beyond*: Leiden: Brill, pp. 125–140.

Gallé, M. (1989), One for the Road. MSc Thesis, University of Amsterdam, Department of Human Geography.

Ghannam, F. (2002), *Remaking the Modern. Space, Relocation and the Politics of Identity in a Global Cairo.* Berkeley: University of California Press.

Jones, G.A. & M. Moreno-Carranco (2008), Liminal Cities: Global Spaces, Everyday Lives, in: M.M. Valença, E. Nel & W. Leimgruber (eds) *The Global Challenge and Marginalization*. New York: Nova Science, New York, pp. 209–225.

Leduc S. & D. Wilson (2012), *Roads to Prosperity or Bridges to Nowhere? Theory and Evidence on the Impact of Public Infrastructure Investment*. NBER Working Paper No. 18042, Issued in May 2012.

Mazzucato, V. (2008), The Double Engagement: Transnationalism and Integration. Ghanaian Migrants' Lives Between Ghana and the Netherlands. *Journal of Ethnic and Migration Studies* 34(2): 199–216.

Ndulu, B.J. (2006), Infrastructure, Regional Integration and Growth in Sub-Saharan Africa: Dealing with the Disadvantages of Geography and Sovereign Fragmentation. *Journal of African Economies* 15 (suppl. 2): 212–244.

Noll, G. (2003), Visions of the Exceptional: Legal and Theoretical Issues Raised by Transit Processing Centres and Protection Zones. *European Journal of Migration and Law* 5(3): 303–341.

Owuor, S.O. (2006), *Bridging the Urban–rural Divide: Multi-Spatial Livelihoods in Nakuru Town, Kenya*. Leiden: African Studies Centre.

Taaffe, E.J., R.L. Morrill & P. Gould (1963), Transport Expansion in Underdeveloped Countries: A Comparative Analysis. *Geographical Review* 53(4): 503–529.

Van Weesenbeeck, L. (2014), Mapping the Food Economy in Sub-Saharan Africa, in: A. Akinyoade *et al.*, *Digging Deeper: Inside Africa's Agricultural, Food and Nutrition Dynamics*. Leiden & Boston: Brill, pp. 19–54.

Vanke, J. (1988), Roads to Prosperity? *The Planner*, December: 426–431.

PART 2

Zones of Transit

∴

CHAPTER 4

Wenela, Katima Mulilo, a Zone of Transit in Barotseland: The Development of a Holding Zone for Migrants on the Extreme Frontier of the South African Empire

Jan-Bart Gewald

As a child I lived for a while in Francistown, Botswana. During the school holidays I would roam around the bush and scale the *kopje*[1] with its water tower near our house. There, in the shade of the water tower and in the small patch of verdant greenery facilitated by the water leaks of shoddy piping, I would dream, eat sweets, and watch aircraft roar over my head. I knew that they were Wenela (Witwatersrand Native Labour Association) aircraft and that they were bound for 'Africa'. One day, while driving home from boarding school, we stopped off at the Wimpy Bar in Bulawayo. There, while eating Vienna sausages, hamburgers, and chips, my parents read the *Rhodesia Herald* and suddenly started chattering among themselves. One of the aircraft that I had watched from my *kopje* had crashed near Francistown, killing nearly everybody on board.[2] Back in Francistown, my chums and I cycled for days, looking for the crash site. Thankfully, we never found it.[3]

Between 1952 and 1974, Wenela transported no less than 1,857,231 men by air. Migrants from all over southern Africa travelled to the mines of South Africa in search of profit, status, and manhood. Over the years, historians such as Van

---

1 In South Africa, a small hill.

2 On 4 April 1974, a Douglas DC 4 with 80 passengers and 4 crew: fatalities were 75 passengers and 3 crew. The aircraft crashed shortly after take-off, owing to fuel contamination.

3 Police Officer Atomic Mosinyi, one of the first witnesses on the scene, described it as the most traumatic experience in his 32 years of service: 'We spent the whole week smelling with the charred remains and we had no desire for meat.' Richard Moleofe, 'Dark Cloud Hangs Over Francistown Again', *Mmegi*, Friday, 5 July 2013, vol. 30, no. 99.

© KONINKLIJKE BRILL NV, LEIDEN, 2015 | DOI 10.1163/9789004306059_005

Onselen,[4] Beinart,[5] Harries,[6] Alexander,[7] and others have worked on and developed a burgeoning literature that has sought to deal with the social, cultural, economic, and political history of migrant labour to the mines of South Africa.[8] The case of labour migrants who remained in Johannesburg and on the Witwatersrand has been extensively studied.[9] Yet few academics have looked at the migrants who, after setting off on their return journey from the Rand, came to be stranded on their way home—the migrants who, in contrast to those of Michael Barrett, did not get to stride home majestically.[10]

Initially, it was envisaged that this paper would deal with the institutional history of Katima Mulilo and Wenela camp in particular. It was intended that the paper would outline the manner in which Wenela camp, on the furthest fringes of the South African empire, became a gateway to South Africa's urban areas and

---

4   Charles van Onselen, *Chibaro: African Mine Labour in Southern Rhodesia 1900–1933* (London, 1976).

5   Although not dealing with the mines of South Africa, important in that he shows the extent to which people moved within southern Africa: William Beinart, 'Cape Workers in German South-West Africa, 1904–1912: Patterns of Migrancy and the Closing of Options on the Southern African Labour Market', Collected Seminar Papers. Institute of Commonwealth Studies, 27, (1981), pp. 48–65. ISSN 0076–0773; William Beinart, 'Transkeian Migrant Workers and Youth Labour on the Natal Sugar Estates, 1918–1940', Collected Seminar Papers. Institute of Commonwealth Studies, 42, (1992), pp. 119–136. ISSN 0076-0773.

6   Patrick Harries, *Work, Culture, and Identity: Migrant Labourers in Mozambique and South Africa, c. 1860–1910* (Portsmouth, NH, 1994).

7   Peter Alexander, 'Culture and Conflicts: Witbank Colliery Life, 1900–1950', University of Johannesburg Sociology and Anthropology Seminar, Wednesday, 14 May 2008.

8   Ruth First, 'The Gold of Migrant Labour', *Africa South in Exile*, vol. 5, no. 3, April–June 1961, pp. 7–31; Peter Warwick, 'African Labour During the South African War, 1899–1902', Collected Seminar Papers. Institute of Commonwealth Studies, 21, (1977), pp. 104–116. ISSN 0076-0773; Richard M. Levin, 'Class Formation, Ideology and Transition in Swaziland', Collected Seminar Papers. Institute of Commonwealth Studies, 37, 1988, pp. 164–175. ISSN 0076-0773; G.E. Stent, 'Some Reflections on Migratory Labour in South Africa', *Theoria, A Journal of Studies*, (1947), pp. 22–27; Baruch Hirson, 'Rural Revolt in South Africa: 1937–1951', Collected Seminar Papers. Institute of Commonwealth Studies, 21, (1977), pp. 115–132. ISSN 0076-0773; David Massey, 'Black Workers' Struggles in the Mines of South Africa, and the Response of Management', *Ufahamu: A Journal of African Studies*, vol. 9, no. 3, (1980), pp. 5–22.

9   Mark Stein, 'Black Trade Unionism During the Second World War: The Witwatersrand Strikes of December 1942, Collected Seminar Papers. Institute of Commonwealth Studies, 26, (1981), pp. 94–102. ISSN 0076-0773.

10   Michael Barrett, '"Walking Home Majestically": Consumption and the Enactment of Social Status Among Labour Migrants from Barotseland, 1935–1965', *The Objects of Life in Central Africa: The History of Consumption and Social Change, 1840–1960* (Leiden, 2013), eds. Marja Hinfelaar, Iva Pesa & Robert Ross. The exception is Warwick's descriptions of

was, in effect, urban South Africa in all of its modernist manifestations. However, the paper has morphed into a work in progress, dealing with the migration of migrants from south Angola and Bulozi via Katima Mulilo to South Africa, migrants who failed to return home at the end of their contracts and who—by force of circumstance and history—came to be stranded in Katima Mulilo, never to return to the lands of their birth. In effect, this paper attempts to examine and provide a context for these men, men who are literally betwixt and between.

Migrant Labour from Western Zambia and Southern Angola

In 1874, two years after the diamond rush centred on Kimberly had started, V.L. Cameron crossed central Africa and described slaves being bought by Lozi from Garanganze.[11] He speculated that some of these men could end up as labourers in the diamond fields in South Africa. Hunter George Westbeech, who, if the evidence provided by Cameron is to be believed, was not averse to trading in slaves, exported 'a large contingent of Africans to work in the newly opened gold mines at Klerksdorp' in the Transvaal in 1888.[12] From at least the early 1900s, thousands upon thousands of young men made their way southwards from Bulozi to the farms and mines of Southern Rhodesia and ultimately the mines of the Witwatersrand.[13]

The defeat of the Boer republics in the South African War (1899–1902) heralded an enormous programme of economic and political reconstruction, in what would become the Union of South Africa, under High Commissioner Sir Alfred Milner, who had established himself in Johannesburg in early 1901. Milner's plans, which emphasized the reconstruction and development of South Africa's mines and agriculture, led to an enormous demand for labour throughout southern Africa.[14] When the South African War began in 1899, the

---

impoverished migrants who walked home following the outbreak of the South African War in 1899: Warwick, 'African Labour', p. 106.

11   Vernon Lovett Cameron, *Across Africa* (London, 1885), p. 390. 'Only a small proportion of the slaves taken by the caravans from Bihé and the West Coast reach Benguella, the greater part, more especially the women, being forwarded to Sekélétu's country in exchange for ivory. And it is not improbable that some of these eventually find their way to the diamond fields among the gangs of labourers taken there by the Kaffirs.'

12   Eugenia W. Herbert, *Twilight on the Zambezi: Late Colonialism in Central Africa* (Basingstoke, 2002), p. 68. As regards Cameron and Westbeech's role in slaving, see Cameron, *Across Africa*, p. 449.

13   G. Caplan, *The Elites of Barotseland 1878–1969* (London, 1970), p. 145.

14   T.R.H. Davenport, *South Africa: A Modern History*, 2nd ed. (Johannesburg, 1978), pp. 148–150.

gold mines employed approximately 90,000 African labourers; by 1910, this had
doubled to 183,793 men, drawn from all over southern Africa.[15] Indeed, so desperate was the demand for labour that, to overcome the shortfall, the Transvaal
Chamber of Mines imported no less than 60,000 indentured Chinese labourers
between 1904 and 1906, at salaries lower than those paid to African labourers.[16]
By 1904, mining had recovered to pre-war production levels and expanded
thereafter, while the value of gold mined rose from £1 million sterling in 1901 to
£32 million sterling in 1910.[17] Nonetheless, the demand for labour remained
high, and the Witwatersrand Native Labour Association (Wenela), founded in
1900 by the Chamber of Mines, actively recruited labour for the mines throughout southern Africa, until its demise in 1978. Wenela was prohibited from
recruiting for mine labour in Zambia only in 1966.[18]

The area that comprised the Zambezi floodplain and its surroundings had long
constituted an area where people had sought refuge from slaving—and where
people had been enslaved.[19] It was an area in which affiliation and association
with the Lozi kingdom had previously provided a modicum of protection and
security from slaving in exchange for labour. With the coming of colonial rule,
new forms of taxation and labour came to be introduced to the region. In lieu of
annual labour pledges on behalf of the Litunga, taxation that could be paid only
in cash came to be introduced and wage labour became the norm. Initially, men
were recruited in the Zambezi Valley by representatives of (i) the Rhodesia Native
Labour Bureau (RNLB), which recruited primarily for the mines and farms of
Southern Rhodesia; (ii) Robert Williams and Company/Tanganyika Concessions
Limited (TCL), which recruited specifically for the mines of Katanga, in southern
Congo; and (iii) a wide variety of independent labour recruiters and touts, whom
Jon Lunn referred to as 'settler contractors'.[20]

---

15   Davenport, *South Africa*, p. 358.
16   Peter Richardson, 'Mobilizing Labour for the South African Gold Mines: The Recruiting
      Operations of the Transvaal Chamber of Mines in South China, 1903–1905', African History:
      postgraduate seminar papers / (University of London. School of Oriental and African
      Studies and Institute of Commonwealth Studies) 1976; Davenport, *South Africa*, p. 357.
17   Davenport, *South Africa*, p. 149.
18   Jonathan Crush, Alan Jeeves & David Yudelman, *South Africa's Labor Empire: A History of
      Black Migrancy to the Gold Mines* (Boulder, 1991).
19   Joseph C. Miller, *Way of Death: Merchant Capitalism and the Angolan Slave Trade*
      (Madison: Wisconsin, 1988); Achim von Oppen, *Terms of Trade and Terms of Trust: The
      History and Contexts of Pre-Colonial Market Production Around the Upper Zambesi and
      Kasai* (Hamburg: Lit Verlag, 1994).
20   Jon Lunn, *Capital and Labour on the Rhodesian Railway System, 1888–1947* (Macmillan,
      1997), refers to these 'settler contractors' in the following manner: 'Relatively little attention

In the 1890s, with the establishment of the German South West African Protectorate, the southern marches of the Lozi kingdom were excised from Bulozi. However, it was not until 1909 that the German empire actually established an on-the-ground presence in the Eastern Caprivi Zipfel.[21] Essentially an enormous triangle of land defined by the Rio Cuando (under its multiple names of Mashi, Linyanti, and Chobe) as it flows south and then northeast to its confluence with the Zambezi, the Eastern Caprivi Zipfel is an enormous area of land that consists of forested Kalahari sands and extensive marshes subject to annual flooding. Not surprisingly, the area was and is host to extensive stocks of wildlife, and the territory was long contested between various powers anxious for control and access to the area's bountiful hunting products. Also known as the Linyanti, the territory has come to form the basis for innumerable hunting and trading legends.[22]

While both the Bulozi and Batawana kingdoms contested access to the Linyanti in the second half of the nineteenth century, numerous European hunters made names for themselves in the area.[23] Frederick Courtney Selous's companion, French, died in a hunting accident in the Linyanti in the 1880s. In 1906, Arnold Hodson (at that stage Assistant Resident Magistrate but later Governor of Sierra Leone) accompanied Resident Commissioner Sir Ralph Williams on a hunting trip to the Linyanti.[24] On this trip Hodson's party came upon a hunting party led by Europeans that had been hunting in the Linyanti, essentially territory subject to imperial Germany, albeit that there was no

---

has been paid to date to the role of the settler contractor in the Rhodesias. Contractors were to be found particularly on the mines, in the building industry and on the railways. The contractor was part of that fluid stratum of the white settler population [...]. Struggling, not always successfully, to establish themselves within the white middle class, these settlers flitted from one activity to another, or combined several at once, depending upon the economic climate and their own inclination' (p. 107).

21   For the intricacies of the German presence in the Eastern Caprivi, see Maria Fisch, *Der Caprivizipfel während der deutschen Zeit, 1890–1914* (Köln: Rüdiger Köppe Verlag, 1996).

22   Hugh Macmillan notes how the establishment of German and British rule 'complicated the Susman brothers' trading relations with people in the two territories where trade had been unregulated'. Hugh Macmillan, *An African Trading Empire: The Story of Susman Brothers & Wulfsohn, 1901–2005* (London: I.B. Tauris, 2005), p. 102.

23   Thomas Tlou, *A History of Ngamiland 1750 to 1906: The Formation of an African State* (Gaborone: Macmillan 1985). Barry C. Morton, *A Social and Economic History of a Southern African Native Reserve: Ngamiland, 1890–1966*, PhD, Department of History Indiana University, 1996.

24   Arnold W. Hodson, *Trekking the Great Thirst: Sport and Travel in the Kalahari Desert* (London: Fisher Unwin, 1912), pp. 148–173.

official German presence in the area.[25] The hunting must have been particularly good, for four years later, in 1910, Hodson guided the highest British official in southern Africa, High Commissioner Lord Selbourne, to the Linyanti, and once again the British officials crossed over and hunted in what was, strictly speaking, German territory.[26]

In 1914, the Eastern Caprivi was occupied by Rhodesian troops, becoming 'the first Allied occupation of enemy territory in the Great War'.[27] Administration was undertaken by the British authorities in Bechuanaland Protectorate, with the area falling under the District Commissioner at Kasane. Throughout the 1920s and early 1930s, the area remained bereft of any form of colonial administration. In 1939, the Native Affairs Department of the Union of South Africa assumed control over the Eastern Caprivi, and Major L.F.W. Trollope was appointed Magistrate and Native Commissioner of the area, which in 1940 was formally declared to be a 'native reserve'.[28] In the same year, Wenela built its airstrip directly adjacent to the ford on the Zambezi at Katima Mulilo.[29]

Wenela

A long line of Africans, neatly dressed in a drill uniform, were drawn up on the airfield perimeter when I arrived. Two Europeans [...] were checking off their names.

These were the new boys for the mines, recruited by the Witwatersrand Native Labour Association Ltd., the organization of the Transvaal Chamber of Mines. Their destination was Francistown in Bechuanaland. From there, they would be taken on the twenty-four-hour train journey to the golden city, Johannesburg.

They had come from Nyasaland, and neighbouring lands, these eager young men. Some of them, from the remoter tribal areas, had turned up for their preliminary interviews in loincloths.

---

25   Hodson, *Trekking the Great Thirst*, pp. 169–171.

26   Hodson, *Trekking the Great thirst*, pp. 264–347.

27   Major L.F.W. Trollope, 'The Eastern Caprivi Zipfel', *The Northern Rhodesia Journal*, no. 2, vol. III, (1956), p. 113.

28   *Ibid*. 114. On Trollope, see J.-B. Gewald, 'Beyond the Last Frontier: Major Trollope and the Eastern Caprivi Zipfel', in: Mirjam de Bruijn & Rijk van Dijk (eds) *The Social Life of Connectivity in Africa* (New York: Palgrave Macmillan, 2012), pp. 81–94.

29   Wolfgang Zeller, 'Danger and Opportunity in Katima Mulilo: A Namibian Border Boomtown at Transnational Crossroads', *Journal of Southern African Studies*, vol. 35, no. 1, (2009), p. 143.

They chattered eagerly, laughing and stamping restlessly. These were the happiest exiles-to-be I had ever seen.

The roar of aircraft engines hushed the din. Over the edges of the airfield, a Dakota circled; it turned in to land, touched down smoothly, and skimmed along the runway until it came to a halt less than a hundred yards from the Africans. They remained motionless, in silent fascination.

The gangway was drawn into position, the door was opened and, shortly, an African in a flashy, striped suit came down the steps of the gangway. On his head he was carrying a handsome tine trunk, decorated with what looked like imitation mother-of-pearl. Another African appeared, another and another—all bearing identical trunks. One carried a guitar, as well.

A long-drawn 'Ah-ah-ah' burst from the watching recruits. Again the babble of voices broke out, the excited shuffling and stamping of feet. They could hardly wait to get on to the Dakota. That was their bird of paradise. What were the long years away in the Transvaal, far from home—so long as they returned with one of those gorgeous trunks, packed with new cloths, imitation jewellery, torches and the like?[30]

From 1936 onwards, Wenela was formally permitted to recruit for 'tropical labour' north of the 22 degrees south latitude.[31] Whereas previously migrants from southern Bulozi had made their own way to the mines of South Africa, a new and highly regulated system that facilitated migration came to be established; and before long, thousands upon thousands of young men were on their way to the mines of South Africa.[32] All over southern Africa, effectively on the outer fringes of the South African empire, a highly sophisticated system of offices, depots, holding stations, and airfields came to be established.[33] Countless officials were dispatched to the furthest reaches of the empire to oversee the recruitment, clothing, feeding, payment, and health of millions of labourers.[34]

30   Don Taylor, *Rainbow on the Zambezi* (London, 1953), pp. 102–103.

31   S. Katzenellenbogen, *South Africa and Southern Mozambique: Labour, Railways, and Trade in the Making of a Relationship* (Manchester, 1982).

32   D. Yudelman & A. Jeeves, 'New Labour Frontiers for Old: Black Migrants to the South African Gold Mines, 1920–85', *Journal of Southern African Studies*, vol. 13, no. 1, (1986), pp. 101–124.

33   Alan H. Jeeves, 'William Gemill and South African Expansion, 1920–1950', paper presented at the University of the Witwatersrand History Workshop, The Making of Class, 9–14 February, 1987.

34   Crush, Jeeves & Yudelman, *South Africa's Labor Empire*. On feeding and Wenela, F.W. Fox, 'How South Africa Became Interested in Nutrition', *S.A. Medical Journal*, (20 April 1963),

Initially, Wenela established its depot at Kazungula to tap the labour from Bulozi and the Zambezi floodplain, but this was soon to be overshadowed by the Wenela depot established in the Eastern Caprivi on the ford across the Zambezi formed by the Katima Mulilo rapids.[35] These depots, and northern Bechuanaland in particular:

> [...] became a central corridor for WNLA operations extending into adjacent parts of Northern Rhodesia, Angola, and South West Africa. WNLA's many depots, fleets of passenger lorries, and network of airports gave the agency a presence in the region which, at least initially, dominated that of governments. New villages grew up along its routes; its motor lorries provided the only transport and mail service in many areas.[36]

Within the complicated negotiations that had preceded the establishment of a Wenela depot at Katima Mulilo, it was agreed that labour from the Ovambo and Kavango regions in northern Namibia was reserved for the South West African Native Labour Association (SWANLA), which recruited labour for the mines and farms of Namibia.[37] It was agreed that SWANLA would recruit as far east as Andara, at the beginning of the Caprivi Strip, and that Wenela would recruit labour in the Eastern Caprivi. Nonetheless, the establishment by Wenela of a depot and airfield at Mohembo on the Kavango, directly to the south of Andara and almost immediately adjacent the Caprivi Strip, indicates the stiff competition that existed for labour.[38]

---

pp. 395–398; on health care and Wenela, see Karen Jochelson, 'Tracking Down the Treponema: Patterns of Syphilis in South Africa, 1880–1940', paper presented at the University of the Witwatersrand History Workshop, Structure and Experience in the making of Apartheid, 6–10 February 1990.

35   For a description of the Wenela depot at Kazungula and its impact on local societies, see the work of Thomas Larson—in particular, T.J. Larson, *From Oxford to the Okavango* (London, 2003).

36   Crush, Jeeves & Yudelman, *South Africa's Labor Empire*, p. 45.

37   Allan D. Cooper, 'The Institutionalization of Contract Labour in Namibia', *Journal of Southern African Studies*, vol. 25, no. 1, (March 1999), pp. 121–138; R.J. Gordon, *Mines, Masters and Migrants: Life in a Namibian Compound* (Johannesburg, 1977); K. Gottschalk, 'South African Labour Policy in Namibia 1915–1975', *South African Labour Bulletin*, vol. 4, 1–2 (January–February 1978); R. Moorsom, 'Migrant Workers and the Formation of SWANLA, 1900–1926', *South African Labour Bulletin*, vol. 4, no. 1–2, (January–February 1978).

38   A form of competition that was at times exploited by those who wished to enter into either the South African or Namibian labour system. Although the author does not deal with Zambia or Namibia, he describes similar processes in Zimbabwe, Mozambique, and

The current settlement of Katima Mulilo in Namibia is situated directly opposite the town of Sesheke in Zambia. The Namibian border post between the two states bears the name Wenela, an indication of the fact that the administrative offices developed on the basis of the Wenela facilities already in existence there.[39]

> The Wenela depot at Katima Mulilo is unique as the buildings are in two territories apart from the bungalows. The administrative offices are in Barotseland [...], while the medical examination room lies about a mile inside the Caprivi.[40]

The initial quota agreed upon with the Northern Rhodesian government was for 3,500 men per year. By 1959, this had risen to 5,000 per year for the whole of Barotseland; and by the time of independence in 1964, this had risen to 6,000 men.[41] This number did not include the men who made their own way to the depot at Mohembo, Katima Mulilo, or Kazangula and is likely to have been much higher in real terms. Wenela ceased formal operations in Barotseland in late 1966, after the Zambian government prohibited the recruitment of labour for the South African mines. Although formal recruitment had ceased in Bulozi, migrants still continued to make their way to the Wenela recruitment depots.

Many see migrant labour, and in particular the sojourn of young men in the mines, as a process that involves a major social transformation for the migrants involved. For many, engaging in migrant labour was a way of becoming an adult; it was, in effect, an initiation into manhood. Michael Barrett noted that the goods with which the returning migrants returned were the 'material culture of the industrial world', which 'constituted a focal point in the social and spiritual negotiations between men and women, old and young' during the social transformation of the migrants:

Botswana: David Johnson, 'Clandestine Migration in South Central Africa', Collected Seminar Papers. Institute of Commonwealth Studies, 40. 1990. pp. 1–11. ISSN 0076-0773. This point was recently made and convincingly argued by Andrew MacDonald, *Colonial Trespassers in the Making of South Africa's International Borders, 1900 to c. 1950,* PhD thesis, St. John's College, Cambridge, August 2012.

39   For a concise overview of the history of Katima Mulilo as well as references to the relevant literature, see Wolfgang Zeller, 'Danger and Opportunity in Katima Mulilo: A Namibian Border Boomtown at Transnational Crossroads', *Journal of Southern African Studies*, vol. 35, no. 1, (2009), pp. 133–154.

40   Jonathan Whitby, *Bundu Doctor* (London, 1961), p. 172.

41   Barrett, 'Walking Home', pp. 93–113.

In particular, European clothes and accessories were the goods most coveted and admired. They were also the vital props through which migrants, partly by enacting ostentatious homecomings to their villages, signalled a change in their personal status.[42]

The young men who stepped off the plane at Katima Mulilo had become adults, insofar as they had not been so before, and they bore with them the material goods that signalled this transformation. Elsewhere in Africa, but equally applicable here, in 1933 a commission of enquiry 'itemized' a list of articles contained in the kits of workers returning from the mines. Included were the following: women's dresses, women's head-clothes, shirts, shorts, trousers, singlets, tennis shoes, sweaters, cardigans, socks, ties, sun helmets, caps, puttees, sheets, towels, handkerchiefs, blankets, mirrors, enamel dishes and mugs, and so forth.[43] The researchers also referred to bicycles, gramophone players, and sewing machines being among the goods normally purchased by returning migrants.

The voluntary nature of much of the migration is partly explained by the comparative material wealth that could be acquired through working in the mines.[44] Barrett argues that by the 1940s, 'going to South Africa or Southern Rhodesia for long spells of wage labour had by then been fully incorporated into the expected life career of rural men'.[45]

The reaction of the average repatriate was that of the experienced traveller. He had already written of his first flight to his family, and as a consequence his prestige would offer incentive to others also anxious to gain importance in the village, for they would have a better pick of the women on their return! Now the repatriate would be an important person in the village; he would be able to elaborate on his adventures to the envy of others. He got into the plane, his luggage, bicycle, and other belongings having been loaded for him by the 'menials' on the airfield. All he had to do was to sit down, and this he did with a superior look on his face.[46]

[...]

---

42   Barrett, 'Walking Home', p. 96.
43   J. Merle Davis, *Modern Industry and the African* (London, 1933), pp. 401–403.
44   A point made very forcefully by Wiseman Chijere Chirwa, '"No Teba...Forget Teba": The Plight of Malawian Ex-Migrant Workers to South Africa, 1988–1994', *International Migration Review*, vol. 31, no. 3, (Autumn 1997), pp. 628–654.
45   Barrett, 'Walking Home', p. 98.
46   Jonathan Whitby, *Bundu Doctor* (London, 1961), p. 153.

Though the average tribesman is fond of bright colours he is also practical in his purchases. First of all he will select the box into which his articles are to be put with great care. The box may be of wood or steel, but both are painted in striking colours, those of the wooden box being more decorative; I noticed that red, yellow and green seemed to be favoured most, though two colours predominate: red and yellow. If one cares to go to the little Syrian shop behind the Wenela compound in Eloff Street, Johannesburg, one can watch men selecting their purchases. They are never in a hurry, and they know what they want.[47]

But what of those men who, for whatever reason, chose not to continue home and chose instead to remain stuck halfway between home and their former places of work?[48]

Stuck in Katima Mulilo

Ja, well you know how it goes: I wanted to go home, but I couldn't. I owed money, and I had lost money, so I stayed.... I did not have to speak Afrikaans; and anyway, once the war came I had an excuse and I remained....

    KLAAS, KATIMA MULILO, 22 July 2013

I am an old man now; I am a Namibian; I know everybody here, and they know I do not come from here, but now I am from here and I am here to stay....

    NDINGO, KATIMA MULILO, 23 July 2013

Look, I am not some sort of bushman. I know Johannesburg; I have been to Cape Town; I know the world. Ek bly hierso, dis my plek hierdie. ['This is my home now, this is my life.']

    MATTHEW, KATIMA MULILO, 22 July 2013

Klaas, Ndingo, and Matthew are now men in their 60s, who live in the sprawling border town of Katima Mulilo in northeastern Namibia. Once they were

---

47   Jonathan Whitby, *Bundu Doctor* (London, 1961), p. 154.
48   Wiseman Chirwa has written about the despair and despondency that developed among Malawian migrant workers following the ending of recruitment for the South African mines in Malawi. Chirwa, 'Plight of Malawian Ex-Migrant Workers'.

young men from Zambia and Angola, who walked to Wenela depots and flew to Francistown and travelled by train on to Egoli. They did not die in the mines of the Rand, but nor did they return to their homes; instead, they chose to break off their journey home in Katima Mulilo and to stay on in this town at the furthest reaches of the South African state. History and time have passed them by: once they were great men who had worked in the mines in South Africa; now they are old men who meet at the market in Katima Mulilo and speak to one another in smatterings of Fanagalo. Their stories of the mines are stories they share among themselves and the visiting researcher. Among the people they see around them, the majority know nothing of their past and shared adventures.

Matthew, a devout Catholic, was born in Angola and speaks Portuguese. He claims to have worked with Nature Conservation as a game scout during the South African War, yet his conversations with me often switched into Afrikaans and jargon that I associate strongly with the SADF. Thus, at times he spoke of 'tiffies' (South African Army slang for technical corps) and mentioned construction and road building in what is today the West Caprivi Game Park—an area which during the war was the rear base for SADF and UNITA operations in southeastern Angola. His frequent and vehement denials of being a 'Boesman' implied to me that he had been employed by the SADF as an overseer of labour drawn from among the refugees that had fled the fighting in southern Angola after 1974. Matthew currently lives with his children in Katima Mulilo and sells metal wares at the market.

Klaas suggested that he came from Lukena, north of Kalabo in Zambia, on the border with Angola. He stated that he had lost most of his earnings in the good life associated with his stay in the mines at Western Deep Levels. Gambling debts and protection payments depleted his earnings. At times, Klaas claimed that his trunk, containing the bulk of his goods acquired at the mines, had been stolen on the train *en route* from Johannesburg. Whatever the case, Klaas returned to Katima Mulilo but did not cross over into Zambia; instead, he came to be employed as a cook with the South African Army and later the South African Navy, which had established a base on the Zambezi River on the site of the Wenela depot at Katima Mulilo in the early 1970s.[49] Currently, Klaas lives near Katima Mulilo on a small holding near the river, where he survives from fishing.

---

49 The South African Navy deployed a Marine Company that operated out of Wenela on the Zambezi in 1981. Helmoed-Römer Heitman, *Modern African Wars Vol. 3: South-West Africa* (Botley, 1991), p. 16.

Ndingo came from southern Angola as a refugee in the late 1960s / early 1970s. He was recruited by Wenela at Mohembo and worked on a mine called Ventersdiep, situated near Ventersdorp. Ndingo speaks Oshiwambo fluently and currently works as a assistant cleaner at the University of Namibia Caprivi campus.

It is clear that Klaas did not return to his home village because, as he said, 'I owed money and I had lost money, so I stayed.' Ndingo and Matthew were both prevented from returning home because of the 40 years of war that swept through the area, beginning in the early 1960s. The partial peace in southern Angola, brought about by the death of Jonas Savimbi in 2002 and the subsequent military and electoral defeat of UNITA, came too late for these two men—in addition to which it is probable that Matthew's likely deep involvement with the SADF will always prevent him from returning home.

From the early 1900s thousands upon thousands of young men have made the long journey southwards from southern Angola and southern Bulozi to the mines of the South African Witwatersrand in search of employment and reward and in anticipation of a better life at home. Although most men eventually returned home to 'walk majestically', there were those who never returned home. Many of these died, or chose to remain in the urban areas of South Africa. However, there were also those who very nearly made it home but chose instead to remain in Katima Mulilo. This contribution indicates that personal choices, coupled with historical developments in southern Africa— in particular the Angolan civil war and the wars of liberation for South Africa and Namibia—effectively prevented a number of migrants from returning home. Instead, they became part of a new urban centre that developed on the furthest reaches of the South African empire.

CHAPTER 5

'Trapped' in the North: Southern Migrants in Northern Nigeria, 1908–1970s

Shehu Tijjani Yusuf

The Development of the Railway System in Northern Nigeria

Northern Nigeria, which is the focus of this chapter, was that geographical region that fell under British rule from 1900. The region is peopled by Hausa and Fulani and other smaller ethnic groups. It formerly comprised the Sokoto caliphate and other polities. At the turn of the century, when the British imposed their rule on northern Nigeria, the region was considered backward, characterized by an agrarian economy and primitive transport systems based on human and animal transport. The region was vast, with a land mass covering more than half of the whole country combined, but it had no access to the sea. Its condition was so precarious that it barely survived on annual grants. It was to this underdeveloped territory that Britain looked when it was faced by a raw cotton crisis at the beginning of the twentieth century (Hopkins 1973: 160–161). British interest in the region was imperialist-motivated to transport cotton for its metropolitan industries. Right from 1900, when Lugard, the High Commissioner (1900–1906), hoisted the Union Jack at Lokoja, he was concerned with how to develop the region for maximum exploitation by his home country. He realized very early on that unless a modern transport system was provided, the economic exploitation of the region could not be achieved.

Modern transport was considered essential not only to open up the Northern Territories to British trade, but also to extend the government's control inland. Right from the outset, the call for improved transport, most especially railway, came from the authority in the north and not from private entrepreneurs as in the south. Because of the advantages it has over other transport modes, railway was considered the best means for developing the country. Lugard proposed the construction of a railway from Baro to Kano. Railways, as W.W. Rostow (1960: 180) pointed out, were the single most important cause of industrialization in Europe and the Americas. Railway has the advantage of discounting space, and it can do the work of a thousand carriers without showing any signs of wear (Lugard 1922: 6; Hopkins 1973: 192).

The approval for the construction of the line was sanctioned by Parliament in 1907, and this laid the basis for railway development in the Northern

Provinces. It authorized the construction of a pioneer line from Baro to Kano. It also sanctioned the extension of the Lagos Government Railway—which was built by the Lagos Colony in 1899 and was the first railway in Nigeria—to meet the Baro–Kano Railway to form a through connection to the coast (Yusuf 2015: 27–31).

Labour Recruitment and Railway Construction

Following approval of the rail line by the imperial authority, real construction did not commence immediately as the labour required for building the line had to be mobilized first. African labour was required for the tedious tasks of surveying, bush clearing, and earth and construction works. The work was conducted through forced labour, recruited through the local authorities of the districts where the rail line passed. When labour was required, the European political officers instructed the local authorities on the number of workers required. The local authorities in turn provided the labourers. Forced labour was adopted on the northern railway partly because of a labour shortage in the north, partly because northerners were unwilling to work for *nasara* ('the whiteman'), and partly because it was the best way to build a cheap railway (Tamuno 1965: 33; Anjorin 1970: 11; Oyemakinde 1974: 317; Mason 1978: 60). The labourers were supposed to work for a few weeks, supervised and paid directly by the European political officers, after which they were to be replaced by another group. This, according to the colonial authority, would save them from exploitation; but in practice it exposed them to exploitation, as they worked longer than required and were paid a paltry sum (*ibid.*).

This labour recruitment method differed from the one employed on the Lagos Railway and its extension northward. Whereas a contract method was applied for the Lagos Railway, in which private contractors supplied the labour, the local authorities acted as the contractors in the north. Instead of allow-ing labour to voluntarily come to the site, they raided villages along the rail line to recruit labour for surveying, bush clearing, and earth and construction works. Previously, it was claimed that reactions to the labour recruitment on the railway did not go beyond ordinary flight (Anjorin 1970; Mason 1978: 76). New evidence from a *wakar diga* (song of *diga* or railway), a 70-verse poem composed by Aliyu Dansidi, the emir of Zazzau (ruled 1902–1924), indicates that the reaction was rather a mixed one of *tsoro* ('apprehension and fear') and *mamaki* ('awe') (Northern Nigeria Publishing Company 1980: 28–29). As has been argued elsewhere, the labour recruitment, the movement of construction materials, and the aura which marked the construction of the railway provoked far more mixed reactions than have been previously recognized. This is because people did not understand the railway's import. However, as soon as they discovered its benefits in the form of wages, they quickly participated in the work to acquire the colonial currency (Yusuf 2014: 153–214; Yusuf 2015: 35–40).

In addition to the forced labour employed on the railway, free labour and domestic servants, as well as prisoners whose sentences were commuted to hard labour, also found employment on the railway construction (Pedraza 1960: 105; Lovejoy and Hogendorn 1993: 219–231; Yusuf 2014: 154; Yusuf 2015: 41). Previously, it has been assumed that only men worked on the line. New evidence—the *wakar diga* mentioned above—suggests that women and children were also employed on the railway (Northern Nigeria Publishing Company 1980: 28–29). The labourers were of mixed ethnicity, comprising Hausa, Nupe, Gwari, and Yoruba. This was the beginning of southern Nigerian migrancy to the north. This is not to suggest the Yoruba were not in the north before this time, but railway work and the opportunities it presented brought them more and more to the north in search of a livelihood, contrary to Wale Oyemainde's (1974: 315) claim that the Yoruba were not employed on the railway's construction. The same source he used indicates that the work 'originally start[ed] with about 1,200 men comprising Yoruba, Hausa and Nupe'. There is no indication to suggest the Yoruba were from the Northern Provinces[1] (Further Correspondence 1909: 134). The Ibo did not feature in railway construction until later. In 1908–1911,[2] 1911–1914,[3] and the 1920s–1930s,[4] railway construction continued to draw large pools of labour from the communities along the rail line and beyond. As Wale Oyemakinde noted, working on the rail line provided able-bodied men with the opportunity to earn the colonial currency. Railway work not only facilitated the circulation of the colonial currency; it also made the labourers independent.

Real construction did not commence until 1908. The construction began from two opposite directions, namely from Baro on the Niger and from Ilorin where the Lagos line was being extended northward to link up with the Baro–Kano line. Construction followed closely on surveying and earth work. The

---

1   There were Yoruba speakers in Ilorin Province in northern Nigeria.

2   The first railway in the north, Baro–Kano railway, was constructed during this period.

3   The Bauchi Light Railway, a branch of the Baro–Kano railway which stretches from Zaria to the Bauchi tin mines, was constructed during this period.

4   There was a massive expansion of the railway system during the post-World War I period. The branch lines from Zaria to Kaura Namoda and the Kano–Nguru railways were constructed during this period. The extension of the Eastern Railway to Kaduna was also accomplished at this time.

construction was completed in 1911, earlier than was anticipated. The whole work spanned a period of three years and eight months.

The completion of the railway was a watershed in the socio-economic and cultural history of northern Nigeria. The railway brought radical reduction in travel time and increased mobility much more than has previously been recognized. For instance, the railway shortened the travel time between Lagos and Kano to three days. Previously, such a journey would have lasted about three weeks by foot and animal transport. The railway linked the north and south together and increased spatial and physical interactions between them more than was possible in the past.

The railway also stimulated agricultural production and trade, with multiplier effects on the local economy. Although the railway had been constructed to transport cotton, northern Nigerians unexpectedly discovered that it was more profitable to grow groundnuts and other crops rather than the officially favoured cotton crop. For instance, groundnuts could finance tax payments, whereas cotton could not. Within a short period after completing the line, groundnut exports rose from almost nothing in 1911 to 21,900 tons in 1913. By 1914, the export traffic had exceeded the capacity of the railway (Hogendorn 1978: 52, 92–128). The export trade also stimulated employment and commercial opportunities, which attracted a large pool of migrants from the southern part of the country to the north. From 1912 through the 1960s, the export boom, the expansion of the railway system, and the attendant opportunities it presented continued to attract migrant labour to the new commercial and administrative centres which emerged on the rail lines in the north.

Labour Migration and the Road to Prosperity

The completion of the railway opened up many opportunities for employment in the colonial service and the commercial firms. It also provided opportunities for commercial ventures, which attracted migrants from the south and beyond to the railway centres in the north. During this period of increased globalization and mobility, the railway offered adventurous migrants the opportunity to travel and participate in an extensive cultural interaction. The existence of railway stations, and the European firms that came in the wake of the railway and other colonial services, meant that more and more labourers were required to fill the vacancies available in the north. A good Western education and technical expertise were required to secure employment in these organizations. The migrants came with 'cultural capital', a set of skills and educational and technical expertise (Oshin 2004: 118; Bako 2006: 18–20; Yusuf 2015: 135).

At the time of the completion of the rail line to Kano, there was an acute scarcity of labour in the north, and northern Nigeria did not have the required labour to fill its vacant positions. As Ahmed Bako noted:

> [...] the question of finding clerks, accountants, labourers, and other cat-
> egories of workers for both government department and the commercial
> firms [was immediate and paramount]. Technical personnel were [also]
> required to operate the railway line and [...] [the] social service depart-
> ments [...].
>
> BAKO 2006: 18–19

As the general manager of Nigeria Railway pointed out, the northerners 'did not possess the necessary [Western] education to enter even the lowest grades' (Oshin 2004: 119). Like the railway, other colonial services and commercial firms faced similar challenges. They were able to meet their initial manpower requirements by recruiting labourers from among the southern migrants and foreigners in the north. The problem was rooted in northern Nigeria's late contact with the British, missionaries, and Western education. The southern authority did not face the same problem, owing to the existence of Western-educated elites of both Nigerians and non-Nigerians (Bako 2006: 19). The southern government's efforts in education were always complemented by Christian missionaries, who established the earliest schools, while the north-ern authority restricted missionary activity until the 1930s. The first elementary school in the north was not established until 1914 (Ayandele 1979: 159–160; Bako 2006: 18–19). It was in response to the various livelihood opportunities that the north became a 'magnet' to adventurous migrants from the south.

The migrants came in three waves. The first generation were those who came to work with the railway and in the colonial civil service. These groups were predominantly Yoruba from southwestern Nigeria and immigrant workers from neighbouring countries who moved to the new administrative and commercial centres on the rail line, such as Kaduna, Zaria, Gimi, Madobi, and Kano. By 1914, Kaduna had emerged as a transit junction for the Lagos–Kano and the Eastern Railway that was being extended northwards from Port Harcourt (Oshin 2004: 109–110).The second generation of migrants were those who came in the 1920s, following the post-war economic boom, the expansion of the railway system in the north, and the intensification of the activities of the commercial firms. This group, as was the first, was mixed. The extension of the Eastern Railway to Kaduna in 1927 and the completion of the Benue Bridge in the 1930s facili-tated the movement of Igbo to the north. The economic dislocation of the 1930s, the intensification of the activity of the commercial firms, and the scarcity of cultivable land in the south brought more and more southerners to the north (Udo 1970: 417–418; Magbeafulu 2003: 26–27; Oshin 2004: 112; Bako 2005: 36). The railway provided them with an outlet to move in their hundreds. During this period of increased mobility, Kaduna became a major railway junction and the largest transit exchange point whence migrants from the western and eastern part of the country entered different parts of the north (Oshin 2004: 112). The railway towns and commercial centres that emerged along the rail line became the destination and transit points for these migrants.

For many of the migrants, this was their first sojourn outside their home towns. These were characteristically young men seeking new frontiers in the emerging colonial economy. Labour migration, as Reuben Udo noted (1970: 124), is selective in terms of age and sex. Although women engaged in migration, their proportion was insignificant compared with their male counterparts, because of the cultural practice of confining women to the home and also because of the Christian notion of women as the weaker sex (Rogers 1980: 30–40). Field research conducted across the railway towns between Kano and Zaria revealed that migrants heard about the opportunities in their new homes through migration networks. These networks, as Arango pointed out (2000: 291), are interpersonal ties that connect migrants with their friends and fellow countrymen at home.

Migration networks reduce the cost and uncertainty of migration, providing prospective migrants with support and assistance by way of information, financial assistance, and accommodation and also by linking them to employers (*ibid.*). For instance, a Yoruba informant, Theophillus Adeyinka Shittu, commented that his father, Samuel Shittu, a railway worker, came to Gimi in the 1940s on the advice of a younger brother who himself was living in Zaria City. Before he came to Gimi he had lived at Beji, a small railway town in Nupe Province.[5] Another informant, Innocent Opufou, an Ijaw man from the old Eastern Nigeria (now South-South Nigeria), commented that his father, Wellman Warri Opufou, came to Gimi in 1939 on the advice of an elder brother, T.E. Opufou, who was working with the London and Kano firm (L&K) at Dustin Wai, another railway town south of Zaria. The elder brother relocated to Gimi, having secured employment with Messrs John Holt in 1938. Mr. Wellman secured employment with the United African Company (UAC), while his other brother, E.C. Opufou, became a Licensed Buying Agent (LBA) in the 1940s, through the help of the elder brother.[6] As Arango noted (2000: 291), migration

---

5 E-mail communication with Theophillus, January 2012.
6 E-mail communication with Innocent, July 2012.

networks can serve as social capital insofar as they permit access to other goods of economic significance, such as employment or higher wages. Within three decades of the opening of the railway to Kano and the expansion of the line, the migrant populations had increased significantly through migration and natural increase.

This population influx, with its attendant problems, was accompanied by measures from the colonial state to segregate the migrants into special locations known as *sabon gari* ('new town'/'migrant quarters') and *unguwan tasha* ('railway settlement'), as was the case in Kwankwaso, Gimi, and Likoro.[7] These quarters were originally conceived for housing all 'natives' and 'non-natives' working with the colonial civil service and the commercial firms. The practice across the north was such that the quarters were settled mainly by southerners and northerners. Previously, it had been assumed that such quarters were established to protect Islam and the indigenous Hausa population, but recent studies by Ahmed Bako have disputed this claim. According to Bako (2005: 469–477; 2006: 1–9), the fact that the quarters were not exclusively settled by Christians or southerners, but rather by both Christians and Muslims and included Hausa, has weakened the claim. The quarters had a life of their own, as they were administered by representatives of the migrants. Some of the quarters, such as the *sabon gari* in Kano, Zaria, and Madobi, were established as independent village units, with their own chiefs appointed by the colonial authority (Bako 2006: 78; Yusuf 2010: 140–141; Yusuf 2015: 138–139).

Socio-Economic Basis of Diaspora Community

The migrant population engaged in various economic activities, which can be categorized into three types. The first category comprised the colonial civil service, such as the railway, post office, and native administration, and also included the commercial firms. This migrant group were the educated few, often products of mission schools in the south and the Middle Belt, and also the uneducated who, because of their technical expertise, were employed on the railway as permanent way workers. The railway was the main industry in which the migrants were engaged, for it was the main employer of labour in Nigeria during the colonial and post-colonial periods.

---

7   The railway settlements should not be confused with railway quarters. The settlements were for migrants, while the quarters were for railway workers.

The second category were commercial or produce traders, who purchased produce and resold it to the commercial trading firms. These were mostly independent traders, some of whom had worked for the commercial firms as clerks and sometimes as middlemen. Having worked for some time, they saved money to start their own businesses. For instance, Michael Nwankwo, an Ibo from Eastern Nigeria, came to Madobi in the 1920s. He worked as a clerk with Messrs John Holt in Madobi. After saving enough money, he resigned to start his own produce trade. By the 1940s, Nwankwo established his own firm (Nwankwo Ltd), which suggests that the produce trade was lucrative. In the 1950s and 1960s, he was the most prominent produce dealer in Madobi and Kura district (Yusuf 2015: 144–145; Yusuf 2010: 129, 148).

The Opufous mentioned earlier were another household name in Gimi and environs in the 1940s, 1950s, and 1960s. The three brothers first worked with European commercial firms, before saving money to go into the produce trade. For instance, T.E. Opufou and E.C. Opufou first worked with Messrs John Holt as clerks before becoming its LBAS in the 1950s (NAK ZarProf MKT vol. 1). Similarly, in Dangora, a Yoruba man, Abdu Rauf Fashola, started as an ordinary produce buyer and later went on to become a major produce buyer in Kiru District in the 1950s and 1960s. Some of the produce traders also combined produce trade with livestock trade. In addition to the produce trade, many engaged in the trading of consumable goods, such as foodstuffs, cosmetics, and textiles, as well as livestock (Yusuf 2015: 140–149). The third migrant group were artisans who were involved in such trades as tailoring, photography, and goldsmithing (*ibid.*). Despite the attempt by the colonial authority to isolate them into a rigid compartment, their economic activities brought them into direct contact with the host communities, a development which was bound to erode social and official barriers. The increased cash returns in the produce trade placed more cash at the disposal of the migrants, which also influenced their upward social mobility. Although not everyone prospered, many did make money and invested it in their children's education, social networks, and landed properties such as houses and shops in the communities. Some of their social lives were characterized by upward social mobility, to the extent that their names appeared on the wealthy individual tax list (KSHCB KanProf 1/11/11; KSHCB KanProf 1/11/13).

The migrants did not lose touch with home and maintained contact through the home town associations. These associations were established in response to the problems of adjustment to the new environment. They also functioned as channels through which monetary remittances were sent home or invested in development projects at home. Although the remittances were rarely seen physically, the evidence indicates that they were sent through the postal agencies which they themselves had helped to establish (NAK P &T/3; NAK KanProf 4705; KSHCB R. 518; NAK ZarProf 1923/S.1).

In the 1960s, many southerners fled from the north owing to the pogrom against the Igbo. As the evidence from the countryside between Kano and Zaria indicates, there were no attacks in most places, but the passing of fleeing Igbos on trains, the rumours, and also the fear that thugs were coming to attack them caused many to flee from the conflict zones to their homeland. The travails of southerners during and after the crisis have elicited a fair amount of attention in the literature and so require only a comment here.[8] By the time they returned at the end of the civil war they found that the vacuum created by their absence had been filled by indigenous people. By this time also, the export trade and the railway were in serious jeopardy (Douglas 2002; Mgbeafulu 2003: 55–67; Bako 2006: 97–102).

'Trapped' in the Diaspora

Despite the collapse of export trade and the railway system in the 1970s, coupled with the economic recession of the 1980s, the incessant ethno-religious crises, and the challenges of citizenship rights southerners faced in the north, many of them preferred to remain in the north rather than go back home. Although, as noted earlier, many went back home or relocated elsewhere and some died, many were 'trapped'. To be trapped is to be unable to move or escape as a result of an obstruction or dangerous situation.[9] In the case of the southern migrants in northern Nigeria, they were trapped not by danger or obstruction or economic misfortunes, but by familial connection, attachment to place, and the economic prosperity and opportunities in the north. Migrants were lured and held by these factors, despite the challenges they faced.

The frequent ethno-religious crises which occurred in the north since the 1960s have robbed many southern migrants of their properties and hard-earned money, depleting their economic fortunes. Commenting on the travails of the Igbos during the 1970s, Mathias Chinonyere Mgbeafulu pointed out that their landed properties '[...] were confiscated as "abandoned property" and shared [...] as war booty' (Mgbeafulu 62), although some got their properties

---

8   See for instance, A. Douglas, *Poison and Medicine: Ethnicity, Power, and Violence in a Nigerian City, 1966 to 1986* (Portsmouth: Heinemann, 2002); A. Bako, *Sabon Gari: A History of Immigrants and Inter-Group Relations in the 20th Century* (Sokoto: Usmanu Danfodiyo University Press, 2006).

9   http://www.collinsdictionary.com/dictionary/english/trapped.

back after a long time and some were compensated by the government. Those who were unable to get their property returned were left impoverished. The frequency of ethno-religious crises in the north has caused misfortune to many, who instead of returning home decided to stay on in the north rather than go home as failures.

The story of Michael Nwankwo is a pathetic one. Before the Nigerian civil war, he was one of the prominent produce traders in Madobi. As described earlier, he had a produce firm which provided employment to many locals, to whom he advanced cash to buy the produce. Besides the produce trade, he had a chain of businesses, such as beer parlours and provision stores in *sabon gari* in Madobi. When the war broke out in the 1960s, Nwankwo fled, like other Igbo in the north, even though there were no attacks in Madobi. By the time he returned at the end of the war, he had lost all his money. The people he advanced cash to could not account for it and many had disappeared altogether. Although he sold most of his landed properties in Madobi to recoup his losses, the amount realized was very small, as prices in rural areas were much lower than in the city. The produce trade which was the source of his livelihood had declined and had been taken over by the indigenous people. Nwankwo felt he could not go back home. Though his children managed to take him home on many occasions, he always returned to Madobi after a while. He died in his home town in the south in 1980s during one such trip (Yusuf 2015: 148).

As evidence indicates, some were trapped because of their familial linkages and attachment to their new home. For instance, a Yoruba man, Abdul Rahimi Ogunlade from Lagos, came to work with the railway in Madobi in the 1920s. He raised a family in Madobi through a wife he married from the locality. Owing to his marriage affiliation and popularity, he was officiated as the village head of the *sabon gari* village unit in Madobi in 1935. Ogunlade died in the 1950s, and since then his children and grandchildren have continued to live in Kano and beyond, as another generation of migrants who perceive Madobi as 'their home'. The children have become linguistically and culturally integrated not only into the Madobi community but also into mainstream Hausa society, owing to their maternal linkage. Some of the children have even held political positions in Kano.[10] To date, the Rahims are still in Kano and they maintain their link with Madobi, their matrilineal home (Yusuf 2010: 144; Yusuf 2015: 138–139, 152–153).

---

10   For instance, among his children were the late Abdu Abdul Rahim, who was appointed Commissioner for Finance in Kano State during the Second Republic (1979–1983), and Alhaji Usman Abdurrahim, Registrar at Kano State University of Science and Technology.

At a time when many southerners were fleeing from the north because of the crises of the 1960s and 1970s,[11] Malam Laraba (as she is fondly called) refused to flee. Laraba is a wife to the Wellman Opufou mentioned earlier. She stated that she has been living in Gimi since the 1940s, when she came to join her husband. Although there were no attacks in Gimi, many southerners, including her husband, fled, but she did not because, according to her, she has a strong attachment to Gimi: 'We have no other home than Gimi.' Laraba, now advanced in age, still lives at Gimi Tasha (the migrant quarters in Gimi). Her husband, also now aged, lives with their eldest son, who teaches at the Polytechnic in Zaria. Three of their daughters have converted to Islam and were married to indigenous people.[12]

Many who fled during the civil war returned to continue their lives after the war and have not looked back since. Samuel Shittu, mentioned earlier, was one such returnee. He came to work with the railway in Gimi in the 1940s. After retiring from the railway, he lived in Gimi with his family until his demise some years ago. Samuel's children continued to live in Gimi, until his wife was forced to relocate to Offa a few years ago, owing to old age and pressure from siblings. Samuel's daughter was also married to a local, and she still lives there despite losing her husband. Although the Shittus are from Offa in Kwara State, they consider Gimi as their 'first home'. According to Theophillus Adeyinka Shittu, Gimi is home to them; and wherever they go, they must return there. Theophillus now lives in the UK, but he still maintain contacts with Gimi even from faraway Europe.[13]

For many, however, it was economic prosperity that trapped them, as Alhaji Abdul Fatai Tijjani, a native of Ede in Osun State, remarked. He came to Mallam Madori in Jigawa State in the 1970s. At that time, Mallam Madori was a bustling railway town. Alhaji Tijjani was attracted to the town by the economic potential spurred by the railway. Immediately after he arrived, he went into the bakery business, and since then he has not looked back. In April 2010, when he was interviewed by Tafferua Ujora, a journalist with the *Daily Trust Newspaper*, Alhaji Tijjani was the chief baker in Mallam Madori (*Daily Trust Newspaper* 2010: 32).When he arrived in the 1970s, he married a Hausa woman, with whom he had three children—although he no longer lives with this woman and has

---

11   For details on the pogrom against Igbo in the north, see: A. Douglas, *Poison and Medicine*.
12   Interview with Malama Laraba Wellman, 25 May 2011.
13   E-mail communication with Theophillus Shittu, January 2013. Dr Shittu is an architect by profession and lectures at a university in the UK. I came to know him in 2012, when he wrote me an e-mail that he was born and brought up in Gimi and that he had discovered, while researching on the Internet, that I was researching the history of Gimi.

since married a Yoruba woman. Alhaji Tijjani rarely visits home, and his business is running well. For him, migration is a permanent and not a temporary objective (*ibid.*).

Conclusion

This chapter has demonstrated how the railways stimulated movement of southern Nigerian migrants to the north. The migrants were attracted by employment opportunities in the colonial civil service, commercial firms, and trade. As was noted, the migrants concentrated in those centres with greater economic opportunities. After a long sojourn, spanning many years, some had died, many went back home, and many others decided to stay behind in the north, despite the difficulties and challenges. As the chapter has attempted to show, many of those who remained did so not because of danger or economic misfortunes, but because of familial connections, attachment to place, and economic prosperity.

References

Primary Sources
Interviews
Interview with Malama Laraba Wellman, Gimi Dabosa, 25 May 2011.
E-mail communication with Dr. Theophillus Adeyinka Shittu, 5 & 10 January 2013.
E-mail communication with Mr. Innocent Opufou, 11 July 2013.

Archival Materials
KSHCB KanProf 1/11/11 History of Kiru District.
KSHCB KanProf 1/11/13 History of Kura District.
KSHCB no. 68, Inspection Notes vol. 1
KSHCB R.518 Postal Telegraph Dept. Miscellaneous (complaints) and Postal Agency.
NAK P&T/3 Postal Agency at Madobi.
NAK ZarProf 1923/S.1, Postal Agencies 1949–1953.
NAK KanProf 4705, Postal Agency at Kwankwaso.
NAK ZarProf MKT vol. I, Groundnut Buying Stations and Points.

Government Publications
Nigeria—Further Correspondence Relating to Railway Construction in Nigeria (1909).
    London: HMO.

Secondary Sources
Published Materials

Arango, A. (2000), Explaining Migration: A Critical View. *International Social Science Journal* 52(165): 287–288.

Ayandele, E.A. (1979), *Nigerian Historical Studies*. London: Frank Cass.

Bako, A. (2005), Colonial Rule and Residential Segregation: The Sabon Gari Settlements Reconsidered, in: A.M. Yakubu, I.M. Jumare & A.G. Saeed (eds) *Northern Nigeria: A Century of Transformation, 1903–2003*. Kaduna: Arewa House, pp. 469–477.

Bako, A. (2006), *Sabon Gari: A History of Immigrants and Inter-Group Relations in the 20th Century*. Sokoto: Usmanu Danfodiyo University Press.

Daily Trust Newspaper, 29 April 2010, vol. 24, no.19.

Douglas, A. (2002), *Poison and Medicine: Ethnicity, Power, and Violence in a Nigerian City, 1966 to 1986*. Portsmouth NH: Heinemann.

Hogendorn, J.S. (1978), *Nigerian Groundnut Exports: Origins and Early Development*. Zaria: ABU.

Hopkins, A.G. (1973), *An Economic History of West Africa*. London: Longman.

Lovejoy, P.E. & J.D. Hogendorn, (1993), *Slow Death for Slavery: The Course of Abolition in Northern Nigeria, 1897–1936*. USA: Cambridge.

Lugard, F.D. (1922), *The Dual Mandate in British Tropical Africa*. London: William Blackwood and Sons.

Mason M. (1978), Working on the Railway: Forced Labour in Northern Nigeria, 1907–1912, in: P.C.W. Gutkind, R. Cohen & J. Copan (eds) *African Labour History*. USA: Sage, pp. 56–79.

Mgbeafulu, M.C. (2003), *Migration and the Economy: Igbo Migration and the Nigerian Economy 1900 to 1975*. New York: iUniverse Inc.

Oshin, O. (2004/2003), Railway and Urbanization, in: T. Falola & S.J. Salm (eds) *Nigerian Cities*. Trenton, NJ: African World Press, pp. 101–126.

Oyemakinde, W. (1974), Railway Construction and Operation in Nigeria, 1895–1911: Labour Problems and Socio-Economic Impact. *Journal of Historical Society of Nigeria*, VII/2, 303–323.

Pedraza, H.J. (1960), *Boriobola-Gha: The Story of Lokoja the First British Settlement in Nigeria*. London: Oxford Press.

Rogers, B. (1980), *The Domestication of Women: Discrimination in Developing Societies*. London: Rutledge.

Rostow, W.W. (1960/1991), *The Stages of Economic Growth: A Non-Communist Manifesto*. Cambridge.

Tamuno, N.T. (1965), Genesis of the Nigerian Railway II. *Nigerian Magazine* 84 (March): 31–43.

The Northern Nigeria Publishing Company (1980), *Wakokin Aliyu Dansidi Sarkin Zazzau*. Zaria: ABU.

Udo, R.K. (1970), Internal Migrations and Development, in: J.S. Ogun Toyinbo, O.O. Areola & M. Filani (1978), *A Geography of Nigerian Development*. Nigeria: Heinemann Books, pp. 124–137.

Yusuf, S.T. (2010), *The Impact of the Railway on Kano Emirate, c. 1903–1960s: The Case of Madobi and Kwankwaso Towns*. Germany: Lambert Academic Publishing.

Yusuf, S.T. (2014), The Development of Baro–Kano Railway as an Aspect of Technology Transfer in Colonial Northern Nigeria. *Kano Journal of History* 1(1): 142–166.

Unpublished Materials

Anjorin, A.O. (1970), 'The Politics of Baro–Kano Railway', a Cyclosted paper read at the 16th Congress of the Historical Society of Nigeria Annual Congress, 1–23.

Yusuf, S.T. (2015), The Socio-Economic Impact of the Railway in Northern Nigeria: A Study in the Transformation of the Rural Communities Along the Rail Lines Between Kano and Zaria, 1908–1970s. PhD thesis, University of Leiden.

CHAPTER 6

Migration and Competition over Commercial Spaces: The Case of Songhay Migrants at the Kumasi Central Market, Ghana 1930–1948[1]

Isaie Dougnon

In the cities of Mali (Mopti, Bamako, Niono, Koutiala, and Sikasso), seasonal workers from the regions of the north are associated, in the last three decades, with the term *koroboro butiqini* ('the small-shop Songhay').[2] This term has passed so much into common usage that small retailers belonging to other ethnic groups accept its use to designate their own trade, and they also accept the attribution to them of the patronymic Maïga, the most widespread Songhay patronymic.

In September 2003, during my research trip in the Timbuktu Region, the bus I was on made a stop of 40 minutes at Sévaré. I took a seat on the bench of a coffee seller, and I asked him which town he came from. 'Rharous,' he replied. He pointed to a long line of coffee sellers: 'All these people are from Rharous.' Indeed, the young ones come from the Rharous Cercle. In certain towns of this larger Cercle of the Timbuktu Region, to speak a foreign language is the distinctive sign of the new identity of 'a man of the world'. For example, in the village of Samar, Ouolof is the language of communication for the youth who commute from their village to Senegal. Whoever does not understand it is considered a *gaoua*, an unenlightened one. These young migrants almost all work in the harbour at Dakar, where they sell coffee or meals.

In the towns of the south of Mali, the increasing number of these small shops and stalls, their quality, and the variety and prices of the products that

---

1 The data used in this paper originates mainly from my investigations in Ghana for the writing of my thesis between 2001 and 2002 and from my postdoctoral research on migrations in the Gourma-Rharous region of Timbuktu in September 2003 and June–July 2004.

2 The term *koroboro* is used for someone who lives in a village—and, by extension, a town. His opposite is *gandjiboro,* someone who lives in the bush. One sees in these dichotomous terms an image of the two principal societies in the north, that of the shepherds or nomads who follow their animals in the bush, and that of the Songhay farmers who live in the towns of the valley and later the political centres that arose in the Middle Ages: Gao and Timbuktu. In reality, the Songhay call themselves *issa boro,* 'the people of the river' or those that exploit the river. One can assume that the terms *koroboro* and *gandjibori* appeared thanks to a political construction.

one finds there have become the major characteristics of the migrant *koroboro* that leave the regions of Timbuktu and Gao[3] for the cities of Mali and those of the coastal countries (Dougnon 2014). Moreover, some among them do not hesitate to proclaim that the Songhay know nothing but trade—an identity previously granted to the Soninké, good farmers at home and good merchants abroad (Whitehouse 2003).

What strikes one are the prejudices that the city dwellers of the south have towards these migrant shopkeepers from the north: they are considered arrogant, have an appearance of laziness, are prone to making quick profits, have a taste for good cuisine, and have an instinct for grouping together on the basis of ethnicity. These labels are often at the root of relations of mistrust or of conflicts between the migrant traders of the north and their customers in the south.

The image of the migrant Maïga was enacted in a sketch which was shown on national television during Ramadan. Improvised with a view to moralizing about the prices of basic necessities, the sketch was played by two actors: a migrant shopkeeper named Mr Maïga and an anonymous customer. The latter comes to buy sugar at the premises of the former, who is saying his prayers in a loud voice. The customer finds that the shopkeeper has illegally increased the price of sugar and shouts into his face: 'Do not pronounce the name of God, for you are taking advantage of Ramadan to cheat customers.' Mr Maïga apologizes to him in recognition that he has acted against God and the law and returns the money to him.

However, field data prove that these prejudices are not based on any objective reality. The petty trade that is the preferred activity of seasonal workers and permanent migrants is not easy work or one that leads to wealth. There is a large divide between this stout-bellied Maïga shopkeeper depicted in a well-furnished shop and the migrant that engages in the trade of door-to-door selling or selling in a market, a divide that very few people succeed in overcoming. Several among those I interviewed never owned shops. They devoted themselves to various activities, from selling water to acting as security guards to extracting sand from the bottom of the river Niger. They engage in these activities just long enough to be able to buy some bags of provisions for their families at home in their village. Their mobility cannot be understood without taking into account the urgency and the necessity of returning to their homes.

It is the specific goal of this paper to place in historical perspective how such prejudices led to the expulsion of the Songhay merchants from the Kumasi

---

3 Until recently, almost all citizens of the north, except the Tuareg, identified themselves as members of the Songhay ethnic group and asserted that they came from Gao or Timbuktu.

Central Market in 1948. Beyond the stereotypes, this expulsion shows the historical context and the politics of competition between natives and migrants around commercial spaces in colonial and post-colonial Ghana.

In this old colonial country, in the migrant quarters known under the name of *zongo*,[4] the Songhay community developed a method of economic adaptation based on the mastery of petty trade. Although predominantly peasants in the valley of the Niger, the Songhay community has become free-market, enterprising, and capitalist to a degree difficult to see in their villages of origin. Founders of an empire that developed thanks to trans-Saharan trade, and heirs to an Islamic civilization, they have responded quickly in the migratory context to become engaged in trade and to prosper therein. Despite their expulsion from the Kumasi Central Market in 1948, the Songhay have lost none of their entrepreneurial spirit.

In terms of employment, every migrant community specializes in the domain in which it feels itself the better placed; the Songhay have done this through their commercial activities. Indeed, the adaptation of a migrant community in a foreign country depends on its economic performance. I described this in a previous article in a comparative study of the case of the Dogon and the Songhay (Dougnon 2012). The Dogon, who favoured colonial work rather than self-employment, have found themselves in the post-colonial period in a lamentable financial situation (chronic unemployment, children lacking education). On the other hand, the Songhay, who excel in trade, have asserted themselves over the course of several years as essential economic actors.

In the city of Kumasi, the Songhay passed from being porters (*kayakaya*) for others to becoming traders in their own right. This new status allowed them to occupy a large part of the Kumasi Central Market and thus to dominate the trade in basic products. How could the natives and their supporters accept that the servants had become masters? In April 1948, a decision by the Kumasi municipal authorities gave the Songhay one month to evacuate the market. According to a widely spread rumour, the Songhay were responsible for the inflation in the prices of essential commodities. And this inflation was supposedly deliberate, for the Songhay abused the monopoly that they held on the trade in food products at the market. In spite of the petitions sent to the colonial and

---

4   *Zongo*, a Hausa word, means 'foreigners' quarters'. In the colonial era, it was the mining companies that, on the basis of instructions from the British colonial government, founded the *zongo* in order to settle the migrant workers that came mainly from the French territories and the British Northern Territories. There are *zongo* areas in all cities in Ghana.

the traditional authorities of the Region of Ashanti and the mediation of the religious and political leaders of the *zongo*, the expulsion order was followed to the letter of the law.

Trade as Migrants' New Social Identity

All the current discussions on mobility, mass migrations, transnational cultural flows, and the concepts of a space, of a people, and of a culture[5] are not in fact new concerns. In Europe, the publications *The Polish Peasant in Europe and America* (Thomas & de Znaniecki 1927) and *Social Mobility* (Sorokin 1927) described the global historical character of urbanization and the movement of rural peoples towards centres of work. These studies showed how the general circulation of population over the earthly globe continually places individuals in countries whose language they do not understand and in social systems in which they do not have a place; and even if they do have a place, this is permanently called into question. It was Durkheim who, for the first time, thematized the relationship between the division of labour and the mobility of people. In *Men and Their Work*, Everett Hughes supports the thesis that the secularized division of work is the most important factor in the mobility of people.[6] In the course of his argument, he refers to this passage from Durkheim:

> For to live by a metier one must have clients, and he must sally forth from his house to find them; he must sally forth also to enter into relations with his competitors, to struggle against them, and to converse with them. Moreover, metiers suppose more or less directly, cities, and cities are always formed and recruited principally by means of immigrants who have quitted their *milieu natal*.[7]

---

5 See Akhil Gupta & James Ferguson, *Culture Power Places, Exploration in Critical Anthropology* (London, 1997); Mirjam de Bruijn, Rijk van Dijk & Dick Foeken, *Movable Africa: Changing Patterns of Movement in Africa and Beyond* (Leiden: Brill, 2001); Catherine Coquery-Vidrovitch, Odile Goerg, Issiaka Mandé, & Faranirina Rajaonah (eds) *Etre étranger et migrant en Afrique au XXe siècle,* especially Volume I, *Politiques migratoires et constructions des identités* (L'Harmattan, 2003).

6 Migration and access to modern business activities are the most important factors for the development of the spirit of rural enterprise in Mali. They allow any peasant to migrate anywhere and to try any job.

7 Emile Durkheim, *De la division du travail social* (Paris 1902), preface to the second edition, 'Quelques remarques sur les groupements professionnels', quoted by Everett Cherrington Hughes in *Men and Their Work* (The Free Press, Illinois, 1958), p. 30.

In pre-colonial Africa, custom and tradition determined the type of work that a man of a given status was permitted to do or not do.[8] In societies where the system of castes exists and where cultural forces attempt to crystallize the forms of institutions and social organization, certain occupations are hereditary (healers, priests, traders, tanners, and so on). With colonization and waves of migration, the local divisions of labour changed abruptly. The upheavals associated with the displacement of peoples, with the methods of production, and with the extension of the frontiers for trade and employment disrupted the ancestral prerogatives of work. My own research on the migrations of the Dogon and Songhay to Ghana illustrate these upheavals (Dougnon 2012). Thanks to migration, the migrant Songhay found themselves earning their living from trading at the Kumasi Central Market, a place which their parents who remained in the village had never heard of before.

In light of the place it occupies in the history of migration in colonial West Africa, Ghana is an appropriate setting to reconsider the specific trajectories of the work of certain migrant communities and the changing relations between migrants and natives in terms of access to work and economic resources.[9]

Of all the professions, trade is the one that demands maximum mobility and contact with others groups. The rivalry between the latter often results in open conflicts. The political management of these conflicts produces a result, in general, which is to the detriment of the least integrated or the most stigmatized migrants.

In the towns in the south of Mali, the activities of seasonal workers from the regions of Gao and Timbuktu were identified with small shops and stalls;

---

8 John Rouche recalls 'la honte du travail' ['the shame of work'] while talking about the migrants of Niger, the zabrama (Gao). According to him, these populations 'considèrent que tout travail, en dehors de celui des cultures, est honteux pour des gens qui ne sont pas de caste servile; un homme libre ne doit pas travailler devant les femmes de son pays. Le migrant, en s'expatriant, peut donc travailler sans honte, à condition de ne pas partir avec sa femme. Il choisit la Gold Coast de préférence à la Côte d'Ivoire, car il sait que personne dans son village ne saura ce qu'il y fait' ['consider that all work, apart from that of their culture, is shameful for people who are not members of a servile caste; a free man must not work in front of the women of his country. The migrant, in emigrating, can therefore work without shame on condition that he does not migrate with his wife. He chooses the Gold Coast in preference to the Côte d'Ivoire because he knows that no one in his village will know what he is doing there']. 'Migration au Ghana (Gold Coast) (Enquête 1953–1955)', Journal de la société des africanistes, XXVI, (1956), p. 195.

9 See Isaie Dougnon, 'Peasant Migration and Labour Codification in the Colonial Era: Emigrants from Dogon Country in the Gold Coast 1910–1950', in: K.S. Jomo & Khoo Khay Jin (eds) Globalization and Its Discontents, Revisited (New Delhi: Tulika Books, 2002), pp. 73–83.

in Ghana, on the other hand, they were known under the curious name of *kay-akaya* ('to carry on the head'). The notion of *kayakaya* was used in reference not only to a particular type of work—portage—but also in reference to the community that exercised this activity. In the 1930s, they were officially called *kayakaya* or *Gao community*. Indeed, *kayakaya* expressed their new identity as migrant workers in Ghana, and their geographic origin as Gao. The word *kay-akaya* had a pejorative connotation because the work it designated was the prerogative of migrants. The stigmatization of the '*kayakaya* community' and of their work is linked to the fact that they were perceived as foreign despite their long stay in the country of the Ashanti. Furthermore, no native of Ghana would accept work as a porter, which was considered a very degrading occupation.

Formerly denigrated, the *kayakaya* community became, over time, a community of respectable businessmen. They passed from being porters for others to being traders in their own right. In this paper I analyse how the migrant Songhay came to 'professionalize' and monopolize a new trade, that of *kay-akaya*. I examine how this supposed monopoly was the reason behind their eviction from the market by the Kumasi municipal authorities. I also describe how the strengthening of their solidarity allowed them to persist in *kayakaya* from generation to generation.

How did they come to discover this distant country to the point of colonizing its market?

Ghana, or the Road to Prosperity

Here, we don't know Bamako, the capital of Mali, but Accra, the capital of Ghana; the people here don't know the banana, but they speak Hausa, English, and Ashanti.

A peasant of Tourchawene, *in the area of Timbuktu*

According to a widespread myth, the Gold Coast road was opened to the peasants of the regions of the north by a local 'explorer'. One day, this ancestor disappeared and his family had no idea where he had gone. After some days of fruitless searching, they concluded that he was lost. One fine day, 'the lost man' returned from his trip. He brought back money, clothes, and many other things. He explained to his friends that the Gold Coast was a place where one could get everything, including products unknown in the country of the Songhay. Through word of mouth, the whole area learned that the Gold Coast was a prosperous country, an Eldorado. The man returned there himself some days later with one of his brothers. 'Among the Songhay, a man goes to where his brother lives,' said Mr Maïga. And this is why everyone followed in the footsteps of the first traveller to the Gold Coast.

However, several testimonies prove that the principal reason is not the presence of a family member but the wealth of the host country. The chief of Kardjiba village, who spent several years in Ghana, describes this country in the colonial era:

> The people left for the Gold Coast because this was the country of good things. The Gold Coast was full of riches that did not exist anywhere else. In Ghana, for instance, one saw a group of people sitting around. Suddenly, a large truck full of merchandise appeared. A member of the group got up to see the owner of the vehicle. He took all the merchandise from him to resell it. He paid what was owed to the owner for the load and kept the profit of the transaction for himself. This is why the people from here preferred to go to the Gold Coast. What's more, the Gold Coast didn't have either politics or lies. There was nothing there but the truth.

How did the Songhay pass from rice-growing to trade in the Gold Coast? According to Agamir Maïga: 'Here, at Kardjiba, we are farmers. When one of us goes to Ghana, an experienced person takes him and initiates him into trading, until he masters it.' The merchandise and the market make the difference between Ghana and the country of the Songhay, as Magazou Haïdara of Gourzougueye explains:

> In Gourzougueye, the people work physically, while in Ghana, there is a lot of merchandise that goes from the towns to the countryside and vice versa. In Gourzougueye, there is everything except merchandise. In Ghana, you can see a man sitting down but he's earning money. A man lends a certain sum to a third party, who then engages in trade and reimburses him his capital plus interest. Migrants that trade in oil or petrol make money by providing these products to retailers, who sell them at the smaller markets.

From the 1930s onwards, the number of young Songhay that left their towns annually for the Gold Coast increased considerably. They worked for the local merchants, both as porters (in the daytime) and as security guards (at night), and this continued for several decades. But as soon as they were trained by the local merchants, they got the better of them.

Goods such as corn, bananas, and yams are cultivated in several parts of the Ashanti Region. However, the cultivators of these products never had a clear policy of transporting them to the Kumasi Central Market. On the contrary, it was the Songhay migrants that travelled to different towns and farming hamlets to transport them, initially in small quantities on their heads and later on transportation trucks.

Moussa Touré of Accra explains why the Songhay migrants have little by little come to dominate the trade in food products:

> Before, a Gaida[10] did not even dare to come to Accra. It was the Sahelian migrants, through their intensive circulation between the north and the south, who opened their eyes. The Gaida cultivated yams in the bush but didn't know that they could bring them to the city and sell them at a profit. It's the Songhay who started it off. It's the same for the market in wood and manual petrol-pumps. The natives understood later that we explored all the routes to monopolize the trade in these lines of business. They said to themselves that the migrants would uproot them from all economic sectors—and even from their women. And the latter liked us so much. Hence, the strategy of their 1948 expulsion policy was to recapture the local markets formerly occupied by migrants.

Mr Halil Touré of the town of Tourchaewene claims that the trade in yams and corn occupied almost 90% of the immigrants of his village. When he arrived in Kumasi for the first time in 1960, his fellow Songhay sold mainly yams. Upon his arrival, the others explained to him how the system worked. Together with an immigrant from his village, he borrowed a sum of 500,000 cedis. He left for the bush to buy yams, which he sold in Kumasi. After three years, he had paid back the loan. Some obtained merchandise in the city, which they sold in the villages. Why were yams and maize favoured by the migrant Songhay? According to Mogazou Haïdara, these products were targeted because of the expected profit. As the local peasants were unaware of the value of their products, they let them go at a very low price. The Rharous migrants who carried these products on their heads to the town made substantial profits.

The Development of the Capitalist Spirit

Fatoumata Mohamed Maïga and her husband returned to their native village in December 2004. Some months later, her husband returned to Nigeria, where he had lived for more than 20 years. When asked why, in her opinion, the

---

10   Gaida is the name given by the Songhay to the inhabitants of Ghana.

people of the valley specialize mainly in small-scale trading abroad, she mentioned the impact of her husband's income on his and her lifestyle:

> In Nigeria, my husband has money every day, every month, and every year. In that country, a woman covers herself with a quality pomade. There is electricity. There is no famine. I eat well. There is no dust.

According to certain seasonal workers, the Songhay do not engage in migration for wage labour but for trading purposes. For many of the migrants interviewed, to work away from home means to count their money at the end of the day or of the month. It is this notion of return on investment that underlies the capitalist spirit of the Songhay migrants of the years 1930–1940. It explains why they all involved themselves in petty trade, from the sale of yams to the rag trade. They opted for self-employment, considering it more rewarding and more profitable than wage labour working for others.

This capitalist spirit is also the case for seasonal migrants, as we have seen earlier. In this regard, the seasonal worker is defined as someone who returns home when he considers that he has earned sufficient funds to provide for his needs and those of his family. These seasonal workers see the market as analogous to their granary in the village. 'When a man eats thanks to the market, he can work only at the market,' as they say. Furthermore, the length of their stay is an important factor for this category of migrants. Someone who migrates for six months will not take the risk of engaging in a job where it requires a year or more to have his income at his disposal. Freedom of movement is also an important factor. Trade allows the seasonal worker to go from one place to another according to its profitability. He can abandon one country, region, town, or market for another if he learns that the commercial conditions there are better. Speed and profitability in a fluid space-time are the two essential dimensions of the capitalist spirit of Songhay migrants in Ghana and in the south of Mali.

The idea of luxury, comfort, and social prestige are to be taken into account in the analysis of their conception of return on investment. The need for money to buy clothes for their wives and for themselves is often underlined. According to them, the seasonal worker that returns must appear beautiful; his body must be glowing. In this regard, one of my interlocutors raised his large boubou, showing off his arms and expressing himself with humour: 'I have just arrived from Sikasso. You see how I shine. But in three months you will no longer recognize me, so pale will I be under the weight of bad conditions.' If the needs of the body are satisfied, the seasonal worker can buy himself a goat or a sheep or even a cow.

However, the migrant does not easily occupy a commercial space without entering into competition with the host country's traders and their customers. And this competition increases with the growing economic power of the migrant.

How the Songhay Migrants Conquered and Lost the Kumasi Central Market

On 3 March 1948, the Songhay migrants or *kayakaya*, originally from the north of Mali, learned through the local press that they had to leave the Kumasi Central Market. The official notice was read and interpreted to those concerned by an interpreter appointed for this purpose. Later, the town crier, Krobo Odusei, publicly announced that all the *kayakaya* would be evicted from the market and asked every customer to settle their accounts before the deadline because, according to him, there would be no *kayakaya* in the market from 1 April 1948.[11] After his public announcement, Mr Odusei hammered home the same announcement in front of Isufu Gao, the leader of the Gao migrant community. In spite of all the negotiations and the petitions sent by the leaders of the migrants to the *Asantehene*, king of the Ashanti, and Charles Owen Butler, colonial governor of the region, the municipal authorities did not revoke their decision to expel the Songhay merchants on 1 April 1948.

The main motive for the eviction was the inflation in prices of basic necessities. In the opinion of the Songhay migrants, the soaring prices were created by the same natives of the region as supplied the market. In their letter to the authorities of Kumasi, the Songhay merchants argued that the inflation was not caused by them but by the local owners of the food products, who entrusted these products to them with strict instructions on the prices. If the natives set the cost prices, the Songhay merchants were obliged to apply them, because it is the owner who decides.

Since the cause of their eviction was supposedly connected with the prices, in their correspondence they asked the colonial and local authorities to furnish them with a price list that had to be applied and to take measures to check and ascertain for themselves whether the Gao migrants violated or complied with the quoted prices. In his correspondence, Isufu Gao, the leader of the

---

11   See 'Petition from Yisifu Gao, headman, Gao now Kayakaya Community in Kumasi, for himself and behalf of the Gao Community', addressed to Otumfo, king of the Ashanti, 23 February 1948, in: *ARG1/2/1/218*, Archives of Kumasi.

Songhay community, did not hide his astonishment and his anger at such an abrupt eviction. According to him, his community had never before been criticized for wrong actions or bad behaviour at the said market. It was particularly surprising given that all the Songhay migrants that lived in the country of the Ashanti or in the city of Kumasi were under the protection of local and colonial jurisdiction.

His anger was all the stronger because the time granted to the merchants to quit the market was only 25 days, while many among them that possessed large stocks of products could not evacuate them in this time period. He asked the authorities to grant the right to oversee and to protect their goods before the final decision was taken. In a second petition, he sought a favourable response from the traditional and colonial authorities on the basis that justice and the law are sacred under the English flag and that the Songhay subjects of the British empire shared the same privileges and rights as other British subjects.

Another line of argument to avoid the eviction was based on the fact that the Songhay migrants maintained that in the matter of sale of food products, they were led by the locals. In addition, they knew no other business or occupation than the market and did not know how to earn their living if they had to leave the market. This was the reason—in the interests of the Songhay community, justice, and fair play—for asking the British governor to do everything to prevent the application of the decision of the Kumasi Town Council.

Another source of complaint was that the Songhay merchants were viewed entirely as foreigners. They considered themselves, however, as people that lived in this country for many years and that paid duties and taxes to the authorities. Consequently, they saw themselves, more or less, as naturalized citizens of the country, and in return they should enjoy the same privileges as the other peoples of the country.

On several occasions, the leaders of the Songhay community insisted on the fact that they were under the jurisdiction of Great Britain and should be protected by the laws of the Crown. As long as they were in the country of the Ashanti, they considered themselves British subjects and asked to be protected by the British government, whose system of justice was widely known throughout the world.

Being merchants with trading licences issued by the municipal authorities, the Songhay traders possessed extensive stocks of rice, groundnuts, beans, maize, and many other products. All this involved large sums of money. The notice that demanded that they had to quit the market not later than 1 April 1948 was a great injury, because they did not know where to go and where to stock all this merchandise in order to sell it and recover all the sums invested in it.

To prove the importance of the products that they possessed at the Kumasi Central Market, they drew up a complete list of products and their owners (Table 1). After the end of this list, the leaders drew the attention of the Town Council to the fact that in every community there are both bad and honest

TABLE 1   *List of merchants and their products at the Kumasi Cental Market before the dead-line for eviction, 1 April 1948*[12]

Name of merchant	Number of bags	Products on sale
1. Isufu Gao	104	Rice, maize, salt and beans
2. Adamu Gao	154	Rice, maize, salt and beans
3. Kadjo Gao	100	Rice, maize and smoked bananas
4. Saidru Gao	120	Rice, maize and smoked bananas
5. Aboagye Gao	100	Rice, maize and salt
6. Allasan Gao	100	Rice, maize, salt and beans
7. Almahadi Gao	160	Rice, maize and yams
8. Aboagye No. 2	250	Rice, maize and sweet potatoes
9. Amadu Gao No. 2	300	Rice, salt, beans and yams
10. Amadu Gao No. 3	300	Rice, maize, beans and sweet potatoes
11. Garba Gao	250	Rice, maize and barrels of palm oil
12. Souma Gao	300	Rice, salt and palm oil
13. Allasane No. 2	500	Rice, salt and smoked bananas
14. Dourata Gao	86	Maize, beans and salt
15. Allasane Diato	300	Maize, beans, salt and rice
16. Younoussa Gao	98	Maize and yams
17. Isufu Gao No. 2	120	Bananas and yams
18. Issa Gao	100	Rice, salt and bananas
19. Mamane Gao	150	Rice, maize, bananas and yams
20. Sewatan Gao	200	Rice, maize, bananas and salt
21. Arachahite Gao	100	Rice, maize and yams
22. Almotaoha Gao	160	Beans, salt, maize and rice
23. Kata Gao	200	Beans, salt and palm oil
24. Salifu Gao	200	Rice, salt and beans
25. Mamane Gao	145	Bananas, yams and maize

12   See the letter 'Humble Petition of Gao Community, Kumasi', signed by Isufu Gao, Headman, Gao Community of Kumasi, 31 March 1948, *ARG1/2/1/64*, in: Gao Community Affairs, Archives of Kumasi.

TABLE 1   *List of merchants and their products at the Kumasi Cental Market before the dead-line for eviction, 1 April 1948* (cont.)

Name of merchant	Number of bags	Products on sale
26. Servato Gao	200	Salt
27. Mustapha Gao	160	Maize, salt and rice
28. Kata Gao No. 2	200	Salt
29. Asara Gao	150	Salt
30. Yams Gao	2,000	Rice, salt, maize and plantains
31. Malam Gao	120	Rice and salt
32. Isufu Gao No. 3	120	Beans, rice and palm oil
33. Issa Gao	100	Maize and salt
34. Suleyman Gao	101	Maize and salt
35. Bio Gao	58	Beans and smoked bananas
36. Alasane Gao No. 3	87	Beans and smoked bananas
37. Izaru Gao	107	Maize, salt and cocoyams
38. Alasane Diato No. 2	400	Maize, salt and beans
39. Almadi Gao	225	Maize, salt and beans
40. Aldu Gao	40	Salt and rice
41. Abadi Gao	45	Salt and rice
42. Isufu Gao No. 4	104	Salt, rice, beans and yams
43. Abogye Gao No. 3	256	Salt, maize and palm oil
44. Yams Gao No. 2	1,350	Rice, smoked bananas and maize
45. Aldu Gao No. 2	300	Rice, smoked bananas and maize
46. Duraba Gao	87	Rice and salt
47. Amidu Gao	300	Rice, salt and maize
48. Kan Burgni Gao	100	Rice, salt and maize
49. Garba Gao	200	Maize, salt and yams
50. Sidi Gao	60	Maize and smoked bananas
51. Amdu Gao	100	Maize, salt, beans and oils
52. Yams Gao	1,000	Salt, rice, beans and yams
53. Allasane Gao	100	Salt and maize
54. Yams Gao	300	Salt, maize, rice and beans
55. Kojo Gao	25	Salt
56. Yaya Gao	200	Salt, rice and maize
57. Amadu Gao	35	Maize and salt
58. Okuyo Gao	38	Salt
Total	13,265	

men. If in the Songhay community of Kumasi there were some bad apples, they were outnumbered by those that were honest businessmen; and they hoped that the conduct of a few bad apples would not influence the municipal authorities to decide to prevent honest citizens from conducting their business and earning a living.

In the face of the Songhay merchants' resistance to leaving the market by the deadline, a special commission was set up on 18 February 1948 to investigate the activities of the 'Gao traders' at the Kumasi Central Market, in order to eliminate the monopoly they exercised. The commission was composed of a chairman, three members, and a secretary.

In the secretary's summary, which it was agreed to call 'The Threat of the Gao to the Kumasi Central Market', the following facts were laid before the commission.

1.   The need to organize the group of Songhay porters or *kayakaya* at the Kumasi Central Market had arisen in 1942. The Council had decided to limit the number of itinerant porters, who were causing overcrowding in the market.
2.   At one of the monthly meetings of the Council, on 26 March 1943, it had been decided to control the Songhay porters at the Kumasi Central Market.
3.   To this end, a hundred Songhay porters had been licensed to work at the market.

In the investigation's report, one can read the following allegations, which condemned the Gao migrants:

That the disorder previously complained of by bulk traders was temporary controlled but with the passage of time some Gao manoeuvred to gain the confidence of traders and having secured spaces in Wholesale Section installed themselves as agents for most of the women traders. Working their way up from small beginning these Gao soon became dictatorial in their bargains and virtually commandeered the wholesale trade with the potential original bulk traders (mostly women) playing the second fiddle. By all sorts of tactics these Gao wholesale traders have made tremendous strides towards monopoly of the wholesale trade by intercepting an easy flow into the retail section of the Market of such staple foodstuffs as yam, corn, plantain and the like. It is reported that by such means the Gao wholesale traders unscrupulously tamper with the weight of bagged foodstuffs and [they sell them] at their own prices far above normal selling prices with the result that foodstuffs reach consumers at extraordinarily inflated prices.[13]

Such a report left no chance to the Songhay traders to remain in the market. On all points, the report accused the Songhay community of being at the root of the price inflation for basic necessities. They were also accused of violating the law that forbids people to sleep at the market. Consequently, they alone were the people responsible for the poor state of hygiene and the contamination of the run-off waters, and they were suspected of being at the root of the epidemic of typhoid fever. They were perceived as being very insolent in their negotiations with the women traders and as disputing the tax rates of the city of Kumasi.

During their visit to the market and the automobile park, the members of the commission questioned some Songhay migrants and some native women. One of my interlocutors was himself a trader but was not working in the market. According to him, the members of the Gao community were themselves installed in the wholesale market, like most traders who assisted in the sale of products brought from the villages. The women generally gave them the products at a fixed price, and they in turn sold them at whatever prices they could get. Acting as intermediaries, they received a commission of 1% on every bag of groundnuts, corn, yams, and so on. According to my interlocutor, the migrant traders from the north of Mali worked in close relationship with the women and therefore had good relations with them. Several interlocutors told the same story as this one. They think that all the Songhay migrants sold the women's products on the basis of an arrangement and at a commission of 1% per bag.

The following statement of the president of the saleswomen of the Kumasi Central Market drove the point home and dispelled any hope of the Songhay migrants maintaining the places they occupied at the market.

> I speak as the head of all the women around me here. Many years back we found the Gao porters very useful and we employed them as carriers for haulage of foodstuffs from lorries to our stalls and to help in stacking. As far as I remember they were then about thirty in number but soon after the size of the Gao porters in the central market became unwieldy and an

---

13   See: 'Report of the Special Committee appointed to enquire into the functions of the Gao Traders in the Central Market and to make recommendations for the elimination of the alleged trade monopoly exercised by them,' ARG1/2/1/64, in: Gao Community Affairs, Archives of Kumasi.

inclination to install themselves in trade as competitors became notice-able. We complained to the Otumfuor Asantehene and the District Commissioner, Kumasi, who saw to it that their number was limited and licences issued accordingly. Some of these licensed porters have been act-ing as our agents on commission basis to facilitate quick sales of our stock. Usually we allow 1% on the bag of foodstuffs. It appears that by some foul means they have amassed substantial capital and have now become chal-lenging in trade, domineering in attitude and almost intolerable within the market area—a change of events which calls for restraint if women traders in the market are to be guaranteed a further lease of time to earn their livelihood. Prices of foodstuffs have soared up because of these Gao intermediaries. They are more of masters than servants and often times do not scruple to use their hands on defenceless women over trade dis-putes. We desire that something be done to curb their activities.[14]

As a result of the deposition of the president of the saleswomen, the commis-sion took drastic measures to definitively expel the Songhay traders from the market. It required that the portage licences for the traders not be extended further from the date of expiration on 31 March 1948. It also required that their security permits be cancelled and that they be allocated new permits. The members of the Gao community could henceforth be employed only as occa-sional porters and could no longer be licensed to install themselves in the mar-ket for the purpose of selling. The commission also proposed that the number of security guards be increased in order to denounce any Songhay that infringed the laws in force.

The three main recommendations of the commission were as follows: (a) to eliminate the Songhay monopoly with a view to facilitating the supply to the market of less expensive products; (b) to destroy the nuisance created by the presence and the habits of Gao people in the public market; and (c) to eliminate any threat to the native traders coming from the Songhay migrants.

Table 1 above clearly illustrates the success of the Songhay migrants at the Ashanti market. Monopoly and profit: these were the two reasons used by the Kumasi Town Council to put an end to the reign of the Songhay merchants at the Central Market. The deadline for their eviction was set for 1 April 1948. How and where to go with more than 13,000 bags of produce? The authorities had pointed to Bantama, a peripheral market not frequented by inhabitants, as a new site for the Songhay merchants.

---

14   'Report of the Special Committee'.

Facing this certain eviction by the Kumasi municipal authorities, the Gao community addressed a letter to the Honourable Charles Owen Butler, Governor of the Ashanti Region. This was the last resort. The leaders of the community pointed to the law and to the unfair and discriminatory character of the eviction decision. They described for him in detail the history of their arrival at the market and the conditions in which they had begun to trade. According to them, the Songhay arrived at the market when the stalls were not yet constructed. They initially paid two pence per day to sell yams at the market and later the price was increased to three pence per day. When the stalls were constructed, a portion was allocated to each community. Some stalls were given to Ashanti women and only 15 to the Songhay traders, who, like all these women, sold their yams. In contrast to these women, the Gao journeyed to the Northern Territories to stock up with food products and bring them to the market at Kumasi. They did not understand why they had to go to the Bantama Market while the Ashanti women were going to retain their position at the Central Market. The preservation of their stalls at the market was vital for the Gao traders, who were considered the yam salesmen of Kumasi. But now, the stalls were to be removed from the Gao traders and given to Ashanti women, and the traders were obliged to sell off their yams at a very low price.

According to the wise men among the Songhay community, the objective sought by the commission was to remove the trade in yams into their own hands and give it to the Ashanti women. They implored the English governor to use his power to annul the decision of the city. From that date onwards, the taxes of Gao people were never accepted either by the municipal authorities or by the banks, the latter acting on the instructions of the former. The wise men said it was unfortunate that, at a time when the word 'democracy' was on everyone's lips throughout the Gold Coast, the Town Council treated the people of Gao in such an undemocratic way.

It is necessary to underline that the conflict between the Songhay migrants and the municipal authorities had repercussions for other migrant communities. This is illustrated by the petition of Mallam Adam Sokoto Zerikin of Kumasi-Zongo and of the leading imam of the Muslim community of Kumasi. Their petition requested the British governor to annul the 5 June 1948 decision according to which only porters of Ashanti nationality had the right to have portage contracts at the Kumasi Central Market. All the workers working at the market were under the leadership of the Zerikin Zongo, and it was therefore the duty of the Zerikin to defend the Muslims who were working at the market. At this meeting the representative of the *zongo* was outvoted. As a result of this decision, a mass protest was organized in the Kumasi *zongo* and the crowd called on the governor to annul the decision before the situation got worse. The protest of the imam and Zerikin was based on the following arguments: the city of Kumasi was a municipality and all the inhabitants paid taxes; no non-Ashanti was exempted from this tax. The decision to evict the Songhay was a case of selfishness, a suppression of the rights and liberties of people who were considered foreigners.

Conclusion

Migrations on the African continent have proven themselves to be one of the means used by citizens, groups, and states to regulate tensions, exploit opportunities, or manage difficulties on a collective as well as individual level. This is evidenced in recent years by what occurred in South Africa, in Equatorial Guinea, in Angola, in Côte d'Ivoire, and recently in the conflict between Senegalese and Chinese traders at the Sandaga Market in Dakar. In these countries and in many others, representations and markers of identity therefore have a crucial importance, because they very often determine the attitudes of people and justify the exploitation of foreigners by the powers that be. Today, economic crisis and chronic unemployment, and the emergence of networks of smugglers have turned the question of immigrants in Africa and Europe into a political game. This was the case in the colonial era for migrants who left one colonial empire for another, as the Songhay did, leaving the French empire for the British one. The problems arise from the fact that governments engage in excessive politicization of the issue of immigrants (e.g. the question of the *banlieues* in France and the relations between natives and Sub-Saharan immigrants in the Maghreb) or pretend to be unaware of these questions, instead of defining a social policy that is acceptable to all sides.

As we have seen in this paper, migrant traders are vulnerable to abuse from municipal authorities when they come into competition with natives in the vital sectors of a national economy. All the arrests and expulsions that immigrants have been subjected to since the colonial era are nothing but the consequences of an employment crisis whose logical result is the emergence of latent or open conflict between foreigners and natives.

For more than 50 years, researchers working on migration in Africa have placed the accent on migrants in search of wage labour with white or black employers and the process of their proletarization and their temporary or permanent urbanization (Cooper 1987; Macmillan 1993; Ferguson 1999; Dougnon 2002). The categories of migrants that work for themselves have been widely ignored by researchers in the social sciences. However, it is in the employment sector which is not under the control of the state or large private companies that migrant communities have acquired new identities as workers.

When Jean Rouch published his *Migrations au Ghana* (*Gold Coast*) in 1956, he suggested that researchers working on migration in Africa could raise the question of how different groups of migrants specialized in particular activities—specifically those in which they had a comparative advantage.

I have attempted to show that despite the constraints they encountered in Ghana, the Songhay migrants there developed a strong capitalist spirit. For them, to work meant to count money at the end of the day. Their choice of trade was based on their notion of return on investment (a capitalist spirit) and the feeling of self-esteem that comes from being self-employed. These two economic conceptions imply that freedom of movement was an important factor for these northern communities in the emergence of new identities of mobility or sedentarization. Trade allows a migrant to visit several places, according to their degree of profitability. He can leave a country, a region, or a city for new horizons or for reportedly better trading conditions.

Since the two major droughts (1973 and 1984), mobility is best adapted as a survival strategy, for it assures young seasonal workers a larger choice of employment or self-employment in the informal sector, a sector which overtook the formal sector at the end of the 1970s owing to the closure of state enterprises. The informal sector (catering, petty trade, security, and so on) provides daily or weekly income often sufficient to allow workers to send supplies to relatives at home in the village. These seasonal workers end up settling permanently in a city or in favourable agricultural zones, when they get married, have children, and take note of the fact that the spectre of famine does not retreat from their native villages.

References

Cooper, F. (1987), *On the African Waterfront: Urban Disorder and the Transformation of Work in Colonial Mombasa.* New Haven: Yale University Press.

Dougnon, I. (2002), Peasant Migration and Labour Codification in the Colonial Era: Emigrants from Dogon Country in the Gold Coast 1910–1950, in: K.S. Jomo & Khoo Khay Jin (eds) *Globalization and Its Discontents, Revisited.* New Delhi: Tulika Books, pp. 73–83.

Dougnon, I. (2012), Comparing Dogon and Songhai Migrations Towards Ghana, in: B. Mohamed & H. de Haas, *African Migrations Research: Innovative Methods and Methodologies.* Trenton, New Jersey: Africa World Press, pp. 211–236.

Dougnon, I. (2014), Klimaveränderung, Bäuerliche Mobilität und ländliche Entwicklung in der Region Timbuktu in Mali, in: Illker Ataç et al., Migration und Entwicklung. Vienna: Promedia, pp: 133–152.

Ferguson, J. (1999), *Expectations of Modernity: Myths and Meanings of Urban Life on the Zambian Copperbelt*. Berkeley: University of California Press.

Macmillan, H. (1993), The Historiography of Transition on the Zambian Copperbelt: Another View, *Journal of Southern African Studies* 19(4): 681–712.

Sorokin, P. (1927), *Social Mobility*. New York: Harper.

Thomas, W.I. & F. Znaniecki (1927), *The Polish Peasant in Europe and America*. New York: Knopf.

Whitehouse, B. (2003), Rester Soninké: La migration, la multilocalité et l'identité dans une communauté sahélienne. MA Thesis, Brown University, Providence Island, USA.

CHAPTER 7

Resettlement in Zimbabwe: Final Destination from the Zones of Transition?

Marleen Dekker[1]

Introduction

One of the main features of African history has been the almost continuous migrations of people across space and time in response to the changing conditions on the continent. Similarly, the population of Zimbabwe (former Southern Rhodesia) has been characterized by a high degree of mobility (Kay 1982). Despite various policies aimed at stimulating the entrance of black workers into the labour market,[2] Southern Rhodesia suffered from a shortage of willing and semi-skilled workers, especially in the agricultural and mining sector. Therefore, labour was imported from neighbouring countries in the form of short-term, circulatory labour migration of predominantly male workers, organized by the BSA Company. The circulatory labour migration was either formally organized through Wenela (see Gewald in this volume) or forced labour (see also Van Onselen 1980), but also through informal, own-account initiatives from prospective migrants who looked for greener pastures, exploring a road to prosperity.

For considerable periods of time up until the late 1950s, the number of foreign workers outnumbered the number of local workers in the white agricultural farming areas (Kay 1982: 86). The 1961 census of employees was the first to show that Rhodesian-born employees (57%) outnumbered those of foreign birth (43%). Yet, alien Africans, as they were often referred to, remained a very significant element within the European Farming Areas and the Urban Areas.[3]

---

1   This paper could not have been written without the invaluable research support of Michael Shambare and Nyaradzo Dzobo, who interviewed the respondents in Zimbabwe and shared their insights in our discussions on this topic. Support from and access to the survey data collected by Bill Kinsey and lineage data collected by Abigail Barr are kindly acknowledged.

2   For example, the hut tax or poll tax requiring the availability of cash in households that were otherwise mainly self-sufficient, and the discouragement of economic development in the Tribal Trust Lands (TTL), areas which were held in trust for indigenous peoples.

3   European Farming Areas and Urban Areas were designated for white Zimbabweans only. Black Zimbabweans were allowed to live there only with a permit, which was to be obtained through employment in white-owned farms, households, or businesses.

In this workforce, men predominated: for every 100 female foreign workers there were 288 males (Kay 1972).

Although migration was intended to be circulatory and it was assumed migrants would go back to their home country either upon retirement or before that, many circulatory migrants stayed in Southern Rhodesia. During fieldwork for my PhD research, which followed a group of farmers who participated in Zimbabwe's first resettlement programme just after the war of independence in 1980, I came across a fair number of first- and second- (or second-plus-)generation migrants who acquired a plot in two resettlement schemes. Initially, I considered the presence of these settlers of foreign descent in these newly created villages remarkable, but I soon realized that foreign descent is not uncommon—see, for example, the accounts of Spierenburg (2003) and Nyambara (2001). It is difficult, however, to capture this presence in figures, since children born in Zimbabwe from first-generation migrants are recorded as Zimbabwean-born. Thus, besides a presence of first-generation migrants from neighbouring countries, a considerable number of Zimbabweans are second-, third-, and fourth-generation, with the most notable example being President Robert Mugabe, who was born in Zvimba, Zimbabwe to a Malawian father and Shona mother (Holland 2010). Yet, in the literature on the first-generation resettlement programme and the background of the settlers (Kinsey 1982; Harts-Broekhuis & Huisman 2001), this issue is not referred to—perhaps simply because it was not an issue at that time, with the euphoric independence mood and high hopes for building new lives for all Zimbabweans irrespective of descent. At the same time, I was intrigued by the question of how these first-, second-, and second-plus-generation migrants ended up in the newly established villages in the early 1980s, to what extent they perceived this to be 'their final destination', and whether first- or second- (or second-plus-) generation migrants had different perceptions. Based on survey data collected from these resettled farmers, I could derive some basic information about their migration histories. This information was used to revisit these settlers in December 2013 and January 2014 and to discuss their life histories, with a specific focus on their migration patterns.

These accounts show that most farmers who participated in the first resettlement programme after independence were highly mobile before they settled. Many reported work experiences across the country and various moves in search of better pay or better company. For this reason, I consider a workplace a zone of transition and argue that the settlers had many zones of transition before settling on their own plot in the schemes that I studied. When they established themselves in the resettlement villages in the early 1980s, non-Zimbabwean settlers reported having occupied more zones of transition compared with Zimbabwean settlers and tended to agree more fully with statements suggesting the resettlement experience provided stability.

This chapter paper is structured as follows. The next section provides more context on circulatory migration processes in Southern Rhodesia and its consequences for the population make-up. The third section explains the sources of data and provides some descriptive statistics on the non-Zimbabwean migrants in the two schemes under consideration. The fourth section discusses the migration histories of the settlers and compares Zimbabwean with non-Zimbabwean settlers. The fifth section explores the extent to which resettlement has provided an opportunity to leave the zones of transition, both for Zimbabwean and non-Zimbabwean settlers, and distinguishes first- from second- or second-plus-generation migrants.

Context of Circulatory Migration

Based on the account of Kay in the early 1970s and 1980s (Kay 1972, 1982), this section explains in more detail the prevalent migration patterns into Southern Rhodesia. Until the 1960s, Malawi had consistently been the main supplier (almost 50% of the 406,000 foreign-born Africans in Rhodesia in 1969), followed by Mozambique (30%) and Zambia (15%). Malawians were dominant in Harare (Salisbury) and the Midlands, while Mozambiquans went to Mutare and the eastern part of Manicaland. Zambians were prevalent in the western part of the country, with some 22% of the population in Wankie[4] (Kay 1972).

Although foreign workers work in all occupational groups, in 1969 they were working particularly in agriculture and domestic services, both with the lowest cash wages and the longest work hours and sometimes in unattractive locations. Foreign workers were concentrated in (present-day) Harare, in some mining settlements, and on some large estates. Usually there were longstanding connections between mines and farms demanding labour and supply areas abroad (Kay 1982). These longstanding relationships, however, did not guarantee stable employer–employee relations. Typically, labourers, both of Zimbabwean and foreign descent, on commercial farms and in the mines change jobs

---

4   Using figures from the CSO, Kay (1972) shows that in 1962 and 1969, 11.3% and 7.5%, respectively, of the Rhodesian population were alien or foreign-born Africans. In 1969, popular towns were Wankie (22% of all Africans in the town were alien), Redcliff (19%), and Salisbury/Harare (17%). The European Farming Areas Darwin (34.2%), Mrewa (31.2%), and Mazoe (31%) had the largest proportion of aliens. Golden Valley/Patchway (44%), Arcturus (40%), and Mtoroshanga (39%) were the mining settlements where alien Africans were prominent.

frequently, looking for new opportunities, leaving places where they do not feel comfortable, following friends, relatives, bosses, etc. To the extent that labourers are constantly in transition, their workplace can be considered a zone of transition.

From 1965 onwards, international sanctions on Southern Rhodesia decreased agricultural exports and led to the widespread retrenchment of labour, especially on labour-intensive tobacco farms (Zinyama & Whitlow 1986). At the same time, a higher degree of mechanization and increasing demand for work from the black Rhodesian population meant the demand for foreign labour decreased, and the colonial administration made it more difficult for aliens to come in/stay and work in the country. Many 'aliens' became reluctant to give up their jobs, fearing they could not re-enter Rhodesia, and they therefore visited their home areas only infrequently or briefly. By 1973, foreign Africans occupied almost 30% of the African labour force in Southern Rhodesia. Later, the escalation of the civil war (and consequent war-related insecurity) in rural areas resulted in displacement of the population within the country (to towns) as well as to adjacent countries, notably Mozambique. This further added to the position of the non-Zimbabwean labour force as being 'in transition'.

In this context and with increasing age or upon retirement, a considerable group of labourers did not go back to their home countries but decided to leave their zones of transition and establish themselves 'more permanently' in Zimbabwe. As access to land in Zimbabwe was and still is mostly arranged through patrilineal descent (i.e. sons of lineage members are allocated land by village leaders), foreign labourers had to find alternative routes to gain access to land. This is illustrated by Nyambara (2001), for example, who documented how numerous retired labourers from Mozambique, Malawi, and Zambia joined the post-World War II influx of immigrants in Gokwe, where they were able to obtain land to establish homes and spend the rest of their lives in their 'final destination'. Since they were retired and did not have rural homes of their own, they applied for a plot of land, sometimes because they married women from Gokwe. The Ministry for Internal Affairs (through the district commissioner) mostly turned down these applications, on the grounds that the TTL Board had passed a resolution in 1965 that the TTL should not be occupied by Africans who were not descendants of tribes ordinarily resident in Rhodesia. Yet, some exceptions were made—for example, for a Malawian from the Rhodesian Armed Forces, who came to live in Zimbabwe when he was three and whose application was supported by a high-ranking government official. Bride service (working on the fields of your in-laws for a couple of years, another way of paying bridewealth) was also a strategy to later obtain land, as was documented for a Mozambican migrant worker who worked on his in-laws' fields for five years before being allocated his own plot. And when powers over land allocation were given to the chiefs under the 1967 Act, many aliens found their way to the land through bribes, gifts, or purchases (Nyambara 2001).

Data

In the early 1980s, just after the war of independence, the first phase of resettlement also offered foreign-born migrants an option to leave their zones of transition and establish themselves more permanently [see Box 1]. To explore this option in more detail, I use data from the Zimbabwe Rural Household Dynamics Survey (zRHDS), a panel study that followed the same households in three resettlement schemes over a period of 20 years.[5] The three resettlement areas, Mupfurudzi, Sengezi and Mutanda, are located in three different

MAP 1   *Locations of the resettlement schemes*

---

5   For more information on the survey and the resettlement schemes, see Dekker & Kinsey (2011).

BOX 1 *Resettlement programme land reform*

Just after independence in 1980, the Government of Zimbabwe embarked on a land reform programme to redistribute land from the commercial farming sector to smallholder farmers. The land reform programme had four components: the establishment of family farms (model A); collective farms (model B); individual cultivation on a core estate (model C); and extensive ranching (model D). In the model A schemes in our study, individual families were settled into villages and allocated with (i) a residential plot to build their houses; (ii) 12 acres of arable land; and (iii) the right to use grazing land on a communal basis. Settlers received permits to use the residential, arable, and grazing land, but the actual ownership of the land was not transferred to them and remained with the state. The resettlement programme was based on voluntary resettlement, and interested settlers applied of their own choice. The 12-acre arable land was a considerable asset; the mean land holdings in the African farming areas in the early 1980s were considerably lower. Various studies have demonstrated the positive effects of resettlement on farming and livestock holdings (see for example Deininger *et al.* 2004), suggesting the allocation of land in such schemes provided the settlers with a potential road to prosperity.

agro-ecological regions and differ in terms of their suitability for crop production. In 1997, communal areas adjacent to the three resettlement areas were added to the sample for comparative purposes. Specifically, I use data on respondents' reported migration histories and their perceptions of the resettlement process (both datasets collected retrospectively in 2000 and 2001). I combine this with data from in-depth interviews conducted with the same settlers with non-Zimbabwean totems in November 2013 and January 2014. The in-depth interviews were conducted in two of the three resettlement schemes covered in the ZRHDS dataset.

There are various ways to identify someone's descent. In Zimbabwe, a common question when people first meet is to ask for someone's totem, as this provides a trace to a person's geographical origin. Someone's totem is made of three elements: their Mutupo, Chidao, and Dzinza. These terms refer to the patrilineal clan, sub-clan, and sub-section of the sub-clan, respectively. Both Mutupo and Chidao have religious and symbolic connotations. Someone's Dzinza simply traces their family roots and refers to the fourth male ancestor up the family tree (Bourdillon 1976). It also indicates the geographical location of the clan lands upon which an individual's great-grandparents lived. For previous work with this same group of farmers, Barr (2004) collected information on the totems of the heads of households and their wife/wives. This allows us to distinguish between settlers with a Zimbabwean totem and settlers with a foreign totem and also captures settlers whose fathers, grandfathers, or great-grandfathers were original migrants to Zimbabwe.[6]

Of the 543 households in our dataset, 26 (4.79%) have a male household head with a non-Zimbabwean totem; 28 household heads (5.16%) are married to a wife with a non-Zimbabwean totem. Since occasionally both husband and wife have a non-Zimbabwean totem (6 cases), in total 48 households (8.84%) in the resettlement areas in this study have non-Zimbabwean roots.

Zones of Transition

What is the background of these non-Zimbabwean settlers? Are they similar to the Zimbabwean settlers or do they have specific migration trajectories that suggest they indeed left their zones of transition when they settled? This section describes the trajectories of settlers who established their homes in the resettlement schemes in the early 1980s. It compares the trajectories of settlers with a non-Zimbabwean totem with those with a Zimbabwean totem.

In 2000, the ZRHDS included a question on the occupational and geographical trajectories of resettled farmers. The question asked the respondents to list each place the head of the household had lived or worked since leaving school or since age 16, including the place of current residence. Responses varied from 0 (i.e. those who were born in the scheme and were currently head of a household) to a maximum of 10. The following was reported by BN, who was born in Malawi. In an in-depth interview, he remembered his zones of transition.

> In 1921, I was born in Mlanje, Malawi. I stayed there for 28 years with my parents, and I used to work as a general hand on tea plantations. In 1949, I became interested in buying a bicycle. However, no bicycles were available in Malawi, and I heard bicycles used to come from Johannesburg to Harare. With three friends, I walked from Malawi to Harare (it took us three weeks), and when we arrived there we found a car looking for labourers at Mtoko. We were taken straight to Saimona farm in Bindura, where I worked as a general hand. Although life was good at the farm, I left Saimona to look for better pay elsewhere. I met a builder from Cooper Farm in Glendale at a church service and moved to

---

6   This method is preferable to the identification of non-Zimbabweans based on their migration histories, as the latter would capture only first-generation migrants.

Cooper Farm to become an assistant builder. The pay was better there. From Cooper Farm another builder helped me to get a building contract at King Farm near Concession, again for better pay. My friends went back to Malawi, but I stayed in Zimbabwe and went to Kachera Farm near Mazowe to work as a builder. I also got married there to a Zimbabwean girl. Then my in-laws asked me to come to Mushowani to stay on their plot. Then I came to Green Dry Farm [this area] to work as a builder and later to Odendella and Makaki Farm, also around here. The war was getting hot, and the white farmer I was working for left for Macheke. I did not want to follow him, and the white man wrote a letter to Madziva council to ask for a plot on my behalf. I then got a plot with village head Manyika and established my home there. When things got really hot in the war, I went to Keep Number 7 [security camp created during the civil war]. When the war ended in 1979, word went around that people could apply for a plot in the farms. I applied and that is how I got my plot in this village.

Interview in Mupfurudzi Resettlement Scheme, February 2014

BN's account as well as the answers to the survey question nicely illustrate the mobility in the Zimbabwean population. On average, a settler lived in more than three places before he/she settled in the resettlement areas in the ZRHDS study. This pre-settlement mobility is highest in the agro-ecological area with highest agricultural potential and is demonstrated by both resettlement and communal area farmers.

When we look in more detail at the number of moves reported by households with non-Zimbabwean totems, an interesting picture emerges. Non-Zimbabwean heads of household report a significantly higher number of moves compared with the Zimbabwean heads of household.[7] On average, non-Zimbabwean household heads had 4–5 previous workplaces, while Zimbabwean household heads reported 3–4 such places (Table 1).

Although circular migration was certainly not restricted to non-Zimbabwean labourers, the fact that they did not have a *musha*, or rural home, meant that each job, and each farm or workplace, was in fact a new zone of transition. And this zone of transition was left for a new one when looking for better conditions, leaving a situation of forced labour, following bosses, friends, and so on.

This is also nicely illustrated by the case of Chenai, to whom I spoke in Sengezi resettlement scheme.

---

7   Similar results are found when considering the difference between households with wives of non-Zimbabwean descent or the variable that combines non-Zimbabwean husband or wife.

TABLE 1   *Number of moves prior to resettlement in 1980, disaggregated according to descent of the head of household*

	Total sample (N = 543)	Sample non-Zimbabwean heads (N = 26)	Sample Zimbabwean heads (N = 517)	p-value difference
Number of moves before settling in 1980	3.36	4.46	3.31	0.0001

SOURCE: ZRHDS 2000 DATA

Chenai is the wife of Nicholas, whose father was born in Malawi and married a Zimbabwean girl. At the time of resettlement, Nicholas's father was working as a private builder at Oklahoma Farm near Marondera. He resigned from this farm and moved to the resettlement area, with his wife and children. Chenai was born in 1964 in Zimbabwe and her parents came from Durban. Her parents are of Zulu origin and had four children in Durban. They left three children there and took one with them to Bath Farm in Hwedza, where Chenai's father worked as a shopkeeper in 1962. Her father would go back to Durban from time to time but continued to work in Zimbabwe. When his white employer got a shop at Imire Game Park, Chenai's father moved there to work for him. Later on, when his employer moved to Karimba shop, he followed as well. When his employer stopped running shops, Chenai's father changed employers and worked as a shopkeeper for Mr Gerry at Bath Farm. When Chenai's father died in 1979, they could not stay at Bath Farm and went back to Imire. Her mother started to look around for her own plot, and a friend helped her to get one in the communal area. Although she stayed there ever since, Chenai's mother is now considering to go back to South Africa. Chenai married Nicholas in 1982 and came to live on this plot together with Nicholas's brother when their father died.

Interview in Sengezi Resettlement Scheme, February 2014

Although most settlers with a non-Zimbabwean totem had an impressive track record when it came to the number of places they had lived and worked before settling in Sengezi or Mupfurudzi in the early 1980s, we also came across one family originating from Mozambique who never worked for a white farmer or mine, but directly obtained land in a communal area before applying for resettlement in 1980.

> Rowesai's parents came from Rushinga. Her grandfather came from Mozambique. The grandfather was called Chari Gwaka. He had four young brothers. These also came to Zimbabwe. They came on foot and they came to settle here. He found a plot at Mahomba in Rushinga, where he farmed. He got married in Zimbabwe and was known for being a good farmer. He had a lot of black pigs. He never went back to Mozambique and never worked for a white man. He stayed with his children in Rushinga, where he died, leaving behind four wives.
>
> Interview in Sengezi Resettlement Scheme, February 2014

Interestingly, we also came across a few settlers with a Zimbabwean totem who had ventured into the neighbouring countries to look for work or land, as was explained by some residents from a village in Mupfurudzi:

> Sarah was born in Masvingo and grew up in Mvuma, where she married Mujere, who lived in the next-door village. Mujere was a cook on a white farm. Mujere then heard of land in Mozambique from his uncle who was already there. Together with two other families, they went to Mukumbura on the Mozambican side to obtain a permit to settle there. At that time they had three children and they obtained a good farm. In Mozambique there was no limit to the number of acres one could till. Farming was successful; he had over ten head of cattle *and* bought a Scotch cart and used to have lots of maize. After ten years, the Frelimo war disturbed them and they decided to go back to Mukumbura on the Zimbabwean side. When Zimbabwe was born, Mujere and his family moved to this resettlement village, together with one other family who came back from Mozambique.
>
> Interview in Sengezi Resettlement Scheme, February 2014

The Resettlement Experience

In a context of circulatory migration, migrants are expected to stay in touch with their home areas and eventually go back. The non-Zimbabwean migrants who settled in the resettlement schemes in the early 1980s obviously did not go back; and given their age, they are not very likely to go back anymore. Zimbabwe's resettlement schemes are where they retire and where they will be buried. In their life histories, many report they have never gone back to their home country, sometimes leaving wife and children behind. Second- or second-plus-generation migrants generally did not go 'home'—although there are exceptions, as illustrated by Mr Kaputa:

Kaputa is the son of Mariko who came from Dowa, Malawi where he was farming. With two others, Mariko came to Zimbabwe on foot to look for work. A friend called him to come to Shamva, where Mariko worked in a white man's shop. Then he moved to Bin Farm to work as a tailor. He had a Rhodesian registration certificate with a red X to show that he had to live 10 km out of Harare. From Bin Farm he went to Cawood Farm to earn more money. At Cawood he was both a shopkeeper and a tailor. Later he moved to Madziva Mine shop, where he died after an illness. This was in the 1970s. Mr Mariko returned to Malawi on one occasion to visit relatives. His father came to Rhodesia on three occasions, and on one of these occasions (in 1968) his father took four of his grandchildren to visit Malawi. The grandchildren came back on their own because the grandfather died.

Interview in Mupfurudzi Resettlement Scheme, February 2014

Does this mean that the non-Zimbabwean settlers consider Zimbabwe now their home—have they left the zones of transition (circulatory migration) and 'established' themselves? It is not so easy to answer this question, as they settled not in a 'traditional village' where they had to assimilate in an existing social structure. They settled in a 'new village', composed of 'strangers' to the extent that most people did not know one another at the time they settled.

In 2001, the ZRHDS questionnaire contained questions on the experience of being resettled, addressing the household head, senior wife, or all adults together. The enumerator read 16 statements and asked the respondent's feeling about how the statement applied to them and their family. These feelings were registered using a Likert scale, a scale between 0 and 4 ranging from the statement 'did not at all apply to them and their family' (0) to 'the statement applies perfectly to them and their family' (4).

In Table 2, I compare the scores for these statements in two groups: the second column reports the scores of the settlers with Zimbabwean totems, while the third column reports the scores reported by settlers with non-Zimbabwean totems. The fourth column provides the t-statistics for the difference in means between the two groups. When the t-statistic is below 0.10, I consider the differences between the two groups to be statistically significant. When reviewing the data presented in Table 2, there are not many differences between the responses of households with Zimbabwean totems and households with non-Zimbabwean totems; in most instances, there are no statistically significant differences between the scores on the statements between the two groups. In general, all respondents reported that their resettlement experience had been a positive experience: resettlement provided them with an opportunity to start afresh, and they had settled well with their new neighbours. There are a few

TABLE 2 *Feelings towards the resettlement experience: comparing Zimbabwean heads of household with non-Zimbabwean heads of household*

Statement	Zimbabwean heads of household	Non-Zimbabwean heads of household	p-score difference in means
Important people with whom we lived previously strongly encouraged us to resettle and to move here	2.37	3.27	0.00
If we had not resettled here, we would have had nowhere else to go	2.41	2.89	0.09
When we moved here we were freed from all sorts of obligations and responsibilities	3.30	3.80	0.01
Important people in the place where we lived previously are still today a major influence in our lives	1.47	1.52	0.86
We have made this village our home in every way	3.90	4	0.38
Resettlement gave us an opportunity to take control of our own lives	3.90	4	0.21
It was our own idea to apply for resettlement	3.55	3.37	0.34
We no longer think about the place where we lived previously	3.34	3.36	0.93
All the people in this village have become like kin to us	3.85	3.86	0.85
When we return to the place where we lived previously, we feel like strangers there	2.22	2.59	0.22
We would not be welcomed back in the place where we lived previously	1.95	2.04	0.74
Our obligations and responsibilities towards people where we lived previously are just as strong now as when we lived there	2.86	2.75	0.63

TABLE 2   *Feelings towards the resettlement experience: comparing Zimbabwean heads of household with non-Zimbabwean heads of household* (cont.)

Statement	Zimbabwean heads of household	Non-Zimbabwean heads of household	p-score difference in means
Living here is easier because we are free to make our own decisions	3.9	4.0	0.22
Resettlement provided us with a chance to make a new start	3.89	3.9	0.66
We do not feel as responsible towards our neighbours in this village as we did towards people where we lived previously	0.84	0.61	0.29
We miss the place where we lived previously	0.72	0.27	0.04

SOURCE: ZRHDS 2001 DATA

interesting observations. Settlers with non-Zimbabwean totems unanimously reported having made this village their new home in every way and that resettlement gave them an opportunity to take control of their own lives (the mean score is 4, which indicates this statement fully applied to their situation). This is not the case for all settlers with Zimbabwean totems, but the differences I found in my sample are not statistically significant.

The significant differences in means on certain statements reported in Table 2 suggest that the decision to apply for resettlement was not taken in isolation. Settlers with non-Zimbabwean totems were more likely to report that important people with whom they lived previously strongly encouraged them to resettle and to move to this new place. To some extent, resettlement was a way out, as settlers with non-Zimbabwean totems also were more likely to indicate they would have had nowhere to go if they had not resettled, suggesting they wanted to get out of the zone of transition they were in just before resettlement. This may refer to their physical conditions, such as living in protected villages, but it may also refer to the social circumstances during and just after the war. In that context, resettlement may also have been 'liberating', as settlers with non-Zimbabwean totems are more likely to report they were freed from all sorts of obligations and responsibilities when they moved to the new villages.

In general, the settlers do not miss very much the place where they lived previously, but this was more common among settlers with non-Zimbabwean totems than among settlers with Zimbabwean totems, suggesting that resettlement provided a new home to them. They had successfully left the zones of transition behind.

Conclusion

Given the historical importance of labour migration in southern Africa, it is not surprising that migrants and their descendants have not returned to their home countries and have settled in their host countries instead—either because they could not return home (for example, because ties with their families were cut or the security situation did not allow them to do so), or because they did not want to go home as the host country kept on providing an imaginary road to prosperity. Based on survey data and in-depth interviews, I reviewed the experiences of labour migrants (or their descendants) from Malawi, South Africa, Zambia, and Mozambique who settled in two resettlement schemes established in the early 1980s, just after the war of independence. Survey data shows that both Zimbabwean and non-Zimbabwean settlers had an extensive migration history before they obtained a plot and agricultural land in the resettlement schemes. On average, they had 3–4 places of residence prior to settling in the new villages; they either worked at various farms, mines, or towns, or they had their own smallholder farm. I refer to these as zones of transition, as people moved from one place to another following friends and employers, leaving difficult living/working conditions behind or looking for new opportunities. A comparison of the averages between the two groups shows that settlers with a non-Zimbabwean descent had experienced a significantly higher number of transition zones before settling in the early 1980s. A review of the resettlement experience, provided by the settler families in the early 2000s, suggests that resettlement provided the foreign settlers with 'a way out'.

References

Barr, A. (2004), Forging Effective Communities: The Evolution of Civil Society in Zimbabwean Resettled Villages. *World Development* 32(10): 1753–1766.

Bourdillon, M. (1976), *The Shona Peoples: An Ethnography of the Contemporary Shona, with Special Reference to Their Religion*. Gweru: Mambo Press.

Deininger, K., H. Hoogeveen & B. Kinsey (2004), Economic Benefits and Costs of Land Redistribution in Zimbabwe in the Early 1980s. *World Development* 32(10): 1697–1709.

Dekker, M. & B.H. Kinsey (2011), Contextualizing Zimbabwe's Land Reform: Long-term Observations from the First Generation. *Journal of Peasant Studies* 38(5): 995–1019.

Harts-Broekhuis, A. & H. Huisman (2001), Resettlement Revisited: Land Reform Results in Resource-Poor Regions in Zimbabwe. *Geoforum* 32(3): 285–298.

Holland, H. (2010), *Dinner with Mugabe: The Untold Story of a Freedom Fighter Who Became a Tyrant*. Penguin.

Kay, G. (1972), *Distribution and Density of African Population in Rhodesia*. University of Hull, Department of Geography. Miscellaneous Series No. 12.

Kay, G. (1982), Population Redistribution in Zimbabwe, in: J.I. Clarke & L.A. Kosinski (eds) *Redistribution of Population in Africa*. London Exeter, NH: Heinemann.

Kinsey, B.H. (1982), Forever Gained: Resettlement and Land Policy in the Context of National Development in Zimbabwe. *Africa* 52(3): 92–113.

Nyambara, P.S. (2001), Immigrants, 'Traditional' Leaders and the Rhodesian State: The Power of 'Communal' Land Tenure and the Politics of Land Acquisition in Gokwe, Zimbabwe, 1963–1979. *Journal of Southern African Studies* 27(4): 771–791.

Spierenburg, M. (2003), *Strangers, Spirits and Land Reforms: Conflicts about Land in Dande, Northern Zimbabwe*. Amsterdam: University of Amsterdam.

Van Onselen, C. (1980), *Chibaro: African Mine Labour in Southern Rhodesia, 1900–1933*. London: Pluto Press.

Zinyama, L. & R. Whitlow (1986), Changing Patterns of Population Distribution in Zimbabwe. *GeoJournal* 13: 365–384.

PART 3

Zones of Transference

∵

A Romantic Zone of Transference? Botswana, Ghanaian Migrants and Marital Social Mobility

Rijk van Dijk[1]

Introduction

Looking back on his eight years of marriage to a woman from Botswana, a Ghanaian hair salon owner in his early fifties, living and working in Botswana, reminisces with satisfaction about how his marital life has developed over those years. Marrying in 2006, it had taken him ten years to prepare for this wedding since he first set eyes on the lady. Sitting in his small office at the back of his hair salon, he recounts vividly the various steps that the marital process required him to take, the complexities that emerged—of which he, being a migrant from Ghana, had little advance knowledge—and the emotions that came with a woman whom he loved dearly and who, as he proclaimed, was taking very good care of him. In marrying a local, he had realized that he had to take a lot of advice, but it had resulted in him marrying a good partner, one that has caused him to continue staying in the country, a country he feels he will never leave again as he has become settled. Asked to elaborate on this point, he continued explaining that after moving from Ghana to South Africa and from there trying his luck by moving to Botswana in the early 1990s, the marriage to his Botswana wife had been truly beneficial to his peace of mind and had given him a purpose to stay in the country and not to move back to Ghana, nor to move on and travel to another country. Together, he, his wife, and their children had now built a comfortable life in one of the new, upper-middle-class living areas, a life of reasonable security, prosperity, and status, not least because of the fact that his wife had become well-educated and had secured a good job as well. Whereas his marriage to a Botswana citizen appears not to have been significant in terms of the status of his stay in the country, reaching the level of the relatively successful, upcoming urbanite middle classes in Botswana was definitely supported through this marriage.

This case of a Ghanaian national marrying a local partner in Botswana in the course of the many years of the Ghana-to-Botswana, South–South labour

---

1   I am greatly indebted to Anna Louban and Jan-Bart Gewald for their critical reading of earlier versions of this contribution and the suggestions they made toward its improvement.

migration process is in many ways representative of other cases that have occurred in the manner in which the Ghanaian migrant community came to settle in the country (for a comparative study of this South–South migration, see Van Dijk 2003; Van de Kamp & Van Dijk 2010; Choplin & Lombard 2013; Kastner 2013). Studying such 'mixed marriages', as they are commonly typified in the literature—the term 'mixed' usually referring to the involvement of two different nationalities—can be revealing in relation to the question whether or not marriage can be identified as an institution relevant to an understanding of 'zones of transit' in the way this book defines them and which forms the main framework of the discussion this contribution aims to offer. On the road to prosperity, people pass through zones of transit: places, locales, borders, and boundaries where people stay and interact before moving on; in some cases, the zone of transit becomes a place of settlement and immobility, something Choplin and Lombard have termed a 'post-transit' situation (see Choplin & Lombard 2013; Suter 2013).

Botswana in this sense is part of a long and well-documented history of massive processes of labour migration, involving the passing through of numerous labour migrants on the road to prosperity in the South African mining and industrial complexes—a history that in many ways turned the roads, railway line, and small villages of Botswana into places of transit for migrants coming all the way from present-day Malawi, Zambia, Zimbabwe, the Congo, and so forth.[2] Whereas this geographical mobility has left its marks on Botswana in terms of being a place of transit for many—which nevertheless also became a place of settlement for those who did not continue their transit to and from the mines—the question remains as to how this interlinks with (upward) social mobility. The history of this massive process of labour migration has produced a literature that investigates the effects of return and remittances for individuals, their families, and their communities (Brown 1983; Manamere 2014) and the extent to which this geographical mobility co-produced social mobility; yet, often the zones of transit as such have not been much included in these analyses. Moreover, as this contribution aims to argue, the zones of transit that exist in terms of upward social mobility have often received less attention—that is, those social zones that help to transfer people from one station in life to a higher one. In other words, while in terms of geographical mobility it has become clear that zones of transit are important in understanding how such mobility has been evolving, in terms of social mobility, however, there is usually much less attention paid to the social forms and

---

2 Examples of the historical study of the significance of (labour-) migration for Botswana can be found in such studies as the early work of Schapera (1947), or later that of Parson (1985).

institutions that make people shift from one (socio-economic) level into a higher one.

The example of the Ghanaian hair salon owner moving into Botswana in the hope of a brighter future, and then accessing marriage with a local partner as a way through which also a shift into a higher socio-economic status in terms of standard of living can occur, forms a case in point. While, on the one hand, Botswana for him stopped being a *zone of transit* (there is no longer a transit to somewhere else), on the other hand it became for him a *zone of transference* to a higher socio-economic class, most likely much higher than what he could otherwise have achieved by remaining based in West Africa or in South Africa. This contribution, therefore, intends to argue that in addition to a study of the 'social life' of geographical zones of transit, social spaces of transference also need to be taken into account as being junctures that make people shift from one social status into another. Some of these spaces of transference are well known: school and the educational system are one such obvious point of transference, as education tends to create opportunities for those in lower socio-economic positions to reach higher standards of living. And often a school, as a point of transference in terms of upward social mobility, is related to geographical mobility, in that receiving education requires travel. The example of the hair salon owner, however, demonstrates that marriage can be located in exactly the same manner as a modality in and through which geographical mobility is brought together with social mobility. Yet, at the same time, in the story of the hair salon owner, we find very different motivations and emotions that do not easily translate his relationship into something purely 'instrumental' in nature. Falling in love, romance, affection, and intimacy are very much part of the picture of this mixed marriage; other motivations, such as for instance those related to gaining access to Botswana society, citizenship, or a higher socio-economic status, do not seem to figure much in the reasons he provides for entering a transnational relationship.

Identifying such a marriage as a zone of transference may potentially do injustice to the romantic nature of the relationship. Often, in discussions about mixed marriages, attention to the instrumental significance of marriage as a zone of transference for a foreigner—for example allowing him or her to gain access to the new nation-state and its social goods—seems prevalent. Also, marriage migration may be related to highly unequal, if not exploitative gender relations, which, as Constable (2009) and Charsley (2012) show, mainly affect women. In this sense, exploring mixed marriages from a perspective of romance and romantic migration (see Trundle 2009; Conway & Leonard 2014)—that is, identifying those aspects of migration that focus on the emotional side of the establishment of transnational relationships—may require further strengthening and support. In many cases, marriage migration is not so much explored in terms of its (possible) *romantic* dimensions (those explicitly related to emotions and affections); rather, it is often researched in a literature that investigates nation-state regimes of controlling borders and access to citizenship status or the (potentially) exploitative and often unequal relations between men and women that are part of the migration pattern (see Williams 2010). Hence, among the questions are these: How romantic can a point of transference be? If marriage seems to function as a point of transference to a higher socio-economic status, how romantic is the marriage? And what then is the place of romance in a mixed marriage such as the case of this Ghanaian–Botswana couple?

Romantic Migration: How Romantic or Romanticist is It?

In recent years there has been a remarkable growth of interest in migration involving (romantic) relationships, especially related to marriage and also including these forms of migration from, to, and within Africa. While the works of scholars such as Neveu-Kringelbach (2013) and Rodriguez Garcia (2006) on mixed marriage, citizenship, and the policing of intimacy in contemporary France and Spain relate explicitly to waves of migration from Africa, other publications, such as those of Williams (2010) on *Global Marriage: Cross-Border Marriages and Marriage Migration in Context* and Charsley (2012) on *Transnational Marriage: New Perspectives from Europe and Beyond,* engage in a wider and more cross-cultural comparative perspective on the process. Much of this literature addresses first and foremost the process of migration related to marriage as an issue for nation-states and the control of borders, or the control of exploitative relations, illustrated by the sharp increase of government inspection of relationships, intimacy, love, and sexuality (Maskens 2013). The socio-political control of citizenship, of who belongs and who does not (Meyer & Geschiere 1999), has enormously sharpened nation-states' pursuit of the policing of relationships, and thereby the creation of a discourse of acceptability and justification of the inspection and introspection of the intimate. Literature such as that of Fassin (2010) on *National Identity and Transnational Intimacies: Sexual Democracy and the Politics of Immigration in Europe,* or that of Groes-Green (2014) on *Journeys of Patronage: Moral Economies of Transactional Sex and Female Migration from Mozambique to Europe,* also places the exploration of such migration in this perspective of being a problem of governmentality. Mixed marriages are explored from a perspective that aims to understand how governments turn transnational relationships into being a problematic to the control of citizenship, warranting stiff measures of policing. This provides social scientists with a specific social, political, and economic context for the investigation of such relationships.

In this production of knowledge, developing the concept of romantic migration may be faced with a number of limitations and questions:

1. Romantic migration is usually associated with what are known as *mixed marriages* or *transnational marriages*; that is, marriages of couples of two different nationalities, implying that any other form of what possibly could be perceived as a *mixed* marriage—say of different faiths, classes, ethnicities or generations—does not enter these considerations very often. It is not hard to imagine that explorations of precisely these different categories can be relevant for the study of romantic migration.

2. Furthermore, the 'romantic' in romantic migration can be exclusively understood in terms of an idealization of intimate relations. The interest in romantic migration commonly does not include an interest in *romanticist* elements in migration—that is, in exploring migration as driven by sentiment and emotion relating to the heroic and the anti-establishment—in short, all migration that is not informed by rational choice. In this way the term romantic migration could easily comprise the mobility of artists and intellectuals, or the mobility of political activists and religious ideologists. Yet, in practice, the term is understood to refer to all forms of migration that have to do with the formation of intimate relationships and the idealization of partners, among which there are of course marital relations, but also friendships, courtship, and caring and altruistic relations.

3. Thirdly, while migration studies usually highlight people and the mobility of people, the concept of romantic migration can foster an interest in the understanding of expectations of relationships, romance, and their modelling/styling (see, for example, Trundle 2009). Yet, the manner in which romantic migration implies a (*global*) *circulation of ideas and images of romance* is often much less elaborated upon. The ways in which such ideas and images also travel and insert themselves into localities and local identities commonly deserves greater attention in research that aims to investigate romantic migration.

4. Related to the previous point, studies of romantic migration often perceive migration as resulting from romance, and not the other way around—that is, *romance resulting from migration*. Yet, this point is certainly of great relevance for this contribution on Ghanaian-Botswana relationships, as will be explained in the remainder of this contribution,

since 'locals' may have developed specific fascinations for the 'foreigner', in a context where the new presence of foreigners may have triggered such sentiments where they did not exist before.

If, for the moment, we return to the first point, namely, how the study of romantic migration can be related to the study of migration for reasons of marriage, a focus in the research into mixed marriages often surfaces, in which the complexities pertaining to the legal aspects of such relations seem to receive much attention. This is usually related to the legal provisions that allow for marriage being a route into acquiring a residence permit or citizenship of a country (in European countries such as the Netherlands or Germany requiring a certain number of years of having been in a relationship and having stayed in the country while demonstrating efforts to 'integrate' such as learning the local language). This means that nation-states in parts of the world assume that transnational migration for romantic reasons can have very different motivations from emotions and sentiments, claiming its purpose may also be instrumental. They have thus been putting in place bureaucratic structures that basically perceive mixed marriage with suspicion. While the rise of these structures has been leading to fierce debates concentrating on the question as to the extent to which a nation-state can have the right to control and inspect marital/intimate relations, the political defence of such policies is that the nation-state has the fullest right to know its citizenry, also in bio-political terms. Romantic migration has been subject to a criminalization of forms of marriage in the Netherlands known as *schijnhuwelijken* (lit. 'sham marriages'). As I have argued elsewhere, some groups of migrants can become heavily targeted for bureaucratic policing of their marital relations (Van Dijk 2001). This happened in the 1990s to the Ghanaian migrant community in various parts of the Netherlands, as Ghanaians became increasingly the subject of an inspection of their marriage, bachelor and birth certificates, and an entire bureaucratic procedure of what became known as 'verification' of these documents emerged (Van Dijk 2001: 579). The work of Anna Louban in Berlin on the German control of intimate relations involving romantic migration draws attention to the subtleties of body language, comportment, and performance that becomes part of the interplay between the couple and the border officials. How long and how intimately does the couple hold hands during an interview?[3] If it is for too long, the relation may be deemed 'fake' and 'instrumental' and definitely not

---

3   In a personal communication, Anna Louban added that other questions officials could raise concerning the status of these relationship were, for instance, the following: When does the couple start to hold hands? In front of the gate, or only before entering the clerk's office?

romantic by such an official; yet, if they hold hands too briefly, a couple may be subject to the same verdict (Louban 2014).

Yet, what happens to the concept of romantic migration and transnational marriages if the issues of citizenship and instrumentalized marriage *are not pre-eminently* the immediate context? What if mixed marriages are pursued without having the possibility of access to citizenship and the social, common goods of a particular nation-state that engaging in such a relationship may offer? Will we then have a chance to study romantic migration in ways that will highlight more the romantic ideal as such and in its singularity? An obvious counter to this notion is that any marriage may have instrumental and romantic aspirations, desires, and motivations; furthermore, even 'instrumentalized' marriages can have romantic sentiments, as the one does not by definition exclude the other. I would like to pause here and consider the possibility of studying the romantic, that is, the romantic component(s) of romantic migration where these mixed marriages are concerned. If we do so and venture to identify such components, where will it bring us compared with studying the instrumentalized dimensions of these marriages? I am proposing in this contribution to take romance seriously and perceive it primarily in the way it offers people notions of taking and negotiating a certain distance from calculative, rationalizing, maximizing behaviours in the pursuit of emotional motivations which can certainly be anti-establishment in nature as well.

There are a number of reasons for the importance of this exploration of the romanticist elements in the romantic migration perspective. The first of these reasons is that romantic migration is part of, and relates to, a perspective that perceives migration as diasporic when it develops into a trajectory of settlement-without-full-integration. Clifford (1997) defined diasporic movement as 'living inside with a difference'. Diasporic communities thereby are seen as bent on maintaining their own cultural repertoires (as marking off their 'inside with a difference' from the rest of society), often by emphasizing such forms of life-crisis rituals as marriage. Hence, the following questions arise: If a marriage takes place, how much sentiment is there in terms of maintaining (cultural) difference? Is marriage then turned into a particular moment to stress a particular identity? And even more importantly, is marriage then arranged at a critical distance from the host society, thus strengthening/reinforcing the 'inside with a difference' over a length of time?

In the Ghanaian context of migration to the West, and in this case to Botswana as well, this question quickly became important because of the rise of Pentecostal churches in the migration communities—churches which not only provide for a circulation of people but also for a circulation of ideas, images, institutions, models, and competences. Their notion of the modelling of marriage according to strict moral principles developed into such a 'living inside with a difference' on two accounts: one relates critically to the cultural or ethnic context of the place of origin; the other relates critically to the host society. As some authors have shown (see Van Dijk 2004; Bochow 2012; Cole 2012), these strict moral principles run counter to local cultural traditions both at the places of origin and at the places of destination: Pentecostal leaders often take (moral) control over the marital proceedings and arrangements, inspect the moral conduct of partners and families, and prohibit the use of alcoholic drinks, the services of traditional healers, the performance of 'lustful' dancing, and so forth. And they do so at home *and* abroad in similar terms, thereby making sure that their Pentecostal notions of a respectful marriage travel along the paths of migration. Such a travelling of (Pentecostal) ideas and models can thus have high moral implications and consequences. Romantic migration then can start to serve a particular moral agenda of the Pentecostals in the way they position themselves in a migrant community and *vis-à-vis* the position of the migrant community and transnational faith in a nation-state set-up and an even wider global world.

Furthermore, while such religious groups may circulate particular ideas of romantic migration across borders, help in establishing transactional relations, and contribute to the process (such as sending letters of introduction across the diaspora concerning marital partners and arrangements), they are not the only ones who mediate models across borders. The manner in which middle-class models of companionate love (Hirsch & Wardlow 2006) began circulating worldwide, creating a very popular fascination especially among the young generation for romantic ideas of glamorous weddings and consumerist lifestyles, prompted a 'diaspora' of the 'white wedding', which is certainly a point of study for romantic migration.

The second step is therefore to also understand *the romantic as being romanticist* (see Maskens & Blanes 2013); that is, as a deviation, as anti-establishment, as anti-conventional, and even as a critique of the local and the cultural. Mixed marriages of a local to a foreigner, therefore, can potentially also allow the *local* to create a critical distance from one's own cultural styles and tradition. Here we meet, for instance, the local fascinations for the stranger, for the manner in which the stranger and the foreign produce romantic fascinations with the exotic, the erotic, the sentimental, or the intimate *as a commentary* on what local traditions and conventions may prescribe about the ways in which a marriage needs to be arranged and performed. In a sense, this can indicate a *migrational romance,* produced by locals in a way that inverts the usual manner in which the flow of romantic migration is understood. In my earlier work on the arrival of Ghanaian migrants in Botswana (Van Dijk 2003), I discussed the manner in which Ghanaian women began introducing West African styles of beautification into this southern African country, styles that certainly informed and sparked a great deal of romantic interest on the part of locals, in that these styles of beautification became incorporated, for instance, in the weddings of the newly emerging middle class.

Romantic migration, in its circulation of people, institutional forms, ideas, and images, can thus be seen to be potentially related to romanticist notions as well as to diasporic notions. In both terms, romantic migration can contain an element of transferring critical dimensions and anti-establishment interests, creating a level of independency from the local while at the same time 'tuning in' to globally circulating ideas of the refashioning of marriage and relationships. If we are to understand how the mixed marriage may operate as a 'transference point' in any migration context, we may need to explore in depth precisely how diasporic notions as well as romanticist ideas intersect and interact.

Ghanaians Marrying Batswana[4]

In a recent stint of fieldwork in Botswana, I took up an interest in relating to those Ghanaians in the city of Gaborone who, since the time of their arrival in the country, had married a local partner. My questions of exploration were threefold:

1. To what extent was the mixed marriage impacted by diasporic sentiment as outlined above—that is, as 'inside with a difference', as highlighting a clash of cultures, as pitting a Ghanaian identity/ heritage against Botswana-based notions of the importance of marriage?

2. How much was it romantic and romanticist as counter-establishment, not based on calculation but on sentiment, and therefore a kind of critical reflection of the (moral and other) strictures that would otherwise apply?

3. And how did the diasporic and the romanticist help in producing the mixed marriage as a social point of transference—that is, as a way of becoming relatively independent of one's circle and (previous) social position and station in life?

In Botswana, marriage to a foreigner is not seen (by Ghanaians and others) as providing the foreigner with immediate legal benefits, especially in terms of

---

4 Batswana (sing. Motswana) is a commonly used reference to the people of Botswana.

standing a higher chance of obtaining citizenship.[5] In addition, in terms of the societal conditions of the foreigner, it is important to note that Botswana's general profile in the southern African region is one of being 'xenophobic' in its public culture and administrative rulings and practices (see Nyamnjoh 2002; Campbell 2003). In my talks with Ghanaian migrants who settled in the country, the point was reiterated by many of them that while they have been recruited by the Botswana government to serve in its public service, even after decades of presence in the country their stranger-hood seems perpetual. Naturalization normally takes at least ten years to complete, and the Ghanaian migrants felt that the marrying of local partners as such does not help much in the process if so desired by the Ghanaian national. Therefore, the couples that I spoke to indicated that their Ghanaian–Botswana transnational marriages could not and did not provide them easy access to a firm establishment in the Botswana nation-state, as securing a job is much more important in doing so. Yet, at the same time, firm establishment is attractive to many Ghanaians since Botswana is and has been a fast-growing economy marked by a high level of political stability, by a well-facilitated public domain with a great deal of opportunities for schooling and further training, and by a well-serviced medical system, while a well-established middle class is producing an exceptional living standard with access to a wide range of consumer goods.

The main access foreigners can have to all of these public goods is through labour. This migration regime is much driven, as I have indicated in an earlier publication, by a policy known as 'localisation' (Van Dijk 2003)—meaning that on the one hand, the government is striving towards an economy in which increasingly jobs and positions held by foreigners are transferred into the hands of 'locals', whereas on the other, employers must have very good reasons to employ any foreigner for a particular job. This means that the presence of Ghanaian nationals in Botswana has basically been possible on the basis of having been recruited for acceptable reasons, such as specific educational qualifications and skilled competences.[6] This being the case, it does produce the interesting questions raised above concerning the motive and motif of romance, diaspora, and transference: If marrying a local does not seem to

---

5 I am thankful to Treasa Calvin for clarifying this point to me in a personal communication. The well-known, so-called Unity Dow court case of 1992 only partially relates to this problematic, as she successfully challenged a gender inequality in the manner in which citizenship rights could or could not be transferred to children of mixed marriages: Batswana women if married to a foreign partner could not transfer these rights to their children while Batswana men could.

6 See Oucho (2000) on this element of the Botswana recruitment policies.

surface as a method for gaining the highly sought firm access to Botswana and all its economic opportunities, is it then to be classified as being pre-eminently 'romantic'? And if Ghanaians remain living in Botswana 'inside with a difference', then how much of the marriage with a local is or was styled as maintaining Ghanaian cultural traditions and thereby running against Botswana cultural and/or conventions And if strong issues of love, attraction, and affection have been playing a crucial role from the start in the marital relationship, to what extent can the marriage then still be seen as a point of transference that has made upward social mobility possible?

While meeting a number of Ghanaian–Botswana mixed couples, I began exploring their circumstances of marriage: the issues they had faced in making the marriage happen, especially in cultural terms; the manner in which they had overcome the difficulties; and the sentiments and emotions that had played out in all of this. I met the spouses of eight couples, mostly consisting of Ghanaian men married to local women,[7] and some of their well-informed advisors (18 individuals in total). The couples married between 1985 and 2014, aged mid-30s to 60s, each in a way with their own story to tell: how they came to set eyes on each other and the manner in which a relationship began to develop; how they then had to contact the family and begin to arrange matters; and also how complexities emerged in the process and how much the Ghanaian men especially were expected to be flexible and allow the Batswana to take control over marital arrangements and negotiations. This often led to the question of where exactly space could be found for the expression of more Ghanaian cultural notions of the wedding and the marital (ceremonial) procedures.

In terms of the formulation of the question of romance: on the part of the Ghanaian men, in the interviews with them they were explicitly clear that the beauty and attractiveness of the lady had been an important trigger for them to make the first move, to approach the lady and start a conversation and show

---

7   Most cases concern Ghanaian men who married local women. In the small community of Ghanaian migrants, it is considered exceptional if a Ghanaian woman marries a local, partly because it was mostly men who migrated to Botswana and were recruited there, thereby often bringing their wives as dependents. In my sample of couples, I included one case of a Ghanaian woman who had married locally, and I noticed that this couple's reflections on the complexities of the intercultural exchange between the Ghanaian party and the Botswana party in the arrangement of the marriage differed little from the majority of cases. Despite the fact that in such a case the man is not obliged to pay *lobola* (bridewealth) (though he may still transfer some wealth/items to the Ghanaian representatives), in terms of the negotiations between the parties involved and the couple's ideas concerning their relationship, no significant differences seem to have occurred in how the intercultural exchange actually unfolded.

interest. All this initiative to start and make a first move was seen as entirely theirs.

There was generally also an expectation that many of the Botswana partners the Ghanaians would meet would have an equal or perhaps even better education than they would have themselves. There was no expectation of 'marrying down', but of at least marrying within the same job bracket and class position as they would have reached—or of 'marrying up'. So, a possible marriage could improve their class position in this society, some Ghanaian men being relatively less educated—such as a hair salon owner/businessman or a builder/constructor—and marrying Batswana women with a higher educational profile, including even university training. One could say that this is stretching the romantic question even further.

As to the romantic experience on the part of the local women, several dynamics could be discerned in their answers. A first dynamic in the shaping of the romantic experience was the fascination for the foreign man. As I had already noticed during earlier work on Ghanaian relations in 2002–2004 (see Van Dijk 2003; Van de Kamp & Van Dijk 2010), a high level of romantic interest on the part of Batswana women in Ghanaian men had been noted in the Ghanaian community as well. This was and is explained by them first of all by pointing at the unequal gender-ratio in the country and its long history. The relative absence of marriageable men from Botswana—because of massive labour migration of able-bodied men to the South African mines—has produced a sense of prolonged gender imbalance. This could explain the continuing eagerness of Batswana women to be on the lookout for marriageable foreign partners. Yet, since this has become very much part of history—this massive labour migration no longer takes place since the 1970s—its myth-making must be recognized in this fascination.

However, the most important discourse among the local women about their attraction for Ghanaian men was the trope of 'care', of taking care and providing care, and caring for the relationship (see for examples elsewhere in Africa of this trope of love and care, Cole & Thomas 2009). The Batswana women I spoke to considered Ghanaian men as being extremely good at 'taking care of them'. This they do better than local men, they said. This taking care by local men is a much more uncertain, whimsical factor, something one can never really rely upon, something that may easily disappear, that they can never really be held to deliver, and something one could only hope for but never expect to receive. By contrast, the Ghanaian men were seen as being more romantically equipped while also being more responsible in keeping a relationship alive, and therefore being a better choice than local men. Some of the women expressed this clearly by stressing that they felt that Ghanaian men are much more serious in a relationship. That is, they are less of the *player* type of men than the locals are, and they make an effort to show devotion and commitment. Of course, much of this would still stand to be proven and the actual experiences of women could differ, but this was and is the framework of romantic expectation.

A second dynamic that entered here was that none of the Batswana women I talked to was ever discouraged by their parents or wider family from marrying a foreigner; in a sense, while they were fascinated by doing so, so were their families. They often felt they were strongly supported by their parents and wider family when stepping into this relationship—although in some cases the women had children from earlier relationships, which made it sometimes quite difficult to find local partners, a factor which may have added to their families' interest in the foreigner. They also explained that their families some-times held expectations concerning climbing the social ladder by marrying their daughter to a foreigner, an expectation of the (seemingly) good position the foreigner might have on the local job market, the income he had, and the relative independence he could display *vis-à-vis* (financial) obligations con-cerning his family, far away in Ghana as they usually are. Again, the mixing and balancing of romantic interests and rationalized reasons for the expression of such interests is at play in this context as well.

A third dynamic in marrying a Ghanaian came through the notion of the self-fashioning a marriage to a Ghanaian would provide in terms of a romantic, glamorous, upper-middle-class styling of the wedding. The global attraction of white weddings, of the appeal of class, status, style, and glamour, and of the ways in which all of this can be informed by middle- and upper-middle-class notions of these, provided in a sense a common and shared romantic language. This is a romantic language that appears highly suited to cross and connect transnational and cultural borders. One couple, for instance, who had met each other in Botswana after the Ghanaian man had moved from Zimbabwe from where he had been recruited to come and work in the country's capital, shared clear cosmopolitan ideas of how their wedding and relationship should look by preparing for it as a 'team'. What Hirsch and Wardlow (2006) have called the rise of a global model of *companionate marriage* certainly applies here: a notion of marriage as a companionate affair whereby both partners share in an interest in a certain classy styling of the wedding and the shap-ing of their marital relations. The way couples such as these speak about their relationship, the way they voice their bond and affections, marks this class distinction and can smack of a form of what can be called 'middle-class folk psychology'—that is, indicating their personality, the way they can reflect about their strong points and weak points, how their characters differ and can complement one another. A sense of cosmopolitanism is also important in not wanting to be bound by local traditions but being able to escape these, to create something that is 'international' as some said, something that is superior to local traditions or that shows a distinctive mastery over resources and access to them. A telling example of this 'international code of love' was the use of the phrase 'getting into the dinner phase' to designate a significant step in the development of their courtship. Whereas other steps in making the relationship become 'serious' can have to do with local and cultural conventions—such as, for example, informing the mother's brother (in Setswana, *malome*; in Twi, *wofa*) of the interest in getting married—taking the beloved out for dinner, complete with candle-light and small gifts (perfume, for example), seemed to resonate more on the level of an intercultural understanding of the indications of 'serious intentions'.

The romantic was also evident in the demonstration of intercultural competence. This relates especially to the way in which some couples strengthened their relationship by creating bonds with the families on either side of the cultural divide. Some of the Batswana women, for example, talked about creating affectionate bonds with their Ghanaian mothers-in-law, such as making an effort to travel to Ghana to the place where her husband's family lives so as to stay there for a length of time and send their Botswana-born children to school in that part of Ghana for the duration of the visit. Without unduly overemphasizing the xenophobic sentiments some authors have pointed out in Botswana society (see above), this effort to create intercultural exchange is quite exceptional when looked at from the perspective of Botswana's popular culture. A couple explained how much effort they had made, including covering the financial costs, in flying in the Ghanaian husband's mother so that regular visits to Botswana were possible. Romance is thus a subject of cultural competence, a demonstration of what a good partner brings and the manner in which this facilitates the possibility of investing in wider social relationships through travel and communication. Clearly, this level of cosmopolitanism is not readily available to the lower socio-economic classes both in Ghana and in Botswana, which means that this development of intercultural romance may mark specific notions of (social) distinction and upward mobility.

This feature of distinction by and through the marital relationship operates in a three-tiered model:

1.   On the level of the local, the marriage to a Ghanaian partner allows for a distancing from local cultural practices, creates greater freedom of choice and independence, and supports a vision of a better, more caring, and more responsible partnership than the locals usually allow for.

2. There is also a perception of 'we Africans' as against the West, that is, a notion of the manner in which especially the educated can see the value of cultural practices that have broad currency across the African continent but make it stand out as against the highly individualized West. These educated middle classes thus create space for their elders and families to come in to organize and run the negotiations that have to do with marital formation as a matter of 'African culture', of African understandings of how a respectable marriage should run. This is what makes people understand each other's marital practices, since there is a sense of commonality in the way an individual must submit his or her wish to marry to a larger field of family and social relations that gives a specific moral authority to the relationship. This is a view of culture as creating a concept of consensus. While being part of the middle classes and meaning that both man and wife become companions in a way that must be negotiated, it nevertheless sets the agenda and the framework for this companionate negotiation.

3. There is at the same time the heavy emphasis most couples placed on middle-class self-styling, self-fashioning, being self-made people who manage to equip themselves with things that have universal value, such as education, experience through travelling and exposure, and the acquisition of life skills. While I expected here also religion, especially Pentecostalism, to come in and provide certain cues about things that may give the global access that shapes a modern believer, who can be identified as such all around the world, this context of self-identification did not appear much. Instead, the investment in bonds and bonding—for instance, with the family of the man in Ghana—often became a focus for emphasizing the value of having and creating a family, for using the opportunities that a consumerist society offers for shaping warm relations, for being able to visit and even occasionally send children to Ghana—these were the things that came across most forcefully.

Hence, what we are seeing here is the romantic in the service of creating (middle-class) distinction (see Spronk 2012) and creating identities, interests, and lifestyles that cut across cultural differences and even explicitly supersede such differences. The romantic interest can thereby stand in opposition to local cultural traditions but, interestingly, often assumes something 'African' in the way in which particular communal forms of arranging marriages and of respecting the authority of the wider family come into play.

This 'balancing act' between the romantic interest of being cosmopolitan and African at the same time calls into question the relationship with local

Ghanaian and Botswana styles and cultural conventions; after all, while the couples in their mixed marriage claim such a position and perspective, the dictum remains: 'easier said than done'. How did they negotiate the diasporic element of their Ghanaian (prospective) spouses living 'inside with a difference'? In practice, how far were they able to push this aspect of creating distance and distinction? Were cultural differences of any concern; and if so, how exactly?

Marriage and the Diasporic Experience

The first question here is how exactly did a sense of *cultural difference* play out? How was it negotiated? How were both partners placed *vis-à-vis* their families and communities in negotiating the process of marital arrangements, if we can assume that marriage is one of the specific life-cycle moments at which notions of cultural style, traditions, and conventions are often felt to be important? While Ghana certainly has its particular and sometimes ethnically based conventions about marital arrangements, negotiations, exchanges, and protocols, so too does Botswana. In a diasporic situation, therefore, how is a necessary level of interculturality negotiated when a couple has announced their wish to formalize their relationship?

In general, all the mixed couples that I interacted with pointed at a dynamic which we can term *the interplay between duress and endurance*. Marrying a foreigner in the Botswana context certainly does bring its complexities in terms of crossing not only national divides but especially socio-cultural divides, an experience which can be stressful, protracted, and not without difficulty irrespective of the intercultural competences of the couples themselves.

In general terms, weddings in Botswana require prolonged preparations and arrangements which can easily stretch over a period of two years, if not more (Van Dijk 2010, 2012). Commonly, they are marked as being complicated because of all the resources that are required, not only in terms of a mandatory bridewealth exchange—known as *lobola/bogadi* (usually in the form of livestock, see Kuper 1982)—but also because of the money, gifts, food, transport, and clothes/dresses the elaborate ceremonies require. As I have demonstrated elsewhere (see Van Dijk 2010, 2012), marriage in Botswana has become the subject of high-level forms of conspicuous consumption, which actually means that fewer and fewer people manage to get married.

Furthermore, there are clearly demarcated steps in the entire process that require special care and attention. These are related especially to the start and the bringing to an end of the negotiations over the terms of marriage between the representatives of the two families (the couples themselves are not involved!), the exchange of the bridewealth, and the feast at the wedding. During these complicated processes of negotiation, in which each partner's mother's brother has an especially important role to play, the parties always seem to stumble over an issue, thereby requiring special (linguistic and other) competences to avoid the emergence of conflicts; conflicts that may easily lead to further delays in the entire procedure.

The Ghanaian partners usually did not have family/uncles to represent them formally in the context of these negotiations, usually did not own livestock (in particular, cattle) for the bridewealth payments, and did not have a homestead that could be called 'theirs' as a place where the meeting of the parties for the negotiations could take place or where the wedding celebrations could be held. On top of this relatively disadvantaged position, the Ghanaian men in particular also told me that they usually became increasingly worried, in the course of all these arrangements, about how all of this would allow for some aspects of more Ghanaian cultural traditions to come in before, during, or after the actual wedding so that Ghanaian traditions would also be honoured to some extent. Not only did they increasingly feel confronted by demands and procedures they knew little about and for which they were ill-prepared; a sentiment related to notions of 'manhood', of proud masculinity, also emerged that was little honoured by what they saw at times as the humbling treatment they received from the 'elders' on the side of their prospective wives. Some men became concerned about the ever-extending bridewealth payments that came to be demanded in these negotiations and felt that enough was quite enough and that it began looking as if they were 'buying a wife'. Some were very clear about this: when the wedding negotiations were settled and the wedding itself had been celebrated, they would want to take control— and after getting married, they would take their newly wedded wives to their homes without following the *segametsi* traditions. These are the traditions by which the new wife is prepared to be brought to the home of the husband and his family's home, since the wife marries into the family of the man (contrary to many of the matrilineal family traditions in large parts of Ghana). These traditions of the *segametsi* (lit. 'the bringer of water') include a period of time in which the new wife has to perform a range of household chores, such as cleaning the yard of the parental house, washing the clothes of members of the household, cooking, and fetching bathwater for her husband. The bringing over of the wife to the family of the man is commonly a ceremony in which the bride is accompanied by female kin carrying baskets and bags of clothes, utensils, and gifts. However, a new husband taking his wife home straight after the formal wedding can be considered by the Botswana family to be an offense. Yet some of the Ghanaian men took pride in having done so, as this act demonstrated their masculine authority and power as well as their interest in countering the control of the Botswana elders and their superimposition of Botswana traditions and conventions. In a romantic sense, the act also seems to come close to the idea of *elopement*—that is, whisking the bride away contrary to the consent of the families—but at the same time intriguingly showing off the newly won freedom it seemed to signify. The Ghanaian men in the interviews listed their complaints about the costs of the wedding; the potentially troublesome nature of the wife's family elders; the never-ending stream of demands for goods, food, money, and transport; the complications of turning cattle/livestock into money so that the *lobola* could be paid in hard-earned cash; and the sheer endless complications about setting dates for every step in the process. All of this—something over which their prospective Batswana wives had very little influence—boiled down to an exercise in coping with duress and endurance on the husbands' part.

Yet for many of the couples at the same time—and much to their surprise—in most of these exchanges a particular counter-process also occurred, a counter-process whereby despite these issues and complications a concern usually seemed to emerge, in most cases, between the Botswana family of the bride and the Ghanaian family of the groom. This took the form of the construction of what can be called a *commonality of concerns*, a commonality in the concern with trying to create an intercultural language to ensure that things would run smoothly, a language that would start to signal respect for each other's positions and ensure cultural conventions and obligations could be maintained, such that conflicts arising out of duress would be minimized if not actually prevented from occurring.

The first strategy that emerged in this perspective of a commonality of concerns was the realization that on the Ghanaian side a modus of fictive kin and representation was to be arranged. Although increasingly the couples themselves were made responsible for large parts of the entire wedding procedure, the realization was that in the negotiations about the terms of the marriage and in the acknowledgement that a formal representation of the Ghanaian family was not available in Botswana, a representative had to be 'made' for the Ghanaian partners. Here we meet much of Janet Carsten's (2000) work on fictive kin-relations and the concept of relationality, since some form of trustworthy representativeness in the negotiation process must be constructed and must be made acceptable to all parties involved. In this regard, the men told me, the Ghanaian migrant community began to play an important role, as especially the Chairman of the Association of Ghanaian Nationals in Botswana often came in to represent the groom in meetings with the representatives of the family of the bride. This (in this case surrogate) mother's brother is known in Ghana as the *wofa*. In southern Ghana, however, in the majority of cases the marriage is not patrifocal but matrifocal, in the sense that the husband marries into the family of the bride, making also for a different trajectory of the bride-price exchange. While Ghanaian men in Botswana do not own cattle, the most important task of this surrogate was to negotiate the equivalent value in money, which the groom then has to provide.

Yet although this assigning of a 'constructed' representation was considered a major step forward in the procedures, misunderstandings in the process could still easily arise, since the Ghanaian surrogate representatives were not always conversant with the local language and conventions. This is why, in a number of cases these couples discussed with me, a special person was assigned from the party of the bride to join the virtual party of the Ghanaian man to inform his surrogate mother's brother of the do's and don'ts in the entire process. Some indicated that even a special term appeared to be reserved for this go-between for the two parties: the man appointed as go-between was called a *Rraditselana*, a woman with a similar status and function a *Mmadit-selana*. In fact, this amounts to a form of cultural brokering and cultural brokerage of a special kind, such as conceptualized by Press (1969). This person, being a Setswana speaker, would know more precisely how to address people and issues and could create a better context of language skills for the process of persuasion and decision making. In these cases, the Ghanaian groom could literally place the success of the negotiations into the hands of strangers. The task of this cultural broker between the party of the bride and the party of the Ghanaian groom was to accompany the party of the Ghanaian man to every moment of negotiation that was arranged between the two families, to translate and interpret what was said and done, and especially to inform the Ghanaian party of what to say and not to say, how to act and how to understand the demands that were made. The commonality of concern for the good standing and reputation of the couple and both their families was these brokers' primary objective and responsibility, so that any issue or any chance of misunderstanding and offense was minimized.

In the case of the Ghanaian hair salon owner mentioned earlier, this brokering concerned the negotiations over money and gifts and the long list of demands presented by the party of the bride, including the *lobola* and so many other items. As the groom, he was pressured to spend money, for which he had to save from his earnings over a long period of time, causing a delay in the wedding proceedings. Through the negotiations it came out he had to provide for eight head of cattle and many gifts, while such things as the party and the hiring of a tent remained the affair of the couple. The brokering especially concerned the setting of dates, which have to be set for almost everything in the process, such as the dates for the meeting of the parties in the process of negotiation, the dates for the handing over of the bride-price and all the other gifts, the dates for the feast of the wedding itself, and, last but not least, the dates for the registration and signing of the marriage contract at the office of the registrar of marriages in the Botswana system of civil marriage.

Hoping to speed up the process, in one case a couple decided that since the signing of the marriage at the registrar's office is not the responsibility of the elders of the wife's family, they could just go there, set a date, register it, and then present this as an accomplished fact: the marriage had been given a date to register, so now they better hurry up with finishing their business! While this provoked complaints on the part of the elders, it shows the relative independence of the Ghanaian men, in particular in simply using the administrative system to their benefit and countering the authority of the elders. As this was considered problematic, however, the go-betweens were asked to smoothen and iron things out.

In other cases, such issues requiring the careful treatment and negotiation of cultural difference revolved around the position of the *dingaka*, the traditional doctors, who from the Botswana family's perspective can be considered vital for the success and spiritual protection of the wedding and the marriage. As I have described elsewhere (see Van Dijk 2012), these traditional doctors' services are crucial at several steps in the entire marital arrangement and involve the spiritual blessing, protecting, and cleansing of items ranging from the wedding dresses to the wedding rings, the place where the ceremonies will be held, the tent that will be pitched, and the slaughtering of the beasts for the feast as well as other food that will be consumed. On the Ghanaian side of things, my inter-locutors explained,there was usually great hesitation if not anxiety about invit-ing such traditional healers, and many were adamant in demanding that no 'doctoring' of any kind was going to take place at any stage during the entire wedding preparations. On the Botswana's family's side, the go-betweens were then required to plead for intercultural respect in explaining that things would be conducted in a 'Christian' manner, at times involving some of the Ghanaian Pentecostal pastors to perform the necessary ceremonial and spiritual duties.

A Zone of Transference?

The most important way in which we can perceive these marital arrangements in the context of a mixed marriage as a zone of transference is by defining it as a 'training ground'. The acquiring of skills in terms of transcultural compe-tences, of dealing with cultural brokerage, and of dealing with (consumerist) negotiations can all be seen to belong to a particular kind of social stratification. Any idea of climbing a social ladder, of upward social mobility, requires societal notions of stratification. In the Botswana situation, one can easily perceive the forms of social stratification that belong to the rise of the new socio-economic classes as a fairly recent phenomenon. Apart from the social stratification in terms of socio-economic class positions which became more pronounced after the country's economic boom in the late 1970s, the country is also marked by a stratification in terms of ethnicity and minority positions. As Durham (2002) and Werbner (2002a, 2002b, 2002c) have argued, this socio-political stratification concerned primarily the relative positioning of the 'internal' ethnic minorities *vis-à-vis* the eight 'principal tribes' in the country (who for a long time were exclusively represented in the country's House of Chiefs, dealing with such matters as the allocation of land). 'External minorities', that is, foreigner minorities such as those of the Ghanaian or at a later date Zimbabwean immigrant communities are to be seen as requiring a new positioning in the perspective of this ethnic-based stratification. For the Ghanaians, in particular, this 'mixing' of two different forms of stratification—one based on their socio-economic position, in which perspective many would belong to the higher echelons of society, and the other based on their minority position—means they often have to 'calibrate' (to use the expression coined by Quayson (2003)) their ideas of their place in this, by all measures, small-scale and tight-knit society.

The weddings with local partners were therefore often talked about in terms of calibration, that is, a discourse of 'how to behave'. And for some Ghanaian men, depending on their profession, level of education, and position in the labour market in Botswana, this calibration could be more, and for others less, exacting. The 'go-betweens', the brokers appointed during the wedding arrangements, were therefore crucial in knowing and learning this 'how to behave' in all its tacitness as well. For one Ghanaian this could be a slightly humbling experience, for another an exposure to a form of discourse, negotiation, and reputational politicking that one had never experienced before, but which was nevertheless equally important in the learning process. In the Botswana context's hierarchy of value, one is considered of lesser status and reputation, for instance, if at official functions an adult man does not wear a jacket. In the respectful meeting of families during negotiations over the *lobola* and other requirements of the marital arrangement, men should wear a jacket; and if they do not, the offense taken in not doing so is considered serious and immediately 'de-classifies' the person and his authority. The tenacity of codes of 'how to behave' require this sign of respect and reputation, meaning that if a Ghanaian adult man appears in his traditional costume of cloth draped around the shoulders but leaving one shoulder bare (as the story of a proud Ghanaian father revealed), this de-classification is immediately applied. While there is a long history of the ways in which 'internal minorities' have been treated in Botswana (which I will not go into in the context of this paper), the point is that Ghanaians were required to understand how and where precisely a 'declassification' of their status and respect could be avoided. As some Ghanaians told me: 'Mistakes were made, certainly in the beginning'; but they were soon corrected. Ghanaians who had become more experienced some-times had to step in, take part in the negotiations, and ensure the Ghanaian groom (or, occasionally, bride) did not make 'mistakes' that might jeopardize not only his/her personal position but the public appreciation of the Ghanaian migrant community as a whole. News about such 'mistakes' can travel fast, wide, and far—the intricacy of the Botswana social system is known for this feature of civic life. The Ghanaian community itself would not want to be ranked alongside the 'internal' minorities, marginalized as these appear to be, especially in socio-political terms. Having been recruited into the country's civil service was part of this perspective of being classified differently from these minorities; yet for those Ghanaians who had ventured out into private business (such as the Ghanaian hair salon owner of the opening example), such self-evidence in occupying and maintaining a different position on the social ladder was not at all to be taken for granted. So, while Ghanaians are differently positioned in the labour market, on a hierarchy of social prestige and success, one Ghanaian can be a high-level and well-trained chartered accountant or university lecturer; another Ghanaian can be of a semi-skilled profession, such as a builder or a hair salon owner.

The way I perceive the wedding, therefore, as a calibrating training ground is that irrespective of such socio-economic differentiation, a collective effort was made by the Ghanaians to ensure that the weddings would become a status-elevating experience. 'Knowing how to behave', the recruitment of the go-betweens, and the careful negotiations and treatment of the social reputa-tions by both sides of the family helped to achieve this. Their marriages, all-in-all, became indeed well-respected, firmly established, and recognized. The zone of transference that I am indicating here is thus much more a matter of the collective and of its imagination than of the exclusively individual. These mixed marriages seem to have been placed in a reputational social framework, in which the collective concern was not only with the individual status of the Ghanaian and the Botswana partner, but also with the way in which the mar-riage reflected upon the societal and public reputation of the Ghanaian com-munity and the Botswana family. Both parties in a sense shared in a reputational 'contract' by which the romantic desires of the couple, the demands in terms

of the glamour as well as the expense of the wedding, and the cultural requirements on either side of the arrangement were to be channelled, such that
climbing the reputational ladder could be honoured and achieved by all
involved. For all the Ghanaians involved in these mixed marriages, the zone of
transference that their marital arrangements signalled amounted to a transference into another set of dynamics that this ladder represented. This is a transference of what initially appeared, in their situation of migration, to be their
private and family affair of getting married, to a point in which the wedding
came to have a much wider significance in terms of the positioning of the collective, its public profile, and the manner in which in Botswana these weddings are part of reputational stratification *par excellence*. Whereas some
Ghanaian men, such as the hair salon owner in our example, may indeed have
been 'marrying up' in terms of the socio-economic status of his partner, the
wider significance of his marriage as a zone of transference is related to how
his marriage is still remembered as providing respectability for himself, his
wife, the families, *and* the Ghanaian community as a whole. The cultural divisions and potential conflicts were mastered and negotiated, the formal
Ghanaian representation shared a commonality of concerns between the different parties, the glamorous image of the wedding was demonstrated, and the
go-betweens of the various parties managed to secure a profile of respectability for this entire achievement.

This means that different forms of social stratification—socio-economic,
ethnic, socio-moral, and reputational—were at play at the same time, such
that this mixed marriage formed an institutional zone of transference between
these different 'registers' of stratification. A mixed marriage in this manner
also comes to represent a 'mixing' of different modalities of stratification,
requiring therefore 'zones of transference'—in a sense, 'bridges'—between
these different modalities so as to be able to jump from one form of social
stratification to another. The mixed marriage thus represents such a bridge,
allowing for instance for a jump from a specific ethnic modality of stratification (being part of a 'minority') into a form of stratification that relates to
socio-economic upward mobility.

Conclusion

This contribution has analysed how the mixed marriages of Ghanaian immigrants to local partners in Botswana can be studied along the axes of two particular dynamics: firstly, the romantic interest of the marriage partners in
pursuing the idealization of their relationship by developing romanticist

notions about the quality and significance of this relationship; and secondly, a diasporic notion of the manner in which cultural differences are both present and at the same time bridged by a commonality of concerns. While the first dynamic of the romanticist interest focuses mainly on the couples themselves and the manner in which they ventured to create a critical relation with local conventions, power structures, and cultural requirements so as to pursue their hearts in striving for glamour, love, and commitment, the second dynamic demonstrates how communal, public profile, and status-related issues enter the entire process and how these are negotiated in the interests of maintaining and producing a reputational gradient. In so doing, the mixed marriage emerges as a social space in which a variety of forms of stratification come together. These social gradients relate to the socio-economic positioning and upward mobility of the couples themselves as well as to the status and prestige of the families and communities they represent, while at the same time there are stratifications at play that engage ethnic, cultural, and social hierarchies in a society where these matters have great relevance.

While the mixed marriage can be perceived as a 'non-space'—much as this concept of Augé (1995) indicates a geographical location in which migrants can be perceived to be in transit in their mobility from their place of origin to the place of destination (or vice versa)—this form of marriage as an 'in-between' space of transit requires exploration in terms of the various forms of social mobility that seem to apply. Mixed marriage can be recognized as forming a precise zone of transference. In analysing these mixed marriages, it has become clear how and why this form of transnational marriage became a kind of romantic and diasporic point of transference as it enabled some Ghanaian men to marry local women who are more highly educated than they were themselves, as well as because of the way in which the institution of marriage came to function as a status-marker of distinction over the last two decades, which also in the Ghanaian case came to provide an upward reputational mobility. The question of whether and how such marriages came to function as a romantic zone of transference is therefore to be answered not only from the perspective of offering a 'non-place', but especially in the way they offer a transference in terms of this gradient that, interestingly, is not damaged or jeopardized by the romantic. While the embedded anti-establishment, anti-calculating, anti-conventional impetus of the romanticist aspects of these couples' marital arrangements may otherwise easily have caused concern about the reputation of the families and the communities involved (since in the eyes of many, 'mistakes' about 'how to behave' can be made so easily), such appears not to have been the case. Despite the romantic, and perhaps even because of the romantic, interest, these weddings seem to have provided a good reputation to all involved. Hence, while the weddings made the Ghanaian partners no longer involved in onward migration—Botswana no longer functioning just as a zone of transit for them—an onward mobility in terms of socio-economic status and in terms of reputational mobility was produced. This means, in conclusion, that the forms of romantic migration as have been discussed here can be significant for the manner in which this form of migration is valued both by its subjects and the host society as providing a point of transference in onward social mobility.

References

Augé, M. (1995), *Non-Places: Introduction to an Anthropology of Supermodernity* (trans. from French by John Howe). London: Verso Books.

Bochow, A. (2012), Marriages and Mobility in Akan Societies: Disconnections and Connections over Time and Space, in: M. de Bruijn & R. van Dijk (eds) *The Social Life of Connectivity in Africa.* New York: Palgrave MacMillan, pp. 123–140.

Brown, B. (1983), The Impact of Male Labour Migration on Women in Botswana. *African Affairs* 28(328): 367–388.

Campbell, E.K. (2003), Attitudes of Botswana Citizens Toward Immigrants: Signs of Xenophobia? *International Migration* 41(4): 71–109.

Carsten, J. (ed.) (2000), *Cultures of Relatedness: New Approaches to the Study of Kinship.* Cambridge: Cambridge University Press.

Charsley, K. (ed.) (2012), *Transnational Marriage: New Perspectives from Europe and Beyond.* London: Routledge; pp. 5–22.

Choplin, A. & J. Lombard (2013), Stranded in Mauritania: Sub-Saharan Migrants in Post-Transit Context, in: A. Triulzi & R. McKenzie (eds) *Long Journeys: Lives and Voices of African Migrants on the Road.* Leiden: Brill, pp. 67–92.

Clifford, J. (1997), *Routes: Travel and Translation in the Late Twentieth Century.* Harvard: Harvard University Press.

Cole, J. (2012), The Love of Jesus Never Disappoints: Reconstituting Female Personhood in Urban Madagascar. *Journal of Religion in Africa* 42: 1–24.

Cole, J. & L.M. Thomas (eds) (2009), *Love in Africa.* Chicago: University of Chicago Press.

Constable, N. (2009), The Commodification of Intimacy: Marriage, Sex and Reproductive Labor. *Annual Review of Anthropology* 38: 49–64.

Conway, D. & P. Leonard (2014), *Migration, Space and Transnational Identities: The British in South Africa.* Palgrave Macmillan.

Durham, D. (2002), Uncertain Citizens: Herero and the New Intercalary Subject in Postcolonial Botswana, in: R. Werbner (ed.) *Postcolonial Subjectivities in Africa.* London: Zed Books, pp. 139–170.

Fassin, E. (2010), National Identity and Transnational Intimacies: Sexual Democracy and the Politics of Immigration in Europe. *Public Culture* 22(3): 507–529.

Groes-Green, C. (2014), Journeys of Patronage: Moral Economies of Transactional Sex and Female Migration from Mozambique to Europe. *Journal of the Royal Anthropological Institute* 20(2): 237–255.

Hirsch, J.S. & H. Wardlow (eds) (2006), *Modern Loves: The Anthropology of Romantic Courtship and Companionate Marriage*. Ann Arbor: University of Michigan Press.

Kastner, K. (2013), Nigerian Border Crossers: Women Travelling to Europe by Land, in: A. Triulzi & R. McKenzie (eds) *Long Journeys: Lives and Voices of African Migrants on the Road*. Leiden: Brill, pp. 27–46.

Kuper, A. (1982), *Wives for Cattle: Bridewealth and Marriage in Southern Africa*. London: Routledge & Kegan Paul.

Louban, A. (2014), Immigration Bureaucracy: Who's In and Who's Out in Membership Terms? Paper presented at the Klausur des Exzellenzclusters 'Kulturelle Grundlagen von Integration', Kartause Ittingen, Schweiz, July 2014.

Manamere, K.T. (2014), Majoni-joni; Wayward Criminals or a Good Catch? Labour Migrancy, Masculinity and Marriage in Rural South Eastern Zimbabwe. *African Diaspora* 7(1): 89–113.

Maskens, M. (2013), L'amour et ses frontières: régulations étatiques et migrations de mariage (Belgique, France, Suisse et Italie). *Migrations Société* 25(150): 43–60.

Maskens, M. & R. Blanes (2013), Don Quixote's Choice: A Manifesto for a Romanticist Anthropology. *HAU: Journal of Ethnographic Theory* 3(3): 245–81.

Meyer, B. & P. Geschiere (eds) (1999), *Globalization and Identity: Dialectics of Flow and Closure*. Oxford: Blackwell.

Neveu-Kringelbach, H. (2013), 'Mixed Marriage': Citizenship and the Policing of Intimacy in Contemporary France. Working Papers, no. 77. Oxford: International Migration Institute, University of Oxford.

Nyamnjoh, F.B. (2002), Local Attitudes Towards Citizenship and Foreigners in Botswana: An Appraisal of Recent Press Stories. *Journal of Southern African Studies* 28(4): 755–775.

Oucho, J.O. (2000), Skilled Immigrants in Botswana: A Stable but Temporary Workforce. *Africa Insight* 30(2): 56–64.

Parson, J. (ed.) (1985), The 'Labour Reserve' in Historical Perspective, Toward a Political Economy of the Bechuanaland Protectorate in: L. Picard (ed.) *The Evolution of Modern Botswana: Politics and Rural Development in South Africa*. London: Rex Collings pp. 40–57.

Press, I. (1969), Ambiguity and Innovation: Implications for the Genesis of the Culture Broker. *American Anthropologist* 71(2): 205–217.

Quayson, A. (2003), *Calibrations: Reading for the Social*. Minneapolis: University of Minnesota Press.

Rodriguez Garcia, D. (2006), Mixed Marriages and Transnational Families in the Intercultural Context: A Case Study of African-Spanish Couples in Catalonia. *Journal of Ethnic and Migration Studies* 32(3): 403–433.

Schapera, I. (1947), *Migrant Life and Tribal Life: A Study of Conditions in the Bechuanaland Protectorate.* Cape Town: Oxford University Press.

Spronk, R. (2012), *Ambiguous Pleasures: Sexuality and Middle Class Self-Perceptions in Nairobi.* Oxford: Berghahn.

Suter, B. (2013), Untangling Immobility in Transit: Sub-Saharan Migrants in Istanbul, in: A. Triulzi & R. McKenzie (eds) *Long Journeys: Lives and Voices of African Migrants on the Road.* Leiden: Brill, pp. 93–112.

Trundle, C. (2009), Romance Tourists, Foreign Wives or Retirement Migrants? Cross-Cultural Marriage in Florence, Italy, in: M. Benson & K. O'Reilly (eds) *Lifestyle Migration: Expectations, Aspiration and Experiences.* Aldershot: Ashgate, pp. 51–68.

Van de Kamp, L. & R. van Dijk (2010), Pentecostals Moving South–South: Brazilian and Ghanaian Transnationalism in Southern Africa Compared, in: A. Adogame & J. Spickard (eds) *Religion Crossing Boundaries: Transnational Religious and Social Dynamics in Africa and the New African Diaspora.* Leiden: Brill, pp. 123–142.

Van Dijk, R. (2001), Voodoo on the Doorstep and the Trafficking in Young Nigerian Women for the Dutch Sex Industry and Its Moral Panic. *Africa* 71(4): 558–586.

Van Dijk, R. (2003), Localisation, Ghanaian Pentecostalism and the Stranger's Beauty in Botswana. *Africa* 73(4): 560–583.

Van Dijk, R. (2004), Negotiating Marriage: Questions of Morality and Legitimacy in Ghanaian Pentecostal Diaspora. *Journal of Religion in Africa* 34(4): 438–468.

Van Dijk, R. (2010), Marriage, Commodification and the Romantic Ethic in Botswana, in: M. Dekker & R. van Dijk (eds), *Markets of Well-Being: Navigating Health and Healing in Africa.* Leiden: Brill. pp. 282–306.

Van Dijk, R. (2012), The Social Cocktail; Weddings and the Innovative Mixing of Competences in Botswana, in: A. Leliveld, J.-B. Gewald & I. Pesa (eds) *Transformation and Innovation in Africa.* Leiden: Brill, pp. 191–207.

Werbner, R. (2002a), Citizenship and the Politics of Recognition in Botswana, in: I.N. Mazonde (ed.) *Minorities in the Millennium: Perspectives from Botswana.* Gaborone: Lightbooks Ltd., pp. 117–135.

Werbner, R. (2002b), Introduction: Challenging Minorities, Difference and Tribal Citizenship in Botswana. *Journal of Southern African Studies* 28(4): 671–684.

Werbner, R. (2002c), Cosmopolitan Ethnicity, Entrepreneurship and the Nation: Minority Elites in Botswana. *Journal of Southern African Studies* 28(4): 731–753.

Williams, L. (2010), *Global Marriage: Cross-Border Marriages and Marriage Migration in Context.* London: Palgrave Macmillan.

CHAPTER 9

The Opportunities of the Margin: The Kapsiki Smith and his Road to Prosperity

Walter van Beek

Introduction

Many West African societies harbour an internal echelon of 'special people', usually artisans, who combine two striking features: on the one hand, they have been crucial for the survival of the group; on the other hand, they have a lower social status. In the ethnographic literature they are routinely referred to as 'blacksmiths' (in French, *forgerons*), but the array of specialized services they render is much larger than just iron work, be it smelting or forging. They do a lot more, as we shall see. In West Africa, artisanal tasks tend to cluster, and the resulting 'general specialists' are assigned peculiar slots in society. In this contribution, I will call them 'smiths', reserving 'blacksmiths' for iron workers. Not all work iron, not by far. They are distinct from the non-smith bulk of the village population, in ways that range from a guild-like artisanal organization to a caste-like arrangement in which society is divided into two rigidly sepa-rated echelons.

My case here is an example of the second type, viz. the smiths in Kapsiki/ Higi society in North Cameroon and northeastern Nigeria. With other similar groups in the Mandara Mountains, which mark the border between Cameroon and Nigeria, these smiths (called *rerhɛ*) have all the hallmarks of a small-scale 'caste': they are despised by the majority of non-smiths (called *melu*, who com-prise 95% of the population, with smiths forming just 5%); are feared to some extent as strange and dirty people; are endogamous, so can never marry a non-smith; and have their own food customs, and thus can never eat and drink with their fellow villagers. Yet, without them, Kapsiki society can hardly survive now, and definitely could not in the past. For any iron tool or brass jewellery, one had to go to the smithy; and the smith's compound is still the first stop for medicinal services, for divination, or whenever one needs music at a festival. Few rituals can be performed without a smith, and absolutely no one will get a proper burial without their crucial input, since they are the essential and inevi-table funeral directors for the village (Van Beek 2012a).

From this curious situation the question immediately arises: Why is a sub-group this important relegated to such a low status? That is the conundrum

I address in *The Forge and the Funeral: The Smith in Kapsiki/Higi Culture* (Van Beek 2015). Here I want to focus on the options for economic betterment: What does their curious social station imply for their chances for prosperity? Does their caste-like status hamper their way on the 'road to prosperity'? And what are the specific dynamics of 'smith-modernity'?

The first issue is how tenacious the distinction between the *rerhɛ* and the *melu* appears to be. Viewing the long history of hierarchical organization in West Africa, and of the relation between professional closure and group formation in the region, one surmises a deeply rooted institution. Social hierarchies do not disappear overnight; even the distinction most rejected by our present-day society, the one based upon slavery, has a much longer half-life than often thought (Pelckmans 2011). And professional closure is a phenomenon of all times. Indeed, as we shall see, the deep rift in Kapsiki society between *rerhɛ* and *melu* has not disappeared at all and is still very much present. That means that the smiths enter on their search for prosperity first and foremost as *rerhɛ*, as smiths. Their options in modernity seem to be primarily informed by their social status, their inevitable smith-hood.[1]

I will begin with a portrait.

Smiths on the Move

Speaking in January 2012, Zeme, an old smith from Sir, remembers well the coming of the first Roman Catholic missionaries to his native village about 60 years before. He was a young boy at the time, and those *nasara* (white men) were looking for builders. With two *rerhɛ* friends, he volunteered, finding that other smith boys had done the same. These missionaries started out building a small storehouse, and the project branched out into a dispensary, a house for the nuns, and the mission station; and by then, the *melu* came into the project as well. Zeme worked during the whole project as a mason, learning the craft from six masons the Catholic fathers brought in from outside, and then he stayed on in the mission. Building was not finished by far, as other houses, the chapel, and later the school followed. His family had a smithy, so he was a blacksmith proper and later learned bronze casting from people from Guili, thanks to the missionary father who encouraged him to do so. As he was engaged with the mission since he was 12 years old, he 'never danced with the corpses', the icon of

---

1 For an overview of the smith situation in this area, see Wade (2012), Vincent (1991), and Langlois (2012); and, for a wider area, Schmitz-Cliever (1979), Wente-Lukas (1972), and Rasmussen (2013).

Kapsiki funerals. The school was important—he saw that right away—and he sent all his children to school with the full support of his wife.

Their seven children all went to school and did well. The oldest son finished the 'lycée', married a white woman, and now lives in Germany. His daughter Kwanyè, as one of the first girls, took full advantage of the education possibilities and is now an ophthalmologist at the hospital in Mokolo, the regional city of the Mandara Mountains. The next two are teachers: one in Sir, one in Mokolo. Number five has a tailor's shop, and the others are good cultivators. Zeme is a content man and recognizes he has been lucky: the first ones to enter the mission have all done quite well. 'When the *melu* saw that, they became jealous,' he says, 'and entered the schools as well.' He has never seen his smith-hood as any barrier, though it still enters the situation of his children.

So, the early mission field offered a clear opportunity for vertical social mobility for smiths; and, indeed, smiths joined the mission in sizable numbers. At first the missionaries were pleased with this rather rapid success; after some years, however, they noticed that the growth in *fidèles* halted quite rapidly: the Catholic parish had become a smith-enterprise, and no *melu* would be caught dead in it. The Protestant mission in Mogode, belonging to the Evangelical Lutheran Brethren mission and with Canadian personnel, went through the same initial phase, and both denominations opted later for a policy to reduce the smith numbers in order to be accessible to the majority of the population. This changeover succeeded in the 1970s. However, though the smiths no longer dominate the Christian flock, they did benefit from both the building spree and the enhanced opportunities for education and training.

Early 2012. The first house I lived in in Mogode is being rebuilt by Izac, one of the sons of Timoti and Rebecca, my adopted Kapsiki parents. Izac is a successful businessman, and he has hired a group of *rerhɛ* from Rumsiki, smiths who have specialized in putting corrugated iron roofs on houses. They learned their trade from the smiths of Sir first (the venue of the first mission) and from the Lutheran mission at Mogode later. Building has become a ready niche for the modern Kapsiki smiths: the government is rebuilding the road from Mogode to Sir (which had been cut off for the previous 15 years) with a solid drainage system. The chief mason of the project is a *rerhɛ* from Kortchi.

In order to furnish my assistant's family with some income, I financed a house for them. Just across the road, Luc and Marie's son had a modern house constructed, to be rented out to the teachers at the nearby public school. Most of the construction was done by the family, assisted by some work parties, but one special feature caught our imagination. The missions often built a cistern, as water was becoming ever more scarce and Europeans need an inordinate amount of water. So that is what son François wanted: a guaranteed supply of water through a cistern, also as a boon for his ageing mother, who should not have to wait interminable hours at the well when during the dry season the water runs out. So I financed a cistern, just as expensive as the whole of the house. Characteristically, when we scouted for someone who could build one, we ended up with a smith, a *rerhɛ* from Vite. He made a drawing—a novelty—and a calculation, and now the house waited for two new arrivals: the new tenants and the first rains.

So building-new-style quickly became a smith job, especially the roofing and special items. One option which seemed obvious for smiths was and is work with corrugated iron. In October 1972 a loud blaring music disturbed the relative peace of Mogode, when a strange vehicle came driving along the main road that led from Mokolo to the south. It was a small van completely covered with corrugated iron of all sorts and varieties, plus a loudspeaker, and it came to sell corrugated iron. At that time most of the homes were straw-roofed, the classic African round grass roof, and *en route* to the market the van created quite a spectacle. The van's arrival meant a real happening in the village, as not that much passed along the road and the car was a strange sight, a sort of iron hut on wheels. But it sold sheets of corrugated iron (*tole ondulée*, as it was called in French), and the ones with this new and surprising enterprise were indeed smiths. They came from Mafa country and, as Mafa smiths who share the same social characteristics as their Kapsiki colleagues, had branched out into this new material.

The Way of Brass

Not just in iron (corrugated or not) but also in other fields, smiths branched out from their professions of old. Kapsiki smiths come in three categories: those responsible for funerals (with the chief smith as main functionary), those working in brass, and those associated with iron. Each cluster of *rerhɛ* families has its ritual responsibilities and myths of origin. Some functions, such as divination, are shared by the various smiths even if they use different techniques (see Van Beek 2015). Music is for all smiths, with a few variations.

So let us follow some of the other specializations, to see how they fare in the new times.

First, the 'other metal', brass, as brass casting forms a good example of a developing craft. The Kapsiki form the northern rim of the diffusion area of *cire perdue* casting in the region, even if in fact brass[2] is more important among

---

2   Brass is an alloy of copper and zinc. One of their bracelets I had tested contained about 75% copper and 20% zinc, with 5% other metals and impurities. Tourist brochures mention *'les*

TABLE 1   *Craft associations of the three groups of smiths*

	Chief smith	Brass smiths	Iron blacksmiths
Primary craft or professional responsibility	burial	brass casting	iron forging
Ritual responsibilities	rites of passage, village year rites, village sacrifice	rites for crop protection	individual protection, magical implements
Divination	crab	pebbles, *kwahɛ*	crab
Musical instruments	drums (especially at rituals), guitar and banjo, one-stringed violin	few: drums, one-stringed violin	guitar, flute, one-stringed violin (non-ritual occasions)

their southern neighbours: the Bana, Fali, and Vere. Still, brass is very much part of Kapsiki culture, especially in initiation, and the technique has been flourishing principally at Hya, a village on the southern border of the Kapsiki area. The main caster at Hya died in 2007, and since then his two widows, Masi and Kwada, have continued the business.

Brass objects are used for decoration, as status objects, and for ceremonial objects in boys' initiation, and the market for brass is still predominantly local. Africans usually like the yellow colour of brass: Kapsiki women wear a large array of brass jewellery (Van Beek 2011), while rich men like to show off with a brass sword or a brass tobacco pouch. But absolutely essential are the rather strange brass ornaments for initiands: triangles, bells, X-shaped plaques, and slender vials, all of the coveted yellow metal. Though brass casting is probably not very old in Kapsiki country—smiths have always been on the lookout for new products—it is well ensconced in the local culture, bearing also a curious symbolism, as iron and brass serve as a symbolic pair, highlighting the difference between the girls' initiation (their first marriage) and the initiation of boys. The first is dominated by iron, the second transition by brass: women of iron, men of brass. The symbolic pair is striking and somewhat counterintuitive (Van Beek 2015).

---

bronzes Kapsiki', but the alloy is always brass. Bronze (copper with tin) is not used in this part of Africa. See Wente-Lukas (1972) and Schmitz-Cliever (1979).

But brass also offered a new opportunity. Cameroonian Kapsiki land has become a renowned tourist destination, at least before Boko Haram entered on the scene. 'Les bronzes Kapsiki' (they are still brass!) are well known on the tourist circuit, an attraction that complements the spectacular scenery of the Kapsiki plateau. The Kapsiki tourist experience combines a prime photo opportunity with exposure to a traditional society, or at least one described as traditional in tourist handbooks (Van Beek 2003). The Cameroonian Kapsiki villages—mainly Rumsiki but increasingly other villages that can be accessed from there on a hiking tour—provide a traditional flavour; and, in this way, Kapsiki culture has become more than a side-show in the tourist encounter.

Traditional objects are part and parcel of this tourist experience and are sold in Rumsiki shops and hotels and by the brass caster himself. Tourists habitually make a short *sortie* from their hotel to Hya, some 10 km to the south, where the two co-widows, Masi and Kwada, have cornered the tourist market. Like their late husband, they cast on demand, normally on a regular basis with the tour operators acting as mediators. Small groups and individual tourists can easily order a casting, though most visit the compound to buy directly from the producer. Until 2005, the array of objects was rather traditional: some pipes, bells, bracelets, and knives, together with the brass pouches that dominated the production in the 1970s and 1980s.[3] Over the decades, the widows' late husband had diversified but little—just some more bells.

After his death in 2007, Masi and Kwada established themselves as able casters and are now in the process of diversifying the objects for the tourist market, more eager to take on some new forms than their husband was. Among these new items are a miniature cooking pot, a brass calabash, and also a dancing adze inspired probably by Vere brasses, as well as larger pipes and bells. But the main thrust is a modest first attempt at figurative sculpting of antelopes and a human figurine, a new development away from the purely non-figurative tradition of brass casting in the southern Mandara. They have also reintroduced old Kapsiki objects of some renown, such as a brass cup and a brass sword, and for the first time since long ago have made a *matlaba* (hip plaque for the richer initiates). Thus they now supply the Rumsiki trade with diversified products; and even if still on a small scale, Rumsiki now offers the experienced tourist some objects that fall into the category of 'airport art' (Jules-Rosette 1984).

The two women have no children; however, two sons of their husband's sister are determined to learn the technique and eventually establish themselves as casters. The women's authority in casting is evident, considering the deference paid to them by their younger kinsmen. Well, they do have something to

---

3   See Van Beek 2012b for a visual comparison.

show for their authority: an official recognition by the Cameroonian Board for Artisanal Production, and they have won several prizes for their productions. The commentary of my non-smith Kapsiki friends was telling: 'The blacksmiths have always obeyed their wives.' Indeed, husband and wife routinely cooperate in brass casting and increasingly do so in iron forging as well.

Tourism has, as observed elsewhere, preserved some cultural items and processes that might, without tourist interest and revenues, have gone out of fashion. Whether in the case of the Kapsiki/Higi this holds for much more than brass casting is debatable (Van Beek 2003), but at least Rumsiki and Hya are secure in their brass production. In Guili, the major Bana village to the south of the Kapsiki area, a caster from Daba country (still further to the southeast) has recently set up shop and transformed his entire household, involving three wives and several daughters, into a brass production unit, turning out a steady stream of brass beads for necklaces, all for the internal market.[4] So, even if brass may be relatively marginal among the blacksmith trades, neither knowledge nor practice is dying out. As long they are sought after by tourists, brass items will continue to be available to the Kapsiki. And the Guili smith is also producing for the local market, focusing on the new rich and the desire to stand out with brass jewellery.

The Way of Music

The traditional Kapsiki first wedding for a girl, *makwa*, is the *verhe makwa* (feast of the bride), falling in April just before the boys' initiation. It shows a curious feature of smith work during festivals, that of master of ceremonies. A new custom was introduced in the Kapsiki villages in the early 1970s, called *hirdɛ* (a Hausa term), a ceremony of gift-giving at a wedding, aimed at helping the groom with the large costs of the wedding. At the *hirdɛ*, friends and clients clothed in their festive best gathered in the afternoon in the groom's compound and conspicuously presented money to the groom. A smith had to act as speaker. Each gift of money was widely acknowledged, through the smith speaker.

In the late 1990s, a new fashion, *amalɛa*, arrived on the wedding scene. It is probably also of Hausa origin but in any case came via the Higi part of the Kapsiki area in Nigeria. Here gift-giving has grown into a full-blown festival, with a ceremonial procession of the bride and groom and their respective

---

4 His stylistic array is quite different from the Kapsiki one; but in the Mandara Mountains, stylistic variation on a small geographical scale is quite common. *Cf.* MacEachern (1992).

friends and kinsmen and an evening-long spectacle in a special enclosure. Drumming, dancing, and gift-giving are the main activities, but the proceedings are, to a certain extent, quite formal. A secretariat keeps track of the gifts, speakers use a microphone with loudspeakers, and a band of musicians (smiths) is hired for the whole night. The *amalɛa* draws a huge crowd, though a strict division between the invited and the non-invited is enforced by the use of fences, a gate, and gatekeepers. Only the real givers and some guests of honour are welcome, and the latter have to show their wealth as well.

A group of young smiths is required with tuners and large speakers, a table, chairs, and lights that they set up inside a fenced-off dancing area. The groom's sister's sons will have made the arrangements, and they also need a few 'secretaries' to note down the gifts, including those of food and drink—usually with a mobile phone as calculator (Van Beek 2009)—plus some organizers to keep out the uninvited, and a smith with a whistle to direct the proceedings. The players are paid by the dancers with gifts of money and food.

The real *amalɛa* starts in the late afternoon on the next day after the *verhe*. Two smiths with drums lead a procession of friends, the bride and groom, and some of the bride's friends, dancing slowly out of the house, all dressed splendidly in gowns and dresses but with expressionless faces. On their arrival at the dancing area, chairs await them at the place of honour. The smiths return to the house to collect the groom's father and his friends, plus the groom's mother and her retinue. When all have arrived, the smith-musicians present the bride and groom in the first dance. The guests have arrived now and start giving money to the master of ceremonies, who directs the session with his microphone, while secretaries write down the amounts given. In the older gift ceremony, the *hirdɛ*, the smith would be the one crying out the amounts offered and taking great liberties with the truth, calling out 500 CFA francs as 5,000— but then, that is what a smith is for at a wedding: amusement and flattery, the smith as a jester. In contrast, at the *amalɛa,* the exact amount is written down, as this has become a serious enterprise and should also make money for the groom—real money, not just flattery. The cost of the evening is considerable, with between 20,000 and 40,000 CFA francs for the performing smiths, half of which has to be paid in advance. Whether the event will indeed show a profit depends on the number of friends and kinsmen the groom can muster. The bride's group will give money too, but much less.

The audience is divided into the usual groups in Kapsiki ceremonies: the groom's father with his friends, the groom's mother with her friends, and the same for the bride's side. The groom's kin make a collection with a dish, but most people prefer to give their contribution to the master of ceremonies to have the amount broadcast over the sound system. The bride's mother and her friends mainly give clothes to the bride. Not only do the different kin groups give as one; they also dance together, the groom's lineage and his mother's, the bride's lineage and her mother's. As usual, the village chief takes the microphone to warn anyone with evil intent that no provocation will be tolerated. Most of the money given is in naira, as the Nigerian currency looks more generous than Cameroonian CFA francs: 25 CFA francs is a coin, while the equivalent in naira is a banknote of five naira.

After this huge festival of conspicuous giving, the secretaries count the money, pay the smiths, and give them a few gifts, such as a bottle of whiskey, a case of *Castell* beer, and tobacco. On average, an evening like this can make a profit of some 50,000 CFA francs (about EUR 75).[5] This ritualization of conspicuous giving has important financial consequences, which are part of the total bridewealth picture. In order to illustrate these implications, I will take an example of a *hirdɛ* in 1972 and an *amalɛa* of 2005 for a marriage like the one mentioned above (see Table 2).

TABLE 2   *Weddings, costs and benefits*

1972: Costs	1972: Benefits
Calling the bride: 2,000 CFA francs	*Verhe* contribution of family: 8,000 CFA francs
Verhe hosting: 8,000 CFA francs	*Hirdɛ:* 8,000 CFA francs
Total: 10,000 CFA francs	**16,000 CFA francs**
Net profit:	
16,000–10,000 = 6,000 CFA francs (EUR 9)	
2005: Costs	2005: Benefits
Smiths: 21,000 CFA francs	Uncles: 8,000 CFA francs
Lighting: 3,000 CFA francs	*Verhe* gifts: 4,000 CFA francs
Kweperhwuli: 4,000 CFA francs	*Amalɛa*: 53,000 CFA francs
Meat: 10,000 CFA francs	In kind from in-laws at festival: 33,000 CFA francs
7 basins of grain @ 800: 5,600 CFA francs	
Invitations: 1,500 CFA francs	
Total: 45,100 CFA francs	**98,000 CFA francs**
Net profit:	
98,000–45,100 = 52,900 CFA francs (EUR 80)	

---

5   For an elaborate treatment of the role of these costs in bridewealth, see Van Beek (2014).

The role of the smiths here is purely musical, but absolutely crucial. Without them, no dance; and without dance, no profit. Usually a small group of young smiths performs the music, with a couple of drums and a guitar, but an electric one. Their main asset nowadays is the amplification, and they hire themselves out with their installation. Curiously, often one of them wears a *livu*, the traditional bridal skirt made of iron rings that has always been a central symbol in marriage proceedings; in this wedding soundscape, it adds the very traditional scraping sound on the iron skirt to the more high-tech music production. In any case, it is a lucrative business, and they earn between 20,000 and 40,000 CFA francs (EUR 30–60) for the two nights, plus their nightly fill of beer and—recently—whiskey.

The flipside of this combination of prosperity and scarcity is that the smiths of today, in the eyes of the *melu*, have become cocky upstarts who do not know their place. As my assistant Luc Sunu said:

> Formerly, you could give a smith anything you deemed sufficient for his services, and he could not complain. If he did not perform well, you could hit him. Now they set their own price and have no hawe [shame].

His musing was elicited by the song of a smith boy in Rumsiki at the turn of the century. The young smith sang songs that were in principle just songs of the harvest festival, or so it seemed. But when transcribing the text, it became clear that he had taken quite some liberties, introducing a meta-commentary on his own position:

> I will not drink water in this house.
> Here are the people with the long necks [a sign of beauty].
> I am the real one, I am the leopard.
> I am old enough to go to a woman without children.
> I am in charge of myself.

These lines are more or less standard, but only when sung by *melu*. The point is that this was a *rerhɛ* addressing a *melu* audience, and a young one at that. This message settled, the singer went further:

> At night, the people here cannot get their penis straight.
> When you bent over, what did you put in your vagina?
> I am from the family of the long ones.
> People pay the vagina here;
> What did you find, bald-headed one?
> I counted 700 clitorises inside the vagina.

The sexual element is customary, albeit quite blatant for Kapsiki norms, but the smith now turns all the tables. While the first part inverts the hierarchy of eating, the second one shatters the endogamy hierarchy. During his singing, he played the clown as well, overacting his text and had people laugh, and that, typically, is the kind of cleverness that people expect of a smith. His was a performance with a lot of layers, which could still be fitted into the traditional relations—but in doing so, one fact sticks out: things have changed.

A Costly Road

So smiths have shown themselves eager to take on new crafts, but not all of them still cherish their smith roots. During my first research period (1972–1973), I needed to develop my photos in the field. Sending the exposed negatives home was not an option, and anyway I wanted to see the pictures myself. But even more, my informants wanted to see their own images. Pictures are there to be given away, and for me handing out pictures was and still is a splendid bonding opportunity. So, during my first month in the field, I scouted for a photographer in Mokolo and found one: Mousa Bale. He was recommended to me because he was Kapsiki (there is a Kapsiki ward in Mokolo), and Bale turned out to be a smith from Sir. He was a smith who no longer wanted to be *rerhɛ*, so when I reacted enthusiastically to his identity, he drew back and closed up a little bit. He explained to me that he did not like to be spoken about as a smith and that he had little contact with his family. He had Islamized, married an Islamized woman (yes, also a smith, a Mafa smith's daughter), had shifted his food taboos, and now ate like a *melu* and drank like a Muslim. He had 'left it behind,' he told me. 'Sanscritization', this process is called in India: trying to move up the caste ladder by adhering to the norms of a higher echelon. In North Cameroon it is called Fulanization, as the city culture of the Fulbe is dominant.[6] His change in status, however, was clearer to himself than to his neighbours, who routinely referred to him as the smith from Sir. He was 'passing' as Fulbe, but not very successfully yet.

Why did he choose photography and photograph processing? His interest in cameras and, later, film processing had been kindled at the Catholic mission in Sir, and that was a new opportunity, a new niche using fascinating equipment. Also, a technical job like a photograph studio was an obvious niche for a 'passing' smith. So Mousa used a new opportunity that fitted rather nicely into the array of smith specializations, and he serviced the few photographers of

---

6 For this process see Van Santen (1993).

Mokolo and me. I could now see and hand out my photographs. Yet in my repeated contacts with him I could not escape the impression of deep loneliness, for here was a man who had a respected job, a family, and nothing else: no people in his courtyard, no chitchat with neighbours—a classic case of someone betwixt and between. He was a *rerhɛ* no longer, but a *melu* by no means— and not yet a Fulbe by a long shot. At present, almost all smiths of Kapsiki origin in Mokolo are Fulanized.

Once I heard the chief smith of Mogode speak with some sadness in his voice about one son of his who 'did not want to be a smith any longer', considering him 'lost'. And in a sense, he was right: going against what is both a birthright and a 'birthdoom' demands a heavy price, and it starts with a severe sense of loss, loss of family and loss of social support. Kapsiki is a stratified society in which the ascribed status is very hard to shed. Fitting in, even in the lower ranking that smiths do have in Kapsiki, is easier than fighting the system. A young Kapsiki filmmaker is now producing a short feature film on the topic but from a more romantic angle: a *melu* boy falls in love with a smith girl—a ravishing beauty, of course—and then the couple encounter huge problems on both sides of the family, plus from the whole community. The theme is a well-trodden romantic path, which works well in European royalty marriages, though much less, I think, in the setting of the Mandara Mountains; but it does illustrate the point. The echelon of the smith, as with any caste-like distinction, produces severe problems in the globalizing world of the cities.

Also, in a village like Mogode, with good connections to the outer world, more smiths are moving out, gradually renouncing their position as 'internal others' in the wider society. Recently, the chief smith of Mogode asked some Nigerian *rerhɛ* to come to Mogode to fill the void, as the Higi smiths are still numerous, too numerous in fact to make a good living in their villages (Kodji 2009: 73). Mogode has a large core of Fulanized Kapsiki, plus the Christian ones, and quite a few smiths have found a niche there. Drumming for the *chef de canton* or in their church, they no longer engage in funerals. Or, they just play the drums or *shila* flute and do not carry the corpse. Some just cultivate and have desisted from all smith crafts; and according to the *melu,* these smiths do cultivate a lot, more than anyone else. No *melu* ever said that the smiths did not work hard.

Also, the spectacular professional success of Zeme's daughter Kwanyè as a medical doctor does come with some inevitable social problems: she is still unmarried, as no *melu* will take her as a bride, and there are no smith men with a comparable background. Yet modern Kapsiki (*melu*) women see her car as a sublime symbol of success that makes up for her lack of marriage and even motherhood.

Roadblocks

Though some roads to prosperity have opened for the smiths, others seem to have closed, while a few itineraries remain out of their reach. Healing is one of the mainstays of the gamut of smith functions; and with development, healing is not receding into the background—not at all. Smiths were still the first option in cases of illness when I first went out into the field in 1972. The *rerhɛ* were the essential middlemen between this world and the other, and this position gave them a decisive advantage in the field of medicine.

Traditional healing is primarily a socio-religious process. A therapy addresses not just the illness but also the patient, not only his somatic but also his socio-religious definition of self. Thus, the divination—also a smith prerogative—redefines symptoms into a reconstruction of the patient's past, which is in fact a partial redefinition of his social 'persona'. Diagnosis is discovering secrets about the patient, about his social relations, about mistakes made by or against him, about his relation with the other world. In Kapsiki traditional medicine, as in many African medicinal systems, the struggle is outside the patient's body, not inside as in Western medicine. One line of approach is to reinstate harmony in his social body, in the relations with people, spirits, and gods, with the walls of the compound as one of the cultural shields. Another line is to restore the integrity of the body's limits, the shield of the skin. Treatment thus reinforces that perimeter, and medication is directed at externalizing the affliction, not internalizing it.

The healers themselves successfully compensated their lower status as smiths with their healing expertise, even if they had no absolute privileges or monopoly on healing. The smiths' position as 'special people' helped them to dominate this arena, but they have now lost their virtual monopoly here. The gradual arrival of cosmopolitan medicine, stimulated also by the mission dispensaries and hospitals which appeared in the region from the 1960s, offered an alternative route to health, with a completely different outlook on illness. This did not replace traditional medication, as both systems developed to coexist alongside each other, as almost everywhere in Africa. But it did change the craft of traditional medicine—from an occupation of people 'in-between', with special links to the other world, towards a more technical, somatic, and above all supra-local endeavour. Instead of smith-healers branching out into new healing options, other *melu* healers appeared and took over the lead in the development of traditional medicine. One such healer is Haman Tizhè.[7] He came to healership via a completely different route, being marginalized in

---

7   Haman Tizhè is described at length in Van Beek (2009, 2011).

Kapsiki society through personal events instead of birthright, and now has a blossoming practice both in Mogode and Mokolo. Also, he organized a healers' association and successfully applied for its government recognition.

So in this field, the smiths are losing out and ceding their first place to *melu*. Why? Usually smiths are the ones to pick up quickly on new developments and adapt quickly to new technologies and markets, but not here. I think the answer lies in professional status and its linkages with the outside world. Healing was always important but quite ambivalent: healing in Kapsiki society was associated with marginal status and ambivalence, and the process itself fraught with danger—including danger for the healer. Though not typically a 'wounded healer' type, the Kapsiki smith/healer still ran the risk of attracting the affliction he cured his patient of. With the coming of cosmopolitan medicine, this changed. Healership, all over Africa, has increased in status while diminishing in risk. The link with the dispensaries and hospitals was always tenuous and fragile, but it has grown stronger; and these prestigious institutions now furnish the model, setting the standard to emulate.

Officialization by the government, in the form of registration and the genesis of professional associations, heightens the status even more, drawing it closer to cosmopolitan organizations. Smiths find it difficult to participate in this, let alone lead such official bodies as *rerhɛ*. The other healers, *melu*, will never accept their leadership. Also, prices rise, including those of healing, and being a healer has become a rather lucrative profession, much more so than in the past. The combined effect has been that the status of healer is rising, slowly but surely, out of reach of the smiths, and the advantages of their underprivileged status are not transferable to a higher social echelon, while their lower status remains intact. In short, they lose on the national scene the relative but restricted advantage that their intermediary position as 'in-between' people offers them locally.

That was a road more or less blocked, but some routes have been out of bounds for *rerhɛ* anyway. Usually, the road to riches in this part of Africa is through commerce, but being a *rerhɛ* is a serious obstacle to the kind of contacts and networks a commercial entrepreneur has to rely on. Regionally, the Kapsiki area has become important in trade with Nigeria, as one of the major routes into Nigeria runs from Mogode downhill into the neighbouring Kamale, with a link to Michika, the Higi district centre lying at the tarmac road leading to Yola and Maiduguri. During the Biafra wars, and in the 1980s with energy prices soaring (Beauvilain 1989), this was a major smuggling route, and some Kapsiki gathered flocks of donkeys and grew rich by this 'informal commerce'. From 2007 onwards a motorable road was built—not an easy task considering the sheer mountainside that forms the border, but quite profitable. Mogode has now developed into an administrative centre, with a *sous-prefet*, a police post and—inevitably—a customs officer. But the bulk of the commerce (groundnuts) has been fully legal.[8] The Mandara Mountains form an important centre of production of groundnuts, usually a woman's crop, often grown in between the sorghum, and this is large-scale commerce with a fleet of trucks. To become such a merchant one has to be Muslim, meaning Fulanized, for this is at a social level where national contacts are essential. The Kapsiki of the village call these merchants *el hadj*, as one simply has to have gone on pilgrimage to Mecca in order to generate these kinds of contacts. For any smith, this is way out of his span of control.

Conclusion

In the end, for the marginal people of old, the new options are important but limited. On their road to prosperity, the Kapsiki *rerhε* experience both the advantages and the disadvantages of their special position, as the new division of labour offers them opportunities-with-blockages. The options for branching out are mainly in line with their fundamental definition as craftspeople, in technical skills and jobs. This lifts them out of their ambivalent status in society, but only up to a point. Essentially, they remain craftsmen in a wider world, acceptable for the 'others' as long as they retain something of their 'in-between-ness', and as long as they behave as behoves their lower social status. One's social position is hard to escape; but then, we all experience both a birthright and a birthdoom.

References

Beauvilain, A. (1989), *Nord-Cameroun, crises et peuplement*. Paris: Alain Beauvilain.

Jules-Rosette, B. (1984), *The Messages of Tourist Art: An African Semiotic System in Comparative Perspective*. New York: Plenum.

Kirk-Greene, A.H. (1969), *Adamawa Past and Present: An Historical Approach to the Development of a Northern Cameroons Province*. London: IAI.

Kodji, G. (2009), *Le forgeron Kapsiki*. Yaoundé: Mémoires Université Yaoundé.

Langlois, O. (2012), The Development of Endogamy Among Smiths of the Mandara Mountains Eastern Piedmont: Myths, History and Material Evidence, in: N. David

---

8   For an overview of groundnut cultivation, see Beauvilain (1989), Van Beek & Avontuur (2005, 2006) and, on a larger time scale, Kirk-Greene (1969).

(ed.) *Metals in Mandara Mountains Society and Culture*. Trenton, NJ: Africa World Press, pp. 226–255.

MacEachern, S. (1992), Ethnicity and Stylistic Variation Around Mayo Plata, Northern Cameroon, in: J. Sterner & N. David (eds) *An African Commitment: Papers in Honor of Peter Lewis Shinnie*. Calgary: University of Calgary Press, pp. 211–230.

Pelckmans, L. (2011), *Travelling Hierarchies: Roads in and out of Slave Status in a Central Malian Fulbe Network*. Leiden: African Studies Centre.

Rasmussen, S. (2013), *Neighbors, Strangers, Witches, and Culture-Heroes: Ritual Powers of Smith/Artisans in Tuareg Society and Beyond*. Lanham, MD: University Press of America.

Schmitz-Cliever, G. (1979), *Schmiede in Westafrika: Ihre Soziale Stellung in Traditionallen Gesellschaften*. Munich: Klaus Berner.

Van Beek, W.E.A. (2003), African Tourist Encounters: Effects of Tourism in Two West African Societies. *Africa* 73(3): 251–289.

Van Beek, W.E.A. (2009), The Healer and His Phone: Medicinal Dynamics Among the Kapsiki of North Cameroon, in: M. de Bruijn, F. Nyamnyoh & I. Brinkman (eds) *Mobile Phones: The New Talking Drums of Everyday Africa*. Leiden: Langaa & African Studies Centre, pp. 125–134.

Van Beek, W.E.A. (2011), Medicinal Knowledge and Healing Practices Among the Kapsiki/Higi of North Cameroon and Northeastern Nigeria, in: M. Dekker & R. van Dijk (eds) *Markets of Well-Being: Navigating Health and Healing in Africa. African Dynamics 9*. Leiden, Brill, pp. 173–200.

Van Beek, W.E.A. (2012a), *The Dancing Dead: Ritual and Religion Among the Kapsiki/ Higi of North Cameroon and Northeastern Nigeria*. New York: Oxford University Press.

Van Beek, W.E.A. (2012b), A Touch of Wildness: Brass and Brass Casting in Kapsiki, in: N. David (ed.) *Metals in Mandara Mountains Society and Culture*. Trenton: Africa World Press, pp. 303–323.

Van Beek, W.E.A. (2014), Dynamic of Kapsiki/Higi Marriage Exchanges, in: S. Baldi & G. Magrin (eds) *Les échanges et la communication dans le bassin du Lac Tchad*. Naples: Studi Africanistici, Serie Ciado-Sudanese 6, pp. 105–131.

Van Beek, W.E.A. (2015), *The Forge and the Funeral: The Smith in Kapsiki/Higi Culture*. East Lansing: Michigan State University Press.

Van Beek, W.E.A. & S. Avontuur (2005), The Making of an Environment: Ecological History of the Kapsiki/Higi of North Cameroon and North-Eastern Nigeria, in: Q. Gausset, M. Whyte & T. Birch-Thomsen (eds) *Beyond Territory and Scarcity in Africa: Exploring Conflicts over Natural Resource Management*. Copenhagen: Nordiska Afrika Institutet, pp. 70–89.

Van Beek, W.E.A. & S. Avontuur (2006), Dynamics of Agriculture in the Mandara Mountains: The Case of the Kapsiki/Higi of Northern Cameroon and North-Eastern

Nigeria, in: C. Baroin, G. Seidensticker-Brikay & K. Tijani (eds) *Man and the Lake; Proceedings of the 12th Mega Chad Conference*. Maiduguri: Maiduguri University Press, pp. 335–382.

Van Santen, J. (1993), *They Leave Their Jars Behind: The Conversion of Mafa Women to Islam*. Leiden: VENA.

Vincent, J.F. (1991), *Princes montagnards du Nord-Cameroun: Les Mofou-Diamaré et le pouvoir politique*. Paris: Harmattan.

Wade, J. (2012), The Wife of the Village: Understanding Caste in the Mandara Mountains, in: N. David (ed.) *Metals in Mandara Mountains Society and Culture*. Trenton, N.J.: Africa World Press, pp. 257–284.

Wente-Lukas, R. (1972), Eisen und Schmied in Südlichen Tschadraum. *Paideuma* 18: 112–143.

CHAPTER 10

Migrants' Assessment of Prospects in Migration: A Case Study of Conservancy Labourers in the University of Cape Coast, Ghana

Augustine Tanle, Benjamin Kofi Nyarko and Akinyinka Akinyoade

Introduction

In Ghana, the main pattern of migration is north–south, which is mostly from rural areas in the northern areas (comprising the Northern, Upper West and Upper East Regions) to urban centres in the southern areas (covering the remaining seven regions) of the country. North–south migration was initiated during the colonial era through a policy of forced labour recruitment of men from the then Northern Territories to the mining and construction industries in the southern parts of the country. Since then, migration has become a colonial legacy, as people from the three northern regions continue to migrate voluntarily to the southern sector of the country in search of job opportunities (Anarfi *et al.* 2003; Songsore 2003; Tsegai 2005; Tanle 2010).

In general, compared with the northern parts of the country, the southern possess better natural resources and therefore enjoy increased socio-economic activities, which makes these areas centres of development and growth, while the three northern regions have remained underdeveloped. Also, further socioeconomic developments by successive governments continue to widen the gap between the northern and southern parts of the country (Addo 1980; Tsegai 2005; Kwankye *et al.* 2007; Abane 2008; Tanle 2014).

A number of studies have been conducted on various aspects of north–south migration in Ghana, some of which have focused on remittances from migrants to their home villages, migration as a livelihood strategy adapted by the migrants, migration and agricultural productivity, and migration and development of northern Ghana (Songsore 2003; Geest 2010; Tanle 2010). Although migration has generally been recognized as a strategy aimed at improving the socio-economic status of migrants, little is known about how migrants themselves assess the prospects associated with migration. This paper focuses on the conservancy labourers in the University of Cape Coast who are migrants from the three northern regions of the country. The main objectives of the paper are to assess the motives for migration and the migrants' views on prospects associated with migration. The study contributes to the

current debate on migration and livelihood and also adds to the existing literature on migration.

Conceptual and Theoretical Issues

Migration can be defined as a temporary or permanent change of usual place
of residence from one geographical area to another within a given time period.
It can be classified into various forms, such as internal or international, and
voluntary or involuntary migration. Internal migration is movement within
the same country, while international migration involves the crossing of one or
several international borders, resulting in a change in the legal status of the
individual concerned (International Organization for Migration 2003). This
paper focuses on internal migration from the three northern regions to the
Cape Coast metropolis located in the southern part of Ghana.

The study is guided by the 'push–pull' theory of Everett Lee (1966) and the
theory of the circular process of cumulative causation of Gunnar Myrdal
(1957). In 1966, Everett Lee developed a theoretical framework to analyse factors which predispose people to migrate. The push factors include deteriorating socio-economic conditions in an area of origin, which literally 'force'
people to move out of such localities. The pull factors include the attractions or
the socio-economic opportunities available at a destination (Arango 2000;
Stock 2004; de Haas 2008). One of the merits of the push–pull theory of migration is that it identifies a set of unique factors at origins and destinations that
influence migration. The uniqueness of both places of origin and destination
can inform analysis of motives and patterns of migration (Conway & Cohen
1998). The migration of people from the three northern regions to work in the
University of Cape Coast as conservancy labourers may be a response to the
push and pull factors at the places of origin and destination, respectively.

The theory of the circular process of cumulative causation was first developed by Gunnar Myrdal (1957). It provides a general perspective on the uneven
distribution of development, the concentration of economic activities at one
locality at the expense of another. The theory holds that deepening spatial and
personal income inequalities between periphery and core regions inevitably
marks development that is dictated by market economic forces. Consequently,
internal and external economies of scales will perpetuate and deepen the differences between periphery and core, such that a periphery area will be characterized by general poverty and underdevelopment while a core area
constantly experiences accelerated economic development (Abane 2008; de
Haas 2008). Although the periphery region can benefit from positive 'spread

effects' from the core by way of increased demand for agricultural raw materials and labour, the 'backwash effects' in the form of stagnating growth and limited economic opportunities can outweigh the benefits. The assumption underlying the theory is that there is no government intervention; market forces alone dictate the pace of development between the periphery and core regions.

Relating the theory to internal migration in Ghana, it has been noted that the unequal socio-economic development in the country has created two main economic zones, namely the northern and southern zones. The northern zone is characterized by poor physical conditions, a perceived lack of natural resources, poor health and educational facilities, and widespread poverty. On the other hand, the southern zone is endowed not only with better natural resources but also the presence of quality infrastructural facilities, which have boosted socio-economic development, making regions in the south centres of development and growth while the northern regions remain largely underdeveloped (Abane 2008). Consequently, a migration gradient is established whereby people from the three northern regions tend to migrate to the southern parts of the country for various reasons.

Data and Methods

A qualitative research approach was adopted in order to understand and explain how the conservancy labourers assess prospects associated with their migration. The instruments comprised both in-depth interviews (IDIs) and focus group discussion (FGD) guides. The questions covered background characteristics, factors that influence migration, and assessment of prospects in migration. The field assistants—four National Service Personnel from both the Department of Population and Health and of Geography and Regional Planning—were given a day's training on the instruments. Using the snowball sampling procedure, four IDIs were conducted in each of the six traditional halls of residence in the university, namely Kwame Nkrumah Hall, Valco Hall, Casely Hayford Hall, Atlantic Hall, Adheye Hall, and Oguaa Hall, providing a total of 24 respondents. In addition, two FGDs were conducted: one at the old site of the university, with six participants drawn from Atlantic, Adheye, and Oguaa halls; and the other at the new site of the university, with the same number of participants drawn from Kwame Nkrumah, Valco, and Casely Hayford halls. With the consent of the respondents, the interviews/discussions were tape-recorded and later transcribed. Through content analysis, the relevant sections of the data were teased out and discussed in line with the objectives stated.

Study Area

The three northern regions of Ghana (Northern, Upper East, and Upper West) constitute the places of origin of the migrants. These areas lie in the savannah agro-ecological zone, which is characterized by a mono-modal rainy season defined by an annual estimated mean rainfall of 1,100 mm (Nyarko 2007). Rainfall over this region exhibits temporal and spatial variability. To understand the social and economic value of the annual rains and their effects on migration, it is important to define the period when rainfall is agronomically useful (Laux 2009). A trend analysis of rainfall data revealed no clear pattern as regards onset and cessation of rainfall over these areas. Therefore, with the high variability in the onset of the rainfall dates, farmers in these areas have difficulties in deciding when to start with their sowing preparations. According to Laux (*ibid.*), the onset of rainfall (Figure 1a) and cessation of rainfall (Figure 1b) in the northern part of the country shows a similar pattern.

Aside from the onset of the rainfall, dry spells are an important measure of agriculture activities in this region. Within the rainy season, it has been observed that a lack of rainfall for more than six consecutive days at a site constitutes a dry spell and affects crop physiology. This northern sector of the country is sensitive to climate variability, and farmers and pastoralist have to contend with the extreme conditions caused by *El Niño Southern Oscillation*

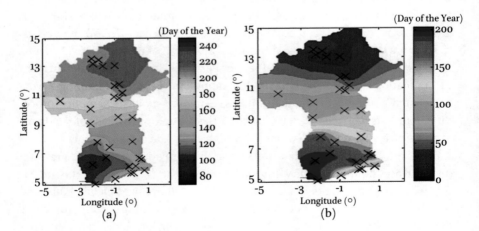

FIGURE 1   (a) Onset of the rainy season (b) Rainy season length.
SOURCE: P. LAUX (2009), STATISTICAL MODELING OF PRECIPITATION FOR AGRICULTURAL PLANNING IN THE VOLTA BASIN OF WEST AFRICA. IMK-IFU, GERMANY.

(ENSO) and extended dry spells. The soils are also generally infertile. Although agriculture is the main livelihood activity in these areas, cultivation is seasonal due to the short duration of rainfall. This encourages seasonal migration to the southern part of the country.

The available socio-economic indicators generally show that the three northern regions together have the worst socio-economic conditions. About 80% of the adult population have never received formal education, poverty is widespread (Tanle 2010), and infant and maternal mortality rates are above the national averages. Owing to inadequate government investment in the area, agriculture constitutes the population's main occupation, with about eight out of ten people engaged in agriculture compared with fewer than five out of ten in other regions (Ghana Statistical Service 2012).

The Cape Coast metropolis, which is the destination of the migrants, is bounded to the south by the Gulf of Guinea, to the west by the Komenda Edina Eguafo Abrem Municipal, to the east by the Abura Asebu Kwamankese District, and to the north by the Twifu Hemang Lower Denkyira District (Figure 2). The metropolis covers an area of 122 square km and is the smallest metropolis in the country. The capital, Cape Coast, is also the capital of Central Region and was the first national capital of the Gold Coast (now Ghana).

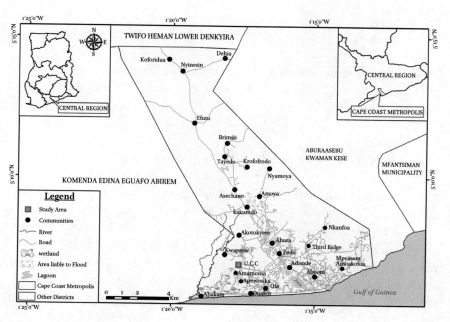

FIGURE 2   *Map of the study area.*
SOURCE: GIS & REMOTE SENSING LAB. DEPARTMENT OF GEOGRAPHY & REGIONAL PLANNINIG, UNIVERSITY OF CAPE COAST, 2015

The Cape Coast metropolis has an estimated population of 169,894, comprising 48.7% males and 51.5% females. The metropolis is 77% urbanized and has 90% literacy rate, which is higher than the national average of 74.1%. Although farming thrives in the northern part of the metropolis, fishing is the main source of livelihood along the southern coastline (Ghana Statistical Service 2012). The Cape Coast metropolis is endowed with historical, traditional, and cultural resources, which have made it a tourism destination of the country.

All parts of the metropolis are connected by roads that are motorable throughout the year. Over 90% of the residents have access to potable water, and the main source of lighting is electricity from the national grid. The metropolis has a wide range of banking and health facilities. The main industry of the town is formal education. Besides the University of Cape Coast, the Cape Coast Polytechnic, and the OLA Training College, it has some of the best first- and second-cycle institutions in the country.

When it became the first national capital of Ghana, it attracted migrants from the three northern regions, and since then people from the three northern regions continue to migrate to Cape Coast in search of employment, particularly in the University of Cape Coast.

Results

This section presents the results, which cover background characteristics of the respondents and factors that influence their migration and assessment of migration prospects.

Background Characteristics of Respondents

The respondents were mostly males aged between 25 and 45 years who were married but had only basic education or no formal education. They hailed from the three northern regions and were mainly of Mole-Dagbani and Gruni ethnic background. Most of them had lived in Cape Coast for at least ten years. The background characteristics of the respondents, particularly their age, sex, and level of education, are consistent with the findings of some previous studies: migrants from the three northern regions are mostly young and illiterates males (Songsore 2003; Geest 2005; Kwankye *et al.* 2007; Tanle 2010, 2014).

Factors that Influence Migration

The factors that influence migration from the three northern regions to the Cape Coast metropolis are analysed within the context of the two theoretical perspectives outlined above.

Push Factors at Places of Origin

Information from the interviews indicates that many varied economic, socio-cultural, and physical factors (such as climate, soil fertility) literally pushed the respondents to migrate from the three northern regions to the Cape Coast metropolis, where they now work as conservancy labourers in the University of Cape Coast. Unfavourable economic situations or factors such as inadequate job opportunities, inability to pay fees at school, and poor rainfall were some of the reasons given for out-migration from the northern sector to the Cape Coast metropolis. The following interview excerpts illustrate these factors:

> I came here to look for a job to better my life but initially I was in Takoradi and later I decided to come to Cape Coast because I couldn't do anything with the school education I had. After school there was no work for me because I didn't get good grades and I couldn't also better my grades because I didn't have money to register the courses again to write the exam. From my hometown, I went to the rubber factory in Takoradi and some of my relatives were also living in Cape Coast, so I told them that I was looking for a job because the Takoradi job was paying less. I had a friend here who was like a brother to me, so I told him also and he told me that the university is looking for conservancy labourers, so he would send my name. After some time, he called to tell me that my name is in the list of names that the university had picked as labourers. (Male, 35 years, senior high school graduate)
>
> When I was in school, issues of money were very hard for my mother. I used to join my brothers to Sunyani to work as a farm labourer so that I can pay my fees and also use some to take care of my mother. That is what my brothers and I used to do till I went to Takoradi and finally to Cape Coast here to work as a conservancy labourer and got money to take care of my mother at home. (Male, 39 years, junior high school graduate)
>
> In the north, we were farmers, and the rainfall pattern was not reliable; and also I have many mouths to feed. Sometimes when we cultivate our

crops they don't do well because the land was not fertile and we would have losses. (Male, 35 years, no formal education)

I was a farmer. When I plant, the rains were not consistent. Sometimes it doesn't rain at all for a long period of time; other times, it rains heavily and the crops are destroyed. This usually results in low yield. The soil was also not very fertile. This is because heavy rainfall washes away all the nutrients in the soil, while absence of rainfall makes the land too hard for crop survival. As the plants lack water, they begin to die. The low yields from my farm compelled me to migrate to Cape Coast. (Male, 31 years, no formal education)

Pull Factors at Destination

The main pull factor or attraction to the Cape Coast metropolis, as reported in the interviews, is the possibility of gaining employment in the formal sector, particularly in the University of Cape Coast. This was the main motive for most people who migrated from the three northern regions to the metropolis, as illustrated in the following interview excerpts:

Well, I migrated to Cape Coast because I was not having any better job doing at my home town; and because I did not have a good formal education, I could not access any good job. In fact, living conditions wasn't easy. I do very tedious work and do not earn much. My brother motivated me when he last visited our home town that he was into clothing business, which at least offered him good money and he could bring me to Cape Coast for us to be doing that together. After working with him for some time, he got a job for me at the sanitary section of the University of Cape Coast. (Male, 32 years, junior high school graduate)

I came to Cape Coast to look for a job. I knew a teacher who comes from the north and works in the university. I went to him to assist me find job and he helped me get a job in the university. I was first at Atlantic Hall and was later transferred to Casely Hayford Hall. I worked for four years in that hall, and later I was taken to Oguaa Hall and I worked there for four years and was brought to Casely Hayford Hall, where I have worked for nine years. (Male, 48 years, no formal education)

I come from [...] in the Upper West Region. When I completed JHS and had nothing doing, I used to visit my people here who motivated me to be here, so that if any chance comes in their workplace [University of Cape Coast], they can help me get the chance to work with them. I finally got a job in the university as a conservancy labourer. It is very difficult getting work to do at our home town, especially when you do not have good formal education. (Male, 34 years, junior high school graduate).

Views about Socio-Economic Status

The ultimate motive of most migrants is to improve upon their socio-economic status. In the study, the migrants were asked to assess their own socio-economic status, whether it had improved, had remained unchanged, or had instead deteriorated. From the results, most of them indicated that their status had improved in a number of ways, including acquisition of durable consumer goods, ability to build a house (either in Cape Coast or their home town) or rent their own accommodation, enrolment of their children in school, and ability to remit funds to relations at home. The following excerpts attest to the diverse ways the migrants reported on improvement in their socio-economic status:

> There has been a significant change in my life compared to when I was in the Upper West Region. I see this change because now I'm married, I have two kids, and I have been able to put up my own house at Efutu, where I currently stay with my nuclear family. I also have everything in my room. I have television, DVD deck, furniture, and so on. My wife is also a food seller at Efutu Secondary School. (Male, 32 years, junior high school graduate).
>
> I have been able to take care of my children in school. One is in the University of Ghana, Legon (Level 300), one is at the Fosu Senior High School (Form 1), and four other children are in the Basic School. Also, I have built a 4-bedroom house; I live in one of the rooms with my wife, and the others have been rented out. I own a television set, a refrigerator, computer, and other material things, but I don't have a bicycle, motor, or a car. (Male, 48 years, no formal education)
>
> Migration has really done to me a lot of good. When I finish taking care of my siblings in school in my home town, my next agenda is to build a small house for myself and my nuclear family. (Male, 28 years, primary school graduate)
>
> Besides caring for my nuclear family, I also cater for children of my siblings in my home town. I pay their school fees and buy clothing for them. Because my siblings are unemployed, they don't have money to take care of their own children. (Male, 34 years, junior high school graduate)

Discussion and Conclusions

From the interview excerpts, inadequate job opportunities at the places of origin (the three northern regions) account for migration to the southern parts of the country, particularly to the Cape Coast metropolis. This is consistent with some earlier studies, which also concluded that north–south migration in Ghana is largely induced by inadequate job opportunities in the northern sector compared with the southern (Plange 1979; Addo 1980; Songsore & Denkabe 1995; Anarfi *et al.* 2003; Songsore 2003; Tsegai 2005; Lentz 2006; Kwankye *et al.* 2007; Abane 2008; Tanle 2010, 2014). It is important to note that both colonial and post-colonial government policies on socio-economic development in Ghana were concentrated in the southern sector of the country at the expense of the northern sector (Plange 1979; Songsore & Denkabe 1995; Anarfi *et al.* 2003; Songsore 2003; Tsegai 2005; Abdul-Korah 2006; Tanle 2010). This was due to the fact that the southern sector is more endowed than the northern sector with precious minerals, such as gold, diamond, bauxite, and manganese, and fertile soils favourable for cash crops such as cocoa and oil palm. Owing to this development gap, north–south migration is a common phenomenon in Ghana; as a result, although the north has 41% of the total land area of Ghana, the population of the three northern regions together has since 1970 been less than 20% of the country's total population (Ghana Statistical Service 2012).

The other economic factor which induced out-migration, as reported by some respondents in the study, is the inability to pay school fees. In Ghana, through the government's Free Compulsory Universal Basic Education policy, pupils in basic schools (primary and junior high schools) do not pay school fees. However, they are expected to pay certain approved fees/levies, such as parent–teacher association fees; information, communication and technology fees; and examination fees. Some pupils from poor homes, whose parents cannot afford these fees/levies, either stop schooling and migrate to search for jobs in the southern sector or engage in menial jobs during holidays to be able to pay their fees/levies—as indicated in one of the preceding excerpts (male, 39 years, junior high school graduate). Consequently, these graduates with low levels of formal education, including those who are illiterate, opt for migration to the southern parts of the country, where they engage in all kinds of menial jobs such as conservancy or sanitary work, like those in the University of Cape Coast.

Although most of the migrants were attracted by job opportunities in the University of Cape Coast in particular, the majority of them recounted that they gained employment as conservancy labourers in the university through various social networks, which usually contain a family relation, a friend, or a known person who hails from the northern sector and lives in the Cape Coast metropolis, and who preferably works in the University of Cape Coast (see some of the preceding interview excerpts under the push and pull factors of migration). In both internal and international migration, social networks have been recognized as an important social mechanism that facilitates the migration process through various means, such as funding the cost involved in migration, arranging jobs in advance, and providing accommodation, food, and general security for new arrivals (Synnove 1999; Ardayfio-Schandorf & Awumbila 2005; Tanle & Awusabo-Asare 2007; Tanle 2010).

The unfavourable physical characteristics of the three northern regions, such as inadequate rainfall and poor soil, were mentioned as some of the major causes of out-migration from the northern to the southern sector. As indicated above, the northern sector is characterized by low, erratic, and seasonal rainfall lasting barely five months, with the rest of the year being hot and dry, and therefore farming becomes impossible without irrigation. It is worthy of note that rainfall patterns continue to change, food security has become unstable, and as a result people in the three northern regions are making efforts in order to improve their survival. Successive governments have, over the years, paid lip service to the need to provide irrigation facilities to supplement the low rainfall. In the Upper West Region, for example, the proposed Kaabaa irrigation project has been on the drawing board for decades, while the Tono and Vea irrigation dam is beset with a myriad problems, such as siltation, low water levels due to high rates of evaporation, and infestation by waterborne diseases such as bilharzia. The soils, which are mainly savannah ochrosols, are generally infertile; moreover, erosion, frequent bushfires, and continuous cropping have made them even more impoverished. Due to these poor physical conditions, the only option for some people, especially the young and energetic ones, is to migrate to the southern sector of the country (Songsore 2003; Lentz 2006). Previously, out-migration from the northern sector was mainly seasonal, but within the last three decades some seasonal migrants have become permanent migrants in the southern parts of the country, a fact which can be attributed partly to the deteriorating physical conditions (Braimoh 2004; Geest 2010). Perhaps this is evidence of climate change in the northern region.

Migration is generally perceived as one option through which migrants can improve upon their socio-economic status (Geest 2010; Tanle 2010, 2014). The views of the migrants were unanimous on the fact that through migration their socio-economic status had improved, through acquiring household durable goods, living in decent rented accommodation, building their own houses (either in Cape Coast or in their home towns), providing quality education for their children, and catering for the education of their siblings and/or their siblings' children at home. Although this finding is based on their own subjective assessment, it is consistent with the findings of some previous qualitative studies: migrants' socio-economic status improves at their destination (Tanle & Awusabo-Asare 2007; Geest 2010; Tanle 2010; Yendaw *et al.* 2013; Tanle 2014). It is instructive to note that conservancy labourers earn the lowest salary among the junior staff of the university, yet they claim that their socio-economic status has improved. This is to be expected if one compares their status before and after migration (see excerpt above from the male, 32 years, junior high school graduate, under views about socio-economic status).

From the findings, some household or family members at the places of origin also benefit from improvement in the socio-economic status of migrants, through remittances and the funding of education of close relations and/or their children. This gesture, which supports children's education in deprived communities at the places of origin, can contribute to poverty reduction, since the three northern regions are the three poorest in the country (Ghana Statistical Service 2014).

In conclusion, the study revealed that the conservancy labourers who work in the various halls of residence in the University of Cape Coast are mostly migrants who hail from parts of the three northern regions of the country. Inadequate job opportunities and the possibility of being employed in the university constituted the push and pull factors at the origin and destination, respectively. Although these migrants fall within the lowest income bracket in the university, from their point of view their socio-economic status has improved, particularly when compared with their status before migrating.

Policy Recommendations

The study revealed that inadequate socio-economic opportunities and poor physical characteristics account for out-migration from the northern to the southern parts of Ghana. Although some households benefit from migration, the three northern regions have over the last three decades remained classified as the three poorest regions in the country. There is therefore the need for conscious efforts by government and other stakeholders to bridge the gap of unequal socio-economic development between the north and the south. In this regard, the SADA (Savannah Accelerated Development Authority) project, which is a development fund initiated by government to bridge the wide socio-economic gap between the northern and the southern parts of the country, is a step in the right direction and needs to be given all the necessary technical and political support.

With the increasing evidence of climate change in the country, the rainfall regime in the three northern regions could become even worse in terms of onset, amount, and duration. This means that irrigation farming will have to be promoted as an alternative to the rain-fed agriculture practised in the area since time immemorial. The other complex natural hazard, which develops slowly, is difficult to detect, and has many facets in any single region, is drought (Morid *et al.* 2006). The three northern regions, and even the entire country's economy, is strongly dependent on rain-fed agriculture; however, droughts pose a potential huge future risk. Droughts have already contributed to human migration, cultural separation, and loss of properties. Several people in northern Ghana have already suffered from the impact of drought; this is exacerbated by health problems such as guinea worm infestation, diarrhoea, and malaria. The economic loss from drought in 1983 in northern Ghana, where agriculture is the mainstay of about 80% of the population, is valued at several millions of dollars (Songsore 2003; Braimoh 2004; Yaro 2006; Tanle 2010).

Migrants could form associations through which they could provide some socio-economic support to schools, healthcare centres, and agricultural inputs to supplement government efforts in the three northern regions. Child fostering should be encouraged among out-migrants resident in the southern parts of the country. Building the human capital of such fostered children, through formal education and/or skills training, could enable them to contribute to the socio-economic development of the northern parts of the country.

References

Abane, A.M. (2008), Poverty and Inequality in Ghana: Focus on the Northern Regions, in: B. Kendie & P. Martens (eds) *Governance and Sustainable Development.* Cape Coast: Marcel Hughes Publicity Group, pp. 160–178.

Abdul-Korah, G.B. (2006), Where is Not Home? Dagaaba Migrants in the Brong-Ahafo Region: 1980 to Present. *African Affairs* 106(422): 71–94.

Addo, N.O. (1980), *Internal Migration, Metropolitan Growth and Socio-Economic Change in Ghana.* ISSER, Legon: University of Ghana.

Anarfi, J., S. Kwankye, O Ababio & R Tiemoko (2003), *Migration from and to Ghana: A Background Paper.* Development Research Centre on Migration, Globalization and Poverty, Working paper C4, 1–38. Available at: http:// www.migrationdrc.org. Accessed February 2009.

Arango, J. (2000), *Explaining Migration: A Critical View.* Blackwell Publishers, Oxford, UK. www.iemed.org/mhicongress/curriculums. Accessed *August 2006.*

Ardayfio-Schandorf, E. & M Awumbila (2005), Migration, Vulnerability and Poverty of Female Porters in Accra, Ghana, in: Awusabo-Asare *et al.* (eds) *The Changing Faces of Poverty in Ghana: Proceedings of the 'NUFU' Workshop.* Cape Coast: University of Cape Coast, pp. 23–33.

Braimoh, A.K. (2004), Seasonal Migration and Land Use Change in Ghana. *Land Degradation and Development* 15: 37–47. http://onlinelibrary.wiley.com/doi/10.1002/ldr.588/full.

Conway, D. & J.H. Cohen (1998), Consequences of Migration and Remittances for Mexican Transnational Communities. *Economic Geography* 74(1): 26–44.

Geest, V.D.K. (2005), Local Perceptions of Migration and Livelihood in Northwest Ghana: The Home Community Perspective. From www.iss.ni/ceres/vdgeest.pdf. Accessed October 2006.

Geest, V.D.K. (2010), Local Perceptions of Migration from North-West Ghana. *Africa* 80(4): 595–619.

Ghana Statistical Service (2012), *2010 Population and Housing Census.* Accra: Ghana Statistical Service.

Ghana Statistical Service (2014), *Ghana Living Standard Survey, Round 6 (GLSS 6). Poverty Profile in Ghana (2005–2013).* Accra: Ghana Statistical Service.

Haas, H. de (2008), *Migration and Development: A Theoretical Perspective.* International Migration Institute, Working paper 9, 1–57. Available at: http:// www.imi.ox.ac.uk/news_store/workin-paper-9-published-migration-and-development-theory. Accessed April 2009.

International Organization for Migration (2003), *World Migration 2003: Managing Migration: Challenges and Responses for People on the Move.* Geneva: International Organization for Migration.

Kwankye, S.O., J.K. Anarfi, A.C Tagoe & A Castaldo (2007), *Coping Strategies of Independent Child Migrants from Northern Ghana to Southern Cities.* Development Research Centre on Migration, Globalization and Poverty, Working Paper T-23. From http:// www.migrationdrc.org. Accessed August 2009.

Laux, P. (2009), Statistical Modeling of Precipitation for Agricultural Planning in the Volta Basin of West Africa. IMK-IFU, Germany.

Lee, E.S. (1966), A Theory of Migration. *Demography* 3: 47–57.

Lentz, C. (2006), *Ethnicity and Making of History in Northern Ghana.* Edinburgh: Edinburgh University Press.

Morid, S., V. Smakhtin & M. Moghaddasi (2006), Comparison of Seven Meteorological Indices for Drought Monitoring in Iran. *International Journal of Climatology* 26(7): 971–985.

Myrdal, G. (1957), *Rich Lands and Poor.* New York: Harper and Row.

Nyarko, B.K. (2007), Floodplain Wetland Riverflow Synergy in the White Volta River Basin, Ghana. *Ecology And Development Series,* No. 53. Bonn, Germany.

Plange, N.K. (1979), Underdevelopment in Northern Ghana: Natural Causes or Colonial Capitalism? *Review of African Political Economy* 6(15–16): 4–14.

Songsore, J. (2003), *Regional Development in Ghana: The Theory and the Reality*. Accra: Woeli Publishing Services.

Songsore, J. & A. Denkabe (1995), *Challenging Rural Poverty in Northern Ghana: The Case of the Upper-West Region*. Trondheim: Reprosentralen.

Stock, R. (2004), *Africa South of the Sahara: A Geographical Integration* (2nd ed.). New York: The Gilford Press.

Synnove, B.S. (1999), Migration and Human Development: A Case Study of Female Migration to Accra, Ghana. *Bulletin of Geographical Association* 21: 157–164.

Tanle, A. (2010), Livelihood Status of Migrants from the Northern Savannah Zone Resident in the Obuasi and Techiman Muncipalities. PhD thesis submitted to the Department of Population and Health, University of Cape Coast, Cape Coast.

Tanle, A. (2014), Assessing Livelihood Status of Migrants from Northern Ghana Resident in the Obuasi Municipality. *GeoJournal* 79(5): 577–590.

Tanle, A. & K. Awusabo-Asare (2007), The *Kaya Yei* Phenomenon in Ghana: Female Migration from the Upper West Region to Kumasi and Accra. *The Oguaa Journal of Social Science* 4(2): 139–164.

Tsegai, D. (2005), The Economics of Migration in the Volta Basin of Ghana: Household and District-Level Analysis. Published PhD Thesis, Cuvillier Verlag Gottingen, Germany: University of Bonn.

Yaro, J.A. (2006), Is Deagrarainisation Real? A Study of Livelihood Activities in Rural Northern Ghana. *Journal of Modern Africa Studies* 44(1): 125–156.

Yendaw, E., A Tanle & A Kumi-Kyereme (2013), Socio-Economic Status of International Return Migrants to the Berekum Municipality, Ghana. *International Journal of Business and Social Science* 4(10): 272–284. www.ijbssnet.com/update/index.php/archive.html.

CHAPTER 11

Coercion or Volition: Making Sense of the Experiences of Female Victims of Trafficking from Nigeria in the Netherlands

Taiwo Olabisi Oluwatoyin and Akinyinka Akinyoade

Introduction

This study examines the claim that Nigerian girls working in the unregulated parts of the Dutch sex market are trafficked victims for commercial sexual exploitation. In the last decade, various discourses (Aghatise 2004; Monzini 2005) have arisen on how women of Nigerian origin are coerced by a madam and her syndicates. The girls are supposedly taken to a shrine to swear an oath of allegiance to comply with all instructions, many of which include, but are not limited to, engaging in forced sex work and other hideous crimes. However, this study aims to systematically produce new and emerging evidence that goes against this notion of coercion leading to or being part of trafficking in the women's journey into sex work in Europe. Close examination reveals that many 'trafficked victims' are sex workers seeking better professional pathways in Europe and, in fact, approach smugglers to assist in transporting them to countries of destination for better opportunities.

Context

Global integration has made an outstanding contribution to development, as many previously inaccessible corners of the Earth are being opened to transnational immigrants with new ideas and capital for investment. But global integration has also caused a 'social exclusion' and 'marginalization' of the impoverished as well as other disadvantageous groups of persons (Elson & Cagatay 2000: 1347). One vulnerable group that has been particularly hard hit are women: the effect of transnational migration has resulted in a large number of them entering the sex market owing to its limited requirement for formal skills or expertise and the huge amounts of money to be earned in a short space of time (Gülçür & İlkkaracan 2002: 411). The migration experiences of women are outcomes of a changeover to 'service economies' by countries of the global North. This has been coupled with the 'structural adjustment policies' of global financial institutions, which have resulted in both drastic cuts in formal institutions (where formerly women earned a living) and in little or no ability to obtain social services (Elson & Cagatay 2000: 1354, 1355; Agustín 2005: 99).

A structural divide exists between women who are tricked into the sex market and those who choose the career path of being sex workers. In this regard, forced sex work is an abuse of free will and is differentiated from free-will sex work, the latter being defined by Doezema (1998) as a labour practice based on women's independent use of their own bodies as a main source of income. The effect of the various discourses has been a major focus on the negative experiences of trafficked women while simultaneously ignoring the necessity for sex workers to seek better socio-economic status outside the shores of their home countries (*ibid.*). The independent decision by many women to migrate is the result of a desire to improve socio-economic status, of a shift in gender responsibilities, and of a high demand for female workers in the infor-mal sectors in many economies of the global North (Phizacklea 1998). In spite of various school of thoughts on forced and voluntary sex work, it is obvious that the marginalization of global South migrant sex workers in Europe estab-lishes a livelihood for these workers that involves increased health dangers, 'violence' and abuse from law enforcement agents, pimps, and customers, and the stigma of being illegitimate migrants (Anthias 2013).

Concerning the status of victims of human trafficking, studies such as those of Aghatise (2004: 1129) and Kelly and Regan (2000: 5) took the position that many trafficked women are in fact naïve about the type of occupation they will be engaged in in a foreign country and, out of desperation to leave their coun-try of origin, they are compelled to swear an oath of allegiance which often involves 'magic juju' sacrifices and the use of private body parts. They empha-sized that these poorly educated and vulnerable women are often not properly enlightened on the terms of 'indebtedness', 'exploitation', and 'control'. The women imagine they can earn huge amounts of money doing any kind of job in a wealthy country and that this will lift themselves and their families out of the trap of impoverishment. Similarly, Plambech (2014: 384) describes traf-ficked women as susceptible persons lured from the security of their homes as a result of impoverishment into 'sexual exploitation' and differentiates them from emigrants who seek better socio-economic status, even though the traf-ficked women can also be described as 'economic migrants' (*ibid.* 385). On the other hand, Agustín (2005: 97) is of the view that many women, in a bid to improve their statuses, decide to travel out of their countries and, on arrival at their destinations, engage in informal occupations to hide and survive as a result of their illegal status. She argues that the debates on trafficking in persons (TIP) in the last decade by supra-national organizations and NGOs in Europe is a component of global debates centring on international crime, national legislation, and citizen safety enshrined in the concept of 'Fortress Europe', dedicated to guarding its territories from unwanted elements (*ibid.* 101). Invariably, TIP and sex work are now components of the combat against international crime, as reflected in the fact that the Year 2000 Palermo Protocol is an appendix to the UN convention against global crimes (O'Connell Davidson 2005). In addition, Agustín (2005: 101) proposes that trafficked women are not deceived, as they are just like any other migrants seeking better economic fortune; their complaints of being tricked are a plea for improvement in their work environments and for better wages (Oude Breuil *et al.* 2011: 40)—a viewpoint that will be explored in this study.

Experiential studies such as those of Brunovskis and Surtees (2008) and Davis (2008) serve as a theoretical backdrop to developing fieldwork for this study, which was conducted between July and August 2014 in the Netherlands. We argue that many trafficked women do not consider themselves as gullible and helpless but as persons seeking good fortune in a foreign land (see Altink 1995). In their bid to access social services, migrant sex workers would prefer to tell what Plambech (2014: 387) describes as the 'trafficking narrative'; this narrative changes the status of these women from commercial emigrants into 'victims of trafficking'. We maintain the perspective that the conceptualization of victims of trafficking as blameless innocents ignores the reasons for their emigration for greener pastures; it also highlights the global focus on the 'sex trafficking of women' as an indication of global gender disparities.

Global governance of control and management of TIP is guided by several conventions and protocols. The first was the 1949 UN 'Convention for the Suppression of the Traffic in Persons and the Exploitation of the Prostitution of Others'. Adopted through a General Assembly resolution (317 (IV) annex), it was the first global document to treat human trafficking in gender-unbiased terms, while also meting out punishment for purchasing sex irrespective of consent in both national and international trafficking (Outshoorn 2005: 142). The convention was enacted as a result of the collaborative determination of the neo-abolitionists, a coalition of feminist evangelical Christians, and took the standpoint that prostitution constituted violence against women and should be eliminated from society (Chuang 2010: 1664). Following this was the 'Year 2000 Protocol to Prevent, Suppress and Punish Trafficking in Persons Especially Women and Children, Supplementing the United Nations Convention against Transnational Organized Crime'. Widely referred to as 'the Palermo', it was the first transnational instrument to comprehensively address trafficking in persons after the 1949 UN convention. This global protocol arose from global pressure to address, as an urgent need, the crime of human trafficking in all its forms (Doezema 2010: 27). The purpose of the protocol was to reduce to the barest minimum TIP for commercial sexual exploitation, with a strong emphasis on women and children and on caring for and assisting victims of human trafficking, as well as aiming to foster cooperation and collaboration among state parties (Defeis 2003: 487). Its enactment facilitated the evolution of a global description and explanation of TIP (Hyland 2001: 38; Akinyoade & Carchedi 2012). The third document was the 2005 Council of Europe (COE) 'Convention against Trafficking in Persons'. The COE convention against TIP, enacted on 16 May 2005 and made operational in 2008, aims at preventing TIP, protecting the fundamental human rights of victims, prosecuting traffickers, promoting the harmonization of federal action and global cooperation, and creating sustainable partnerships with relevant actors to raise global awareness on TIP, thereby reducing it to the barest minimum (Council of Europe 2014). The COE convention is a bold attempt by member states to confront TIP in the twenty-first century, and its ratification offered a new aspect to tackling this global scourge, in addition to complementing existing TIP and human rights protocols ratified by the UN and other transnational organizations (Sembacher 2005: 438).

In Nigeria, there exists the Nigerian 'Anti-Trafficking Policy'. This comes against the backdrop of Nigeria's Parliament passing the 'Trafficking in Persons (Prohibition) Law Enforcement and Administration Act' and setting up the National Agency for the Prohibition of Traffic in Persons (NAPTIP). The Act empowered NAPTIP to synchronize all anti-trafficking laws in Nigeria, enhance mechanisms to boost the effectiveness of eradication of TIP, endorse a witness assistance policy, rehabilitate and appropriately reintegrate rescued Nigerian victims of all forms of trafficking, and strengthen partnerships between important law enforcement agencies in the battle against TIP (Olateru-Olagbegi & Ikpeme 2006: 23; NAPTIP 2014). Nigeria is a hub for TIP activities, continuing to be an origin, transit, and destination country for women and children subjected to forced labour and sex trafficking (Akinyoade & Carchedi 2012). It is an origin country for trafficked women. Foreign nationals from Benin Republic and Republic of Togo are also trafficked into Nigeria or are brought into Nigeria to be transferred to other countries. Nigerian women trafficked overseas are sent to Europe (Netherlands, Germany, Italy, Switzerland, Belgium), West Africa (Mali, Côte d'Ivoire), Central Africa (Gabon, Cameroon), North Africa (Morocco, Algeria), and the Middle East (Saudi Arabia) (see Aronowitz *et al.* 2006: 11, 12). The women are recruited from rural villages, where the level of impoverishment is high and there is a dearth of basic infrastructural amenities.

In Section 11 of the NAPTIP Act a punishment of life imprisonment is prescribed for anyone who brings into the country or sends abroad any person under 18 years of age for the purpose that such person will be compelled or inveigled into prostitution (NAPTIP 2003: 11–12). Furthermore, Section 35(a) of the document directs that any person found guilty of any crime outlined therein must surrender to a Victims of Trafficking Trust Fund all properties which are the subject of a provisional order of the court (*ibid.* 23). Similar to the COE convention against TIP, the NAPTIP Act in Section 50(a) directs that no victim should be treated unjustly as a result of colour, ethnicity, or social origin (*ibid.* 30).

The 2014 annual United States Trafficking in Persons Report (US TIPR) published by the Department of State ranked Nigeria Tier 2 on account of the inability of the federal government to pass into law a draft legal code that would restrain the capability of judges to offer monetary penalties in lieu of prison sentences, as well as the non-execution of a formal process to rehabilitate and reintegrate repatriated survivors of commercial sexual exploitation. A number of rescued trafficked victims in the Netherlands and other European states have been denied residence permits or have had their asylum applications denied on the basis of information from the Nigerian government's NAPTIP that there are adequate mechanisms in place for their rehabilitation (US TIPR 2014: 297–298). The implication is that the women are left idle, thus creating the opportunity to be re-trafficked and exploited and thereby losing hope in the capability of their country to cater for them.

One main criticism of the NAPTIP Act is that it focuses predominantly on the prosecution of traffickers rather than on the preclusion of trafficking and protection of trafficked persons. This frustrates attempts to take legal action against traffickers, on account of lack of cooperation from victims due to fear of revenge attacks. However, the Nigerian government has taken a commendable stride forward, aimed at bolstering the statutory and institutional framework to address TIP in Nigeria (Olateru-Olagbegi & Ikpeme 2006: 24).

Discourses Surrounding Sex Work and Sex Trafficking

The transcontinental characteristics of sex work are a universal, present-day occurrence necessitated as a result of 'global economic restructuring' (Boidi *et al.* 2009: 9). The sex industry is one the most lucrative and thriving industries of the world economy, comprising building companies, media outlets, telephone companies, and the amatory industry (*ibid.* 10). As the sex market in the global North boomed, a huge demand for migrant women from the global South was needed to fill the gap, giving rise in the 1980s to discourses by feminists and supra-national institutions such as the UN and EU on the relationship between sex work and TIP in (Outshoorn 2005: 141).

Sex trafficking is defined as the 'prostitution' of individuals, and victims of TIP are characterized as unlawful migrants, sex workers, or displaced vagrants (Bernat & Zhilina 2013: 1). Anti-sex-work activists, in buttressing their stance on the offensiveness of sex work, have constantly emphasized the dissimilarities between forced trafficking, trafficking, and human migration by insisting that injustice, intimidation, and exploitation are the features of all acts of TIP and sex work (Weitzer 2007: 452). However, the majority of TIP victims are cajoled by the huge sums of money that will supposedly be made and by a desire to create an independent, ostentatious lifestyle, as well as by a dissatisfaction with their current socio-economic status (*ibid.* 453). Despite existing information that many of the victims are deceived, a significant proportion traded in sex in their countries of origin and were adequately informed of the type of occupation they would be engaged in (*ibid.* 454). The causes of TIP are interrelated with the susceptibilities of persons to it (Bernat & Zhilina 2013: 7). These susceptibilities are the outcomes of the lack of legal rights to nationality and rights of abode, compelling vulnerable women to engage in clandestine activities and thus increasing their vulnerability to trafficking (*ibid.* 8).

Three major antithetical feminist views exist on sex work. First are the 'free thinking' feminists under the identity of the Global Alliance against Trafficking in Women (GAATW), who view female sex workers as professionals who choose sex work of their own free will (Chapkins 1997, as cited in Matthews 2008: 29). Second are the 'extremist' feminists in the Coalition against Trafficking in Women (CATW), who are of the view that labelling 'prostitution as sex work' erroneously gives a cleaner image to the sex industry and the male clients who purchase sexual services. The extremist feminist perception of a free choice to engage in sex work is inaccurate, as women are forced into sex work as a consequence of impoverishment, gender inequity, and prejudice. The extremists argue that women are being used by men who regulate and manage the sex industry, while the women also bolster male-controlled establishments which influence women and gender relationships (Raymond 2004: 1157; Sanders *et al.* 2009: 4). These women canvas for the criminalization of sex work for the following reasons: (i) sex working poses a threat to an individual's well-being in addition to exposing the sex worker to assault while waiting on or attending to a client; (ii) the sex worker has no agency, as her activities are determined and influenced by other persons; (iii) the act of sex work is an intrusion into the private arena of the female body; (iv) in the quest to earn money, the sex worker turns her body into a commodity to be bargained for in the capitalist market, thus validating their position that women are pushed into sex work as a result of impoverishment (Nussbaum

1999: 289–291). Nevertheless, both viewpoints are one-dimensional and take into account neither the capitalist economic system nor the inequity affecting gender relations between men, women, and the multiplicity of persons in the sex industry (Sanders *et al.* 2009: 5).

Also worthy of mention are the sex workers under the umbrella body Network of Sex-Work Projects (NSWP), who advocate for their rights in the sex industry and oppose the view that migrant sex workers are victims of trafficking, while also disagreeing on the comparison between voluntary and forced sex work (Saunders 2005: 348). In addition, Giddens (1979) argues that the feminist discourses on sex work reflect an undetermined 'agency/structure' discourse which torments the 'social sciences'. The disconnect between these standpoints reflects how the concepts of trafficking, migration, and sex work are viewed by various groups. In criminal law and jurisprudence, TIP, by reason of its definition as the movement of women across local and international boundaries for sexual exploitation, has basically been linked to sex work (Outshoorn 2005: 146).

TIP was subsequently viewed as being a casual factor responsible for sex work, thus creating a mechanism whereby the most reasonable approach to eradicating TIP for commercial sexual abuse of women was the abolishment of sex work; as the decriminalization and legalization of sex work was viewed as creating more demand for sex workers, thus leading to the TIP of more women to fill the demand (*ibid.*). Proponents of sex work as a professional choice maintain that as a consequence of vulnerabilities, women can be victims of TIP but not all women crossing a boundary to enter another nation state illegally are victims of involuntary sex work. They maintain that the inequality in wealth distribution compels many women to migrate and choose the option of being sex workers to better their socio-economic status (*ibid.* 147).

The decision of women to enter into any form of work in present-day society is hindered by forces operating at the global and economic level. At the economic level, within the capitalist market system, workers are free to engage in any form of labour activity, at a price, in the fragmented labour market, where access to different levels of employment is dependent on education and skills. Access is also differentiated along the lines of social category, age, gender, and location. The majority of women in sex work have low educational levels and poor skills, and their choice in the market is therefore generally restricted and dependent on poorly paid, temporary, and menial jobs (Sanders *et al.* 2009: 10). The decision to sell sexual services is systematized by an ideology which indicates that men have the right to demand sexual services in the market space (*ibid.*).

Methodology

In selecting the appropriate methodology for our research, we agree with Zhang (2009:162), who postulated that a researcher researching on migrant sex workers and the vulnerabilities they are exposed to in the hidden sex market needs to spend a significant amount of time with these persons, in order to elicit appropriate information that will be beneficial for the research. In view of this, during the field work (July–August 2014) participant observation and semi-structured interviews were employed for primary data collection. Observations were made of sex workers in red-light districts, and of sex work advertised on TV screens daily between the hours of 12 a.m. and 4 a.m. on some Dutch television stations. Key informant interviews were held with social workers, a senior Dutch police officer, an Immigration and Naturalization Service Netherlands (IND) official, lawyers, and the pastor of a Pentecostal church. A total of 14 respondents participated in the research. We also engaged with relevant secondary data from journals, books, and publications of government agencies.

This research was conducted with the assistance of two NGOs based in The Hague that assist migrant sex workers, refugees, and victims of TIP with stipends and basic needs in addition to attempts to legalize their residence in the Netherlands. The choice of working with these organizations was due to the fact that they facilitated access to the women and some related NGOs.

Sampling Method

Respondents that participated in the interviews were selected from the population from which the most could be learned and understood from the perspectives of our respondents (Merriam 2002: 3). Hence, the lawyers and social workers were deliberately sampled with the assistance of the project officer of VluchtelingenWerk Zuidvleugel.[1] The police officer and pastor willingly shared their experiences with many of the women they had encountered in the course of their work. The Nigerian migrant sex workers who were interviewed were those who willingly agreed to participate in the research on the basis that their identity would be concealed. An IND official was selected to participate in the research based on his relevance to and knowledge of the subject matter of the research.

---

1 A volunteer organization in The Hague that provides help for refugees and asylum seekers.

Observational Strategy

In order to create a good relationship with our respondent sex workers, one which would enable them to respond warmly to interview questions, Oluwatoyin partook with the women in activities organized by project officers of facilitating NGOs, ranging from house cleaning to sharing of toiletries, cooking, picnicking, summer parties, dancing, and discussions on women's health. This strategy was devised as a result of the sensitivity of the research, as many of the respondents would not openly discuss the unfavourable circumstances they had been exposed to. Partaking in joint activities permitted development of rapport and close observation. It created a level of trust, as the women opened up about their conditions of living, as well as their experiences in the Netherlands and the shame of not being able to return to Nigeria. Some direct observations were made at the premises of VluchtelingenWerk Zuidvleugel from around 10 a.m. to 2 p.m., when the women came to collect basic necessities donated by the church, the Good Samaritans, and other charity organizations.

In-depth Interviews

Vital informant interviews were held with two lawyers, one police officer, one IND official, and five social workers. These interviews often lasted from 50 to 90 minutes, depending on the social dimensions that came up in the course of the discussions. As only the police officer consented to be recorded, the other interviews were transcribed during the discussions. All the interviews were conducted in the offices of the officials, while the interviews and discussions with four of the sex workers were in discussion rooms of the VluchtelingenWerk Zuidvleugel, and the interview with the fifth sex worker was held in an African hair salon, where she learns to weave hair at Holland Spoor in The Hague.

Narratives

Discussing basic issues determined the starting point of the sex workers' narratives, which included their motivations for coming to the Netherlands, their methods of arrival, and their experiences with the IND, law enforcement, and social services of Dutch society. This approach provided a platform for the women to discuss freely their experiences as sex workers in Dutch society, as Kvale and Brinkmann (2009: 2) earlier observed.

Method of Analysis

In selecting the appropriate method of analysis for this study, we concur with Krippendorff (1980) on content analysis being a research technique which is a methodical as well as an unbiased means of interpreting and measuring events and happenings—as the use of this method enabled us to consistently analyse spoken and unspoken communication messages of respondents (*ibid.* 107). In using this method, we were able to analyse and understand our respondents' verbal and non-verbal responses to interview questions. It is worth mentioning that in using content analysis, the aim was to provide a recognition of recurring concepts and themes, with a view to understanding the differentials in perception that Nigerians girls in the Dutch sex industry were or were not coerced into engaging in sex work.

Challenges and Research Limitation

A number of the Dutch NGOs we consulted to facilitate our access to the women declined to participate in the research. In addition, many of the sex workers in the facilitating NGOs vehemently refused to participate in the research, as they expressed their grievances towards the Nigerian government, which they felt was responsible for the refusal of the Dutch authorities to grant them permanent residence permits. The sex workers claimed that a report from the Nigerian government to the Dutch government contained information that Nigeria's NAPTIP has the competence and capability to rehabilitate and reintegrate deported women into Nigerian society without any problems. Thus, the researcher being a Nigerian, the sex workers felt it was an indirect attempt by Nigerian and Dutch authorities to obtain information that could be used to justify their being sent back to Nigeria.

Researchers were also in a disadvantaged position during the observational studies because some of the women did not fully trust the female researcher: they felt inferior socio-economically and thus assumed a posture that the researchers would never understand their reasons for being sex workers. Furthermore, many of the women refused to respond to some interview questions. Many times they seemed lost in thought when they recalled only traumatic experiences and momentarily reflected on what life might have been like had they not embarked on the journey to Europe. All the women refused to be audio-taped, but the promise made to protect their identities relaxed them somewhat for interviews. In addition, the Dutch brothels and Turkish brothels contacted to assist with the research refused outright to cooperate in some cases, as they claimed the researcher could not be trusted.

Finally, as many of the women are now in a foreign country and in the delicate stages of their journey, they were not ready to provide information about their real circumstances: whether they were trafficked, their traffickers' identities and locations, and how they were able to travel abroad with fake travel documents without being apprehended by law enforcement agencies. In view of this, there exists considerable scepticism about the actual identities of these women, and caution is urged in the understanding of their responses.

Background Description of Location of Respondents

The respondents were all based and interviewed in The Hague. Interviews with the sex workers were held in various locations such as a church building, the Holland Spoor train station, and the office spaces of facilitating NGOs. Interviews with the police officer were held at the common room of the International Institute of Social Studies of Erasmus University, The Hague. The interview with the pastor was held in his office at Parkstraat, The Hague, while interviews with social workers were held in their offices.

The IND, VVF, and their Core Activities

The Immigratie en Naturalisatiedienst IND (Immigration & Naturalization Service of the Ministry of Security and Justice of the Netherlands) is the organization that handles the admission of foreigners to the country. This government agency processes all applications for asylum, family reunification, and visas and other residence permits. IND also implements the aliens policy, the Aliens Act, and the Netherlands Nationality Act on behalf of the Dutch State Secretary for Justice.

VVF offer refugees support during their asylum procedure and their integration into Dutch society, as well as providing members of Parliament with information concerning refugee issues, policies, and rights. VVF also supplies information and advice to asylum lawyers, in addition to developing projects to promote the integration of refugees in the Netherlands.

Kariboe Bibi is a centre where Sub-Saharan African women support and inspire each other. It is an organization which is open to all African women in the Netherlands and aims to provide an environment that empowers abused women, who include but are not limited to victims of human trafficking.

Social Construction of the Illegal Migrant

The social construction of particular groups of persons recognizes their social processes as an embodiment of their daily lives (Burr 1995). Being labelled as an illegal migrant by Dutch society means that the women are locked into a cyclic, stereotypical 'logic', as all subsequent interpretations of their actions are in terms of the status to which they have been assigned (Jary & Jary 1995).

The status of the women was a major concern to the NGOs, as many could not be given stipends and were already faced with threats of deportation by the IND. None of the respondents came through the desert or via the Mediterranean Sea, as all claimed to have arrived in Europe by air but with falsified travel documents arranged for them by either a sibling or an acquaintance. All respondents expressed the desire to have travelled with legal documents, as despite being Nigerians they have no proof of their nationality in a foreign land, making them feel stateless.

> I came through Belgium from Lagos with aeroplane and when I arrived Belgium I came by train to the Netherlands with an old friend who assisted me with the travel documents free. Suffering was too much at home, and she said I could make money from sex work. I was not happy about the job, but I was happy coming to Europe.
>
> Interview with sex worker during field work, July–August 2014

> After I arrived here, I thought I would start making money from ashawo work sharp, sharp, but it did not happen that way. I managed to get work in a brothel, but customer will pay manager my fees; when it's time for 'action', he will not use 'balloon'. At least I have to be protected. The last time I insisted, the customer slapped me and reported me to the manager. That was the last day I worked in the brothel. What was my offence? I wanted the use of balloon to protect myself. I later got to know that unprotected sex is more expensive and in order to make profit, brothel manager promotes it. I am more surprised that this experience that cannot happen to me in Nigeria is happening to me in a foreign land. But if I am Dutch, can the man slap me and I will not call police. Is it not because I have no 'paper'.
>
> Interview with sex worker during field work, July–August 2014

The emergence of pluralization and fragmentation of migration is creating a new migration characterized by new geographical patterns of migration, with new kinds of emigrants with illegal statuses who are dependent on means of existence other than formal paid employment or social benefits (Snel *et al.* 2000, cited in Engbersen & Van der Leun 2001: 52). Illegal migrants are considered a social problem in Dutch society (Engbersen & Van der Leun 2001: 54) and regarded as 'undesired illegal migrants' (*ibid.* 55). Simultaneously, they are viewed as villains, social benefits seekers, and criminals (Johnson 2004, cited in Warner 2005: 56). The illegal status of the women makes them susceptible to abuse and exploitation, as in the bordellos where many of them secretly work they have incurred debts on subsistence living and cannot leave until these debts are cleared. And even if they could leave, the possibility of being able to secure another job is slight since they do not have valid residence permits.

One of the interviewed sex workers contended:

> If I had a working permit, I would be able to go uitzenbureau or one of the cleaning services company, and I am sure they would be able to assist me with a job. At least with a good job, then I can pay off my debts. But with no residence permit, I have no choice but to remain hidden and keep paying my accumulating debts.
>
> Interview with sex worker during field work, July–August 2014

Favet and Falch (2010) concur and argue that as a result of the illegal status of migrant sex workers, which places them in a low or no bargaining position, they are more susceptible to assault, intimidation, and injustice.

> Many of these sex workers experience many problems with persons and authorities. Oftentimes a few of them having no one to turn to run to the church for help, such as the payment of fines, financial and psychological assistance.
>
> Interview with pastor of Reconciliation and Restoration Church, The Hague, July–August 2014

However, one social worker argued:

> The problem with many Third World nationals is that they think Europe is a problem-free paradise. I beg to disagree with them. We have an army of problems in Europe, but we have only learned to hide and beautify our problems. Many of the women come here with extremely high expectations of making money, but they are often at a disadvantage because they are not registered and thus have no access to social protection. The stipends we try very hard to assist them with are from the church, and

that does not come regularly. Being a refugee or an illegal migrant in the Netherlands is hard.

Interview with a social worker during field work, July–August 2014

According to a Dutch Senior Police Officer, investigating officers battle with a dilemma in the course of their duties:

Operation Koolvis[2] further revealed that either the women were telling lies or they were giving contradictory and false information about their traffickers. The sad thing is if after the reflection [the moment where investigators indicate to the women that the women are not being truthful] they do not cooperate with law enforcement, they are deported— which is an injustice, considering the myriad problems already encountered by them in the Netherlands. I think it's a huge problem, and more needs to be done by the government of Nigeria.

Interview with a police officer during field work, July–August 2014

Pattern of Exclusion and Intersectionality: Process and Problems

Workplace Conditions

The work environment of migrant sex workers reveals how gender, class, and nationality intersect, thereby marginalizing women in the sex market.

A number of respondents revealed that they had borrowed money to travel to Europe and they are under intense pressure to return loaned money, while at the same time their families left behind in Nigeria expect remittances. Furthermore, they revealed how they wish to work legally even if it means working legally as a window prostitute; but since they are prevented from doing so, as a result of Dutch state policy on sex work,[3] they are left without the

---

2　In 2007 the Netherlands police and prosecution services conducted an extensive investigation of human trafficking from Nigeria to the Netherlands and other European destinations. This investigation, code named 'Operation Koolvis', was conducted in close cooperation with other European destination countries and with the National Agency for the Prohibition of Traffic in Persons and Other Related Matters (NAPTIP) of Nigeria. The investigation led to simultaneous arrests in October 2007 of traffickers in the Netherlands, other European countries (Belgium, United Kingdom, France, Spain, Germany, and Italy), the US, and Nigeria itself. See: https://ec.europa.eu/anti-trafficking/member-states/netherlands-4-eu-and-international-cooperation_en.

3　The Dutch policy on sex work includes a requirement that sex workers must be legally resident in the Netherlands and must fulfil tax and periodic health check requirements.

capability of choosing which clients to attend to or which clients to refuse. They also cannot report any abuse because of their illegal status.

> I cannot believe I have to cheapen myself. I cannot make a choice, as I have to service every customer that shows interest in me, no matter how old or young, because I need the euro. You cannot imagine where I work from: no good mattress, as one time I was servicing a customer and the bed broke. Many times the illegal bordello I work from does not have electricity, as a result of non-payment of electricity bills to ENECO.[4] The house is often dark, so I have to use other instruments to light up my space.
>
> Interview with a sex worker during field work, July–August 2014

A few of the respondents expressed frustration and extreme bitterness that in spite of more than five years working as a sex worker, they had not been able to remit considerable amounts of money to Nigeria, thus wasting their efforts and energy in the Netherlands. They confided that they were better off as a result of giving the false information that they were trafficked to the Netherlands, and with their false identities they had access to food stamps and a subsistence allowance. However, investigations carried out by Dutch NGOs and law enforcement agencies, as well as the strict anti-trafficking policies in place, revealed their real status and leaves the Dutch authorities no option but to deport them back to Nigeria.

Some reasons were tendered to justify the deportations. According to one of the social workers working in VluchtelingenWerk Zuidvleugel:

> The present European Union policy makers do not support migration, as a result of the pressure immigrants put on the social system, and thus are seeking for ways to 'evict' persons out of the EU at all costs. It is a pity that these women have to be deported with nothing from the Dutch government or the IOM [International Organization for Migration] as they are not victims of TIP.
>
> Interview with a social worker during field work, July–August 2014

And it appears that the fear of returning home to Nigeria, either by voluntary or involuntary means, is not about the fear of incurring the wrath of the traffickers it is assumed the girls are indebted to; it is more about societal scorn. As aptly expressed by one of the sex workers interviewed:

---

4 ENECO is the Dutch electricity supply company.

> I have worked for a while with nothing to show for it in Europe. Well, I am
> sad because when I get home and people come to knock on my door to
> ask what I brought back, I have nothing to give them.
>
> Interview with a sex worker during field work, July–August 2014

Another sex worker was confident:

> I know I am going to be deported but I will find my way back to Netherlands
> or any European country. There is no future for me in Nigeria; how will I
> cope without a job or money? In the Netherlands with one euro or 50
> cents at least I can buy bread in Albert Heijn; what will one naira or 50
> kobo buy me in Nigeria? Nothing.
>
> Interview with a sex worker during field work, July–August 2014

Apart from the societal ridicule is the formal coping mechanism and the
absence of an organized mechanism to absorb and reintegrate them back into
society on return to Nigeria.

> The Nigerian government have not been able to find the girls kidnapped
> by terrorists in the month of April nor put an end to incessant bombings,
> coupled with no light and facilities. I want to remain in the Netherlands.
> I am pleading with VVF lawyers to please assist me if I can be allowed to
> stay back on humanitarian grounds because of these children that I gave
> birth to in Netherlands, and they are 'Dutch'. How will they cope in Nigeria?
> At least me and my husband, we have been managing in Netherlands with
> the little allowance and earned money. How will I survive in Nigeria?
>
> Interview with a sex worker during field work, July–August 2014

Some of the women explore and/or use different methods to lengthen or
secure their stay in the Netherlands. Prominent among these methods is starting a family. The women have children with the conviction that the Dutch
authorities will not dare to separate children from biological parents and that
such children represent opportunities to be given residence permits on com-
passionate grounds.

> Many of these women, when they are told they will be deported, they
> 'get married' and they are pregnant and then they plead to be allowed to
> stay on humanitarian grounds because of pregnancy. In the Netherlands,
> we do not work that way; they will be deported to Nigeria and taken to
> NAPTIP. In fact, NAPTIP wrote to the Dutch government informing it that

it has the capability and capacity to rehabilitate and reintegrate rescued sex workers; so we are simply taking them to where they will receive assistance from their country. I wonder why they are so adamant on not wanting to return to Nigeria.

Interview with a social worker during field work, July–August 2014

An official of the IND who was contacted for a viewpoint on this matter revealed that, on the contrary:

In the Netherlands, if you claim you are a victim of human trafficking, there are certain prerequisites that must be met before any 'victim' can qualify for the residence permit: first, a police report confirming this, and also a report from a medical practitioner indicating that a person has been abused and thus needs to be granted a residence permit.

Interview with an IND official, IND office, Den Haag, July–August 2014

Oftentimes, the ability of a woman to prove that she has been a victim of human trafficking is difficult, as the police and NGOs are aware that illegal sex workers often lie that they are trafficked. Thus, obtaining a report from the police or medical practitioner would be difficult since none of these persons wish to write a report that could jeopardize their career.

The problem now is that many NGOs in the Netherlands have stopped working with Nigerian victims, as they do not know if they are real or false victims. There have been many instances where women would come with bruises and tell stories of how they have been victimized; then sometimes in collaboration with other NGOs we put in all their efforts and strengths to accelerate the residence permit process. And once the women obtain the permit, they start working as hidden sex workers; and once this is noticed, a set of investigations start all over, which many times reveals that the women were not actually trafficked victims but sex workers who lied about their true identity. As a result of this, most organizations have stopped working with Nigerian victims.

Interview with social worker in her office during field work, July–August 2014

Many of the migrant sex workers were actually exploited by traffickers in the Netherlands who promised to help them with legal residence permits:

I met him [the trafficker] in Holland Spoor; he was from my tribe, so I felt very at home with him. I told him about my plight and how I was not earning enough money in the Netherlands. He told me there was market in Belgium, so I followed him. I was placed in window prostitution in Belgium, while he was my pimp. He always takes my money. When I tried complaining to him, he assaulted me. That night I took a train back to the Netherlands and went straight to Kariboe Bibi for help.

Interview with a sex worker, in NGO office, August 2014

Migrant sex workers, like victims of TIP, face insecurities in the Netherlands, which ultimately leads them back to the hands of their exploiters for aid, thus facilitating further abuse and exploitation. Examples of such abuse are highlighted in the next section.

Violence Experienced by Migrant Sex Workers

My respondents all recounted how at one time in the course of their work they had experienced violence from customers and, to their surprise, law enforcement agents. Many occurrences of violence were attributed to either a refusal of sexual advances or a refusal by a client to use a condom, and also to an inability to pay a brothel owner for space.

I was raped by a customer because I urged him to use a condom, and there was no one I could tell about it.

Interview with a sex worker, July–August 2014

Many of the women experience violence because they are unaware of their rights, even though they are illegal migrants. Women in the Netherlands are respected. The violence is a result of their not being able to negotiate their stance, coupled with the fact they have a low self-esteem because of their illegal status.

Interview with a social worker during field work, July–August 2014

As a result of their vulnerability, in dealing with workplace violence migrant sex workers experience various challenges, many of which expose them to an increased risk of sexually transmitted infections, rape, assault, HIV, and poor reproductive health (Goldenberg *et al.* 2014: 1). Bodily, economic, and sexual violence experienced by sex workers has occasionally been the focus of general or intellectual interest, and studies (Lowman 2000; Kurtz *et al.* 2004) have confirmed that sex workers experience abuse from pimps, customers, owners of bordellos, and law enforcement officers (Watts & Zimmerman 2002: 1236; Sanders & Campbell 2007: 1). Similarly, Kinnell (2006) asserted that in the last ten years more than 80 sex workers were killed in the UK, which proves that sex workers are more likely to be killed while performing their job than people of any other professional occupation. The reason attributed by researchers is that sex workers are outside the security of legal structures (Kurtz et al., 2004: 358). Violence experienced in all forms by sex workers is multifaceted and linked to gender inequality, neoliberal economic policies, and impoverishment. Interpersonally, violence is caused by underlying factors, which include brothel condom-use policy and level of rapport between sex workers and customers (Choi 2011: 36).

> Most people from home who are now in Europe, once they get to know you are a sex worker, they stigmatize you. I feel terrible when I am looked down upon—not only by clients, who many times want you to engage in unimaginable sexual acts with them, not respecting your choice.
>
> Interview with a sex worker during field work, in a church building,
> July–August 2014

As a result of the clandestine and stigmatized nature of their work and their illegal status, migrant sex workers are rarely able to choose the circumstances under which they will work and the kinds of hazards they will be exposed to, as issues such as drug addiction and housing problems may increase and complicate the likelihood of exposure (Katsulis *et al.* 2015: 2). Furthermore, Ward *et al.* (2004) argue that because of racial bias and their unlawful status as undocumented migrants, negotiating safe sex is problematic for the women. Concerning the health of these women, Sanders (2004) claims that the health dangers the women are confronted with are manifold and intersecting. Psychological damage caused by the objectification of their bodies, as well as the risk of illegitimate pregnancies and abortions, constitute a full range of health risks that sex workers face on a daily basis (O'Connell Davidson 1998).

> It is a sad situation many of the women are either exposed to or have been inflicted with STIs. Getting an appointment with medical personnel is difficult because they many times do not have health insurance; and in this country, without health insurance health care costs are extremely expensive.
>
> Interview with a social worker in her office, July–August 2014

Globally, migrant sex workers are at high risk of contracting HIV infection, as they are often confronted with precarious situations where they do not have access to protective contraceptives, HIV avoidance information, and sexual health services. Factors responsible for their vulnerability include but are not limited to language barriers and illegal status leading to an inability to access health insurance (WHO 2005). Violence experienced by migrant sex workers is, by extension, a demonstration of the prejudice and bias against the sex work profession (*ibid.*).

Conclusion

This study has shown some evidence disputing the general assumption that all women working in the unregulated Dutch sex market are trafficked victims for commercial sexual exploitation. Additional evidence was offered on factors responsible for entry of transnational migrant women into the sex market. Some studies run counter to the trafficking narrative and see these women as economic migrants in search of a better socio-economic status, to lift themselves and their families out of impoverishment.

Furthermore, the issue of being an illegal migrant with no access to any social benefits is enormous for these women, as they do not have the ability to exercise their human functional capabilities. Thus, as noted in Nussbaum (1999: 41, 42), migrant sex workers do not have the ability to complete their life cycles owing to a myriad health-related problems, such as HIV/AIDS, high blood pressure, and mental health illnesses. As a consequence of their illegal status in society, sex workers are unable to seek medical help, which ultimately leads to their inability to enjoy life. Secondly, the women lack bodily strength and comfortable accommodation. Thirdly, they lack quality education, which would endow them with the capability to be creative. Fourthly, they lack freedom to move about without fear of either being apprehended by law enforcement agents as a result of being illegal migrants, or being raped by immoral men who view them as mere sluts with no access to justice in the Dutch state. Added to this is the inability to be loved and respected by society. Lastly, there is the inability of the women to plan their lives as a result of their exclusion from social privileges, and the inability to participate in issues that concern their environment, such as the ability to vote and be voted for. The inability of migrant sex workers to meet these criteria, which are prerequisites for core human functional capabilities, reflects a failure of social justice: a person who falls short in any of the capabilities cannot live a fulfilled and comfortable human life. Those undergoing such anomalies may indeed use any narrative, true or not, to get out of their predicament.

Concerning the denial of residence permits for victims, one of the social workers informed us that there were a number of Nigerian rescued victims of trafficking in the Netherlands, and each time an application is filed for a residence permit in the law courts, it is always struck out on the grounds that Nigeria has the capability to rehabilitate and cater for rescued victims when they are repatriated.

On the other side, evidence obtained in the course of the field work suggests the use of false pretences on the part of sex workers for their labelling as 'trafficked', and highlights the doubts this has introduced into the minds of the Dutch authorities on the subject. It appears also that the negative experiences of sex workers at the hands of their clients and the state has driven sex workers, in some instances, to the relative comfort of traffickers and pimps, who offer them at least hope.

Finally, it should be noted that this is an exploratory study, and certain limitations require that conclusions be treated with caution. Therefore, we recommend a larger (more respondents) and wider (beyond The Hague) study, to tease out factors that will improve our understanding of the phenomenon of trafficking from Nigeria. The outcome of such a study would contribute immensely to enriching academic and programmatic understanding and help eradicate the problems associated with this social phenomenon.

References

Aghatise, E. (2004), Trafficking for Prostitution in Italy. *Violence Against Women* 10(10): 1126–1155.

Agustín, L.M. (2005), Migrants in the Mistress's House: Other Voices in the 'Trafficking' Debate. *Social Politics: International Studies in Gender, State and Society* 12(1): 96–117.

Akinyoade, A. & F. Carchedi (2012), *Cases of Severely Exploited Nigerian Citizens and Other Forms of Exploitation. An Enquiry Conducted Jointly Between Italy and a Number of Nigerian States. Initial Considerations.* Ediese: Rome, pp. 368.

Altink, S. (1995), *Stolen Lives: Trading Women into Sex and Slavery.* Scarlet Press, pp. 180.

Anthias, F. (2013), Intersectional What? Social Divisions, Intersectionality and Levels of Analysis. *Ethnicities* 13(1): 3–19.

Aronowitz, A., N. Fanou-Ako, C. Okojie & A. Amenyedzi (2006), Measures to Combat Trafficking in Human Beings in Benin, Nigeria and Togo. Republic of Benin, Nigeria and Togo: United Nations Office on Drugs and Crime, pp. 6–148.

Bernat, F. & T. Zhilina (2013), Human Trafficking: The Local Becomes Global, in: F. Bernat (ed.) *Human Sex Trafficking.* Routledge: USA, pp. 1–8.

Boidi, M., B. El-Nagashi & B. Karner (2009), A Report on the Intersections of Legislations and Policies Regarding Sex Work, Migration and Health in Europe. Sex Work Migration Health. Netherlands: TAMPEP International Foundation. pp. 5–128.

Brunovskis, A. & R. Surtees (2008), Agency or Illness—the Conceptualization of Trafficking: Victims' Choices and Behaviors in the Assistance System. *Gender Technological Development* 12(1): 53–76.

Burr, V. (1995), *An Introduction to Social Constructionism*. Routledge, pp.198.

Choi, S.Y. (2011), Heterogeneous and Vulnerable: The Health Risks Facing Transnational Female Sex Workers. *Sociology of Health & Illness* 33(1): 33–49.

Chuang, J.A. (2010), Rescuing Trafficking from Ideological Capture: Prostitution Reform and Anti-Trafficking Law and Policy. *University of Pennsylvania Law Review* 158(6): 1655–1728.

Council of Europe (last updated 2014), Action Against Trafficking in Human Beings (a webpage of Council of Europe). http://www.coe.int/t/dghl/monitoring/trafficking/default_en.asp. Accessed 27 August 2014.

Davis, K. (2008), Intersectionality as Buzzword: A Sociology of Science Perspective on What Makes a Feminist Theory Successful. *Feminist Theory* 9(1): 67–85.

Defeis, E.F. (2003), Protocol to Prevent, Suppress and Punish Trafficking in Persons: A New Approach. *ILSA Journal of International & Comparative Law* 10: 485.

Department of State, United States of America (2014), Trafficking in Persons Report, No. 14, United States of America: Department of States, United States of America, pp. 7–432.

Doezema, Jo (1998), Forced to Choose: Beyond the Voluntary. Forced Prostitution Dichotomy, in: K. Kempadoo & J. Doezema (eds) *Global Sex Workers: Rights, Resistance and Redefinition*. Routledge: New York and London.

Doezema, J. (2010), *Sex Slaves and Discourse Masters: The Construction of Trafficking*. Zed Books: London.

Elson, D. & N. Cagatay (2000), The Social Content of Macroeconomic Policies. *World Development* 28(7): 1347–1364.

Engbersen, G. & J. Van der Leun (2001), The Social Construction of Illegality and Criminality. *European Journal on Criminal Policy and Research* 9(1): 51–70.

Favet, L. & C Falch (eds) (2010), Indoor Sex Work: Analysis and Good Practice Manual on Indoor Sex Work Settings in Seven European Cities. INDOORS, Autres Regards, Marseille. www.autresregards.org See: http://tampep.eu/documents/Outreach_Report-Indoors_2.pdf. Accessed 15 July 2015.

Giddens, A. (1979), *Central Problems in Social Theory: Action, Structure, and Contradiction in Social Analysis*. University of California Press, pp. 294.

Goldenberg, S.M., V. Liu, P. Nguyen, J. Chettiar & K. Shannon (2014), International Migration from Non-Endemic Settings as a Protective Factor for HIV/STI Risk Among Female Sex Workers in Vancouver, Canada. *Journal of Immigrant and Minority Health* 17(1): 21-28.

Gülçür, L. & P. İlkkaracan (2002), The 'Natasha' Experience: Migrant Sex Workers from the Former Soviet Union and Eastern Europe in Turkey. *Women's Studies International Forum* 25(4): 411–421.

Hyland, K.E. (2001), The Impact of the Protocol to Prevent, Suppress and Punish Trafficking in Persons, Especially Women and Children. *Human Rights Brief* 8(2): 12.

Jary, D. & J. Jary (1995), *Collins Dictionary of Sociology*. Glasgow.

Johnson, Kevin R. (2004). The Huddled Masses Myth: Immigration and Civil Rights. Philadelphia, PA; Temple University Press, in, Warner, J.A. (2005), The Social Construction of the Criminal Alien in Immigration Law, Enforcement Practice and Statistical Enumeration: Consequences for Immigrant Stereotyping. *Journal of Social and Ecological Boundaries* 1(2): 56–80.

Katsulis, Y., A. Durfee, V. Lopez & A. Robillard (2015), Predictors of Workplace Violence Among Female Sex Workers in Tijuana, Mexico. *Violence Against Women* 21(5): 571–597.

Kelly, L. & L. Regan (2000), Stopping Traffic: Exploring the Extent of, and Responses to, Trafficking of Women for Sexual Exploitation in the UK. Police Research Series, Paper 125. London: Home Office.

Kinnel, H. (2006), Murder Made Easy: The Final Solution to Prostitution?, in: R. Campbell & M O'Neill (eds.) *Sex Work Now*. William Press: Cullompton.

Krippendorff, K. (1980), *Content Analysis: An Introduction to its Methodology*. Sage: Beverly Hills CA.

Kurtz, S.P., H.L. Surratt, J.A. Inciardi & M.C. Kiley (2004), Sex Work and 'Date' Violence. *Violence Against Women* 10(4): 357–385.

Kvale, S. & S. Brinkmann (2009), *Interviews: Learning the Craft of Qualitative Research Interviewing*. Sage: United States of America.

Lowman, J. (2000), Violence and the Outlaw Status of Street Prostitution in Canada. *Violence Against Women* 6(9): 987–1101.

Matthews, R. (2008), *Prostitution, Politics and Policy*. Routledge: Cavendish.

Merriam, S.B. (2002), *Qualitative Research in Practice: Examples for Discussion and Analysis*. Jossey-Bass Inc Pub: Chicago.

Monzini, P. (2005), *Sex Traffic. Prostitution, Crime and Exploitation*. Zed Books: London, pp. 208.

National Agency for the Prohibition of Traffic in Persons and Other Related Matters (NAPTIP) (2003), Trafficking in Persons (Prohibition) Law Enforcement and Administration Act, Amended. Nigeria.

National Agency for the Prohibition of Traffic in Persons and Other Related Matters (NAPTIP) (Last updated 2014), About NAPTIP (a webpage of National Monitoring Center NAPTIP Abuja Nigeria). http://www.naptip.gov.ng/aboutus.html. Accessed 20 August 2014.

Nussbaum, M. (1999), *Sex and Social Justice* (1st ed.). Oxford University Press: New York.

O'Connell Davidson, J. (1998), *Prostitution, Power, and Freedom*. University of Michigan Press: Ann Arbor, p. 9.

O'Connell Davidson, J. (2005), *Children in the Global Sex Trade*. Polity: Cambridge, pp. 224.

Olateru-Olagbegi, B. & A. Ikpeme (2006), Review of Legislation and Policies in Nigeria on Human Trafficking and Forced Labour: Action Programme Against Trafficking and Forced Labour in West Africa. Nigeria: International Labour Organization. pp. 1–52.

Oude Breuil, B., D. Siegel, P. Van Reenen, A. Beijer & L. Roos (2011), Human Trafficking Revisited: Legal Enforcement and Ethnographic Narratives on Sex Trafficking to Western Europe. *Trends in Organized Crime* 14: 30–46.

Outshoorn, J. (2005), The Political Debates on Prostitution and Trafficking of Women. *Social Politics: International Studies in Gender, State and Society* 12(1): 141–155.

Phizacklea, A. (1998), Migration and Globalization: A Feminist Perspective, in: K. Koser & H. Lutz (eds) *The New Migration in Europe: Social Constructions and Social Realities.* Macmillan Press: London.

Plambech, S. (2014), Point of Departure: Life After Human Trafficking in Western Europe. PhD Thesis. Institute of Anthropology, University of Copenhagen.

Raymond, J.G. (2004), Prostitution on Demand: Legalizing the Buyers as Sexual Consumers. *Violence Against Women* 10(10): 1156–1186.

Sanders, T. (2004), A Continuum of Risk? The Management of Health, Physical and Emotional Risks by Female Sex Workers. *Sociology of Health & Illness* 26(5): 557–574.

Sanders, T. & R. Campbell (2007), Designing out Vulnerability, Building in Respect: Violence, Safety and Sex Work Policy. *The British Journal of Sociology* 58(1): 1–19.

Sanders, T., M O'Neil & J. Pitcher (2009), *Prostitution: Sex-work, Policy and Politics.* London, California, India, Singapore: Sage.

Saunders, P. (2005), Traffic Violations: Determining the Meaning of Violence in Sexual Trafficking Versus Sex Work. *Journal of Interpersonal Violence* 20(3): 343–360.

Sembacher, A. (2005), Council of Europe Convention on Action Against Trafficking in Human Beings. *The Tulane Journal of International & Comparative Law* 14: 435.

Snel, E., J. de Boom, J. Burgers & G Engbersen (2000), Migratie, integratie en criminaliteit Rotterdam: RISBO. Cited in: G. Engbersen & J. Van der Leun (2001), The social construction of illegality and criminality. *European Journal on Criminal Policy and Research* 9(1): 51–70.

US Department of State Trafficking in Persons Report (US TIPR) (June 2014), Available at: http://www.state.gov/documents/organization/226844.pdf. Accessed 19 July 2015.

Ward, E., A. Jemal, V. Cokkinides, G.K. Singh, C. Cardinez, A. Ghafoor & M. Thun (2004), Cancer Disparities by Race/Ethnicity and Socioeconomic Status. *CA: A Cancer Journal for Clinicians* 54: 78–93.

Warner, J.A. (2005), The Social Construction of the Criminal Alien in Immigration Law, Enforcement Practice and Statistical Enumeration: Consequences for Immigrant Stereotyping. *Journal of Social and Ecological Boundaries* 1(2): 56–80.

Watts, C. & C. Zimmerman (2002), Violence Against Women: Global Scope and Magnitude. *The Lancet* 359(9313): 1232–1237.

Weitzer, R. (2007), The Social Construction of Sex Trafficking: Ideology and Institutionalization of a Moral Crusade. *Politics & Society* 35(3): 447–475.

World Health Organization (Last updated 2005), Violence Against Women and HIV/AIDS: Critical Intersections. Violence Against Sex Workers and HIV Prevention (a webpage of The World Health Organization). www.who.int/gender/documents/sexworkers.pdf. Accessed 15 October 2014.

Zhang, S.X. (2009), Beyond the 'Natasha' Story: A Review and Critique of Current Research on Sex Trafficking. *Global Crime* 10(3): 178–195.

PART 4

Zones of Transit and Transference

∴

CHAPTER 12

So Be Nya Dagna? ('Is Someone Injured?'): The Evolution and Use of Tricycles in Tamale, Northern Ghana

Samuel Ntewusu and Edward Nanbigne

Introduction

Over the last ten years or so there has been a growing utilization of tricycles for the transport of people and goods in Ghana. In the north of Ghana and especially in Tamale (capital of the Northern Region), this mode of transport is fast replacing other modes of transport such as human-powered porterage and taxis. An important question one may investigate is the reason or reasons behind this phenomenon, especially given the ease with which roads can be constructed in the flat treeless terrain of northern Ghana. The fact still remains that feeder roads are few and badly maintained in the peri-urban and rural areas of northern Ghana. People have to make do with bush tracks to their farms, and these tracks are the only links between many communities. Where roads have been constructed between communities, they are little better than bulldozed tracks that are not motorable to most buses. As a result, the people of these communities first relied on bicycles and then gradually transitioned to motorbikes. Motorbikes, even now, are the popular means of transportation in both the urban and rural areas of northern Ghana. They are so popular that they have become a part of complementary prestation in the marriage system for many families.[1]

This paper discusses the tricycle popularly referred to as 'Motor King'.[2] The paper is devoted to the whole complex of evolution of, access to, and use of the Motor King in Tamale. It will examine the reasons for and implications of the adoption of this tricycle in Tamale. The paper will also examine the local terminologies which have evolved since the adoption of this so-called new technology and how the terminologies relate to the risks associated with this mode of transport. By discussing the evolution of the Motor King, one conclusion is drawn in this paper: the Motor King has offered opportunities for the

---

1   Interview with Salifu Alhassan, lecturer at Tamale Polytechnic, Tamale, 25 February 2013.
2   The name Motor King has been adopted as a generic term for motorized tricycles, even though there are many other brands such as Haojin, Apsonic, Sunny Best, and Luo Jia.

personal development of the owners and for the economic progress of its users.

In order to understand fully the rationale for the Motor King's popularity in Tamale, it is important to give a brief historical background to Tamale. It is also necessary to discuss some forms of transport systems that were operational there before the introduction of tricycles. Such a brief discussion will facilitate our understanding of the uniqueness of tricycles in the city and its surroundings.

A Brief History of the Evolution of Tamale

Tamale is the capital of the Northern Region of Ghana. The region is bounded to the north by Upper East and Upper West, to the west by Côte d'Ivoire, to the east by Togo, and to the south by the Brong-Ahafo Region. The main ethnic groups inhabiting Tamale are Dagomba, Mampruise, Nanumba, and Gonja. Other ethnic groups who are indigenous in the region, such as the Konkomba, Nchumburu, Nawuri, Bassari, Bimoba, and Chakosi, also inhabit Tamale.

As an urban centre, Tamale is also home to southern ethnic groups such as the Akan, Ewe, and Ga. There is also a small number of expatriate nationals, such as the Lebanese, Indians and, lately, Chinese. At the end of the nineteenth century, Tamale was only one of the numerous villages in the Northern Territories (now Northern Region, Upper East Region, and Upper West Region). In 1906 the British authorities, considering a new site for their northern headquarters, decided in favour of Tamale. Prior to that it was Gambaga that was the capital. In 1907, the capital was relocated from Gambaga to Tamale, but the new headquarters was formally opened only in 1908.[3]

At its foundation, traditional political power was still vested in the Ya Na, who resided in Yendi. Nonetheless, the Ya Na had two chiefs who represented him in Tamale, and they were the Dakpema and Gulkpena. At the time of Tamale's foundation, the population there was just 1,435. It was not only small in size but was also economically irrelevant compared with other settlements in the region, such as Salaga, Yendi, and Gambaga. But when it was made the administrative capital, it began assuming importance, with many more people moving into Tamale and thereby redefining the urban demography of the town.[4]

The period 1921–1931 saw Tamale's population more than triple, from 3,901 in 1921 to almost 13,000 in 1931. At that period Tamale's expansion was due to a

---

3   Wyatt MacGaffey, A History of Tamale, 1907–1957. *Transactions of the Historical Society of Ghana*, New Series, No. 10, (2006–2007), p. 110.

4   Wyatt MacGaffey, 'A History of Tamale, 1907–1957', p. 111.

number of factors. The first has to do with the completion of the Great North Road, which linked the south of Ghana to the north. The completion of the road caused traders from the south to move to the north to engage in trade and to settle there.[5]

The second factor was the presence of ex-servicemen who fought in both World War I and World War II. It is a historical fact that most of the people who were recruited into the Gold Coast Regiment were from the northern part of the country, as well as from present-day Togo and Burkina Faso. After demobilization, most of them, instead of moving back to their villages where they had been recruited, chose instead to stay in Tamale. The colonial administration's zoning policy of Tamale tended to favour such ex-servicemen, who were given plots in Moshie Zongo to build houses to live in. They comprised mostly ethnic groups such as Moshie, Grushi, Zabrama, Frafra, and Builsa.[6]

In the 1950s through to the 1960s and 1970s, Tamale's population growth was mainly due to formal employment opportunities that came along with the decolonization of Ghana. Many ethnic groups, such as the Nawuri, Nchumburu, and Konkomba, moved into Tamale to work in some of the government establishments—examples include agriculture, social welfare, banks, Ghana National Trading Corporation, State Transport Corporation, and Omnibus Services Authority. In addition, the attempts by government to industrialize and produce more agricultural goods led to a number of initiatives in Tamale which equally promoted the city's growth. The Botanga irrigation project, for example, employed a number of people who produced vegetables and fish, while the Nasia rice fields employed thousands of people who worked on the farms but stayed in Tamale.

The economic recovery programme of the 1980s also led to a growth in Tamale's population. The period saw the collapse of agriculture, as the programme recommended that all subsidies for agriculture be eliminated. With the subsidies removed, it became much more difficult to produce cereals such as rice and maize and legumes (e.g. beans and groundnuts). Owing to the decay of rural areas, some people moved into urban centres such as Accra and Tamale in search of jobs. Others entered into petty trading, thereby contributing immensely to the distribution sector of Tamale.[7]

---

5   S. Soeters (2012), Tamale 1907–1957: Between Colonial Trade and Colonial Chieftainship. PhD Thesis, University of Leiden, pp. 23–24.

6   S. Soeters, 'Tamale 1907–1957', p. 83.

7   Interview with Emelia Asamoah, Tamale, 17 September 2013. Emelia is a teacher and a businesswoman in Tamale. She owns Nassant Ventures, a supermarket located in the central business district of Tamale.

In 1994, an ethnic conflict broke out between Konkombas, Nawuris, Bassaris, and Nchumburus on the one hand, and Dagomba, Gonjas, and Nanumbas on the other. During and after the war, most ethnic groups such as the Konkomba, Nawuris, Bassaris and Nchumburus fled Tamale.

Tamale bounced back to its former status in the 2000s. According to the 2012 population census, Tamale has 537,986 inhabitants. It is considered in modern times to be one of the fastest-growing cities in West Africa. Its central location has made it possible for it to serve as a hub for all administrative and commercial activities in northern Ghana. As a capital-*cum*-relay city, transport is key to its functioning, and different modes of transport have had significant impact on Tamale's history.

Transport Modes in Tamale

At its foundation in 1907, Tamale relied much on head porterage. Horses were available for transport, but they remained the prestige possessions of chiefs and other titled men. By 1920, however, Tamale was connected to the south via Kumasi through a road that was popularly referred to as the Great North Road.[8] Once motorized transport came to Tamale, other modes of transport, particularly bicycles, followed. Although in comparative terms bicycles got to the south before the north, northerners soon overtook people of the south in the purchase and use of this mode of transport.

Scholars on Ghana's transport history, such as Grieco, Turner, and Kwakye (1994), have provided various reasons or indicators that influenced the use of bicycles in general in the northern part of Ghana. They contend that bicycles were common in the northern part of the country because of the topography or geography of the area. They argue that the flat nature of the north, with fewer mountains and forests, made it possible for bicycles to be easily used. Furthermore, they analysed the use of bicycles based on the economic situation of the north. They were of the view that because bicycles were cheaper than motor vehicles and because the north is an area with appreciable levels of poverty, these factors caused residents to chose the cheapest transport systems available, such as bicycles.[9]

---

8 For more on the Great North Road, see S.A. Ntewusu (2014), The Road to Development: The Construction and Use of the Great North Road in Gold Coast, Ghana. Leiden: ASC Working Paper 114.

9 M.S. Grieco, J. Turner & E.A. Kwakye (1994), A Tale of Two Cultures: Ethnicity and Cycling Behaviour in Urban Ghana, in: *73rd Annual Meeting of the Transportation Research Board.* Washington DC. (January), pp. 1–2.

Besides geography and poverty, there were other factors which equally played a crucial role in the evolutionary history of bicycles in the north. A politico-cultural dimension to the use of bicycles cannot be ignored. As stated earlier, bicycles were an option because horses, which thrive in the north, were the prestige possession of royals and titled men. It was reported, for example, that until 1942 a chief in the north might refuse to allow anyone in his district to buy a horse, unless through his mediation.[10] The horse was the basis of political and military power and a symbol of chiefship. Indeed, in chiefly societies in the north one cannot complete the greeting of a chief without asking after the health of his horse. As it is said in Dagbani: *Ka naa wahu be wula?* ['And how is the chief's horse?']. The monopoly on horses by chiefs made many people choose cycles, which most scholars of transport perfectly described as the *iron horse*.

It was in this context that motorcycles were introduced in Tamale. Even though the history of motorcycles dates back to the 1860s, mass production in the US and Europe began only in the 1900s. And it was owing to colonialism that most parts of Africa were associated with this mode of transport. For example, in Zambia, by the second decade of the 1900s, well-to-do colonial officials had taken to puttering around on a wide variety of motorcycle models that had been produced by British manufacturing firms.[11] In Ghana, the colonial administration imported motorcycles basically for the use of colonial officials who worked in the health and sanitation sector.[12] With time, other colonial staff were provided with motorcycles, both in the south and north of Ghana. But the motor revolution in Tamale occurred only in the early 1960s. Kwame Nkrumah encouraged the Yugoslavian government to develop a TOMOS (abbreviated from TOvarna MOtornih koles Sežana) motorcycle industry in Tamale. Even though a manufacturing company was not established, shops were opened in Tamale to distribute TOMOS motorcycles imported from Sežana, Yugoslavia. It is important to mention that Nkrumah in the early 1960s was ideologically attached to socialist nations in Eastern Europe, and he was developing Tamale as a model city that reflected Eastern Europe both in terms of its residential pattern and economic activities, including transportation. This ideology influenced the popularity of TOMOS motorcycles in Tamale.

---

10   Christine Oppong, *Growing up in Dagbon* (Accra-Tema: Ghana Publishing Corporation, 1973), p. 18.

11   J.-B. Gewald, 'People, Mines and Cars: Towards a Revision of Zambian history, 1890–1930', in: J.-B. Gewald, Sabine Luning & Klass van Walraven (eds) *The Speed of Change: Motor Vehicles and People in Africa, 1890–2000* (Leiden: Brill, 2009), p. 37.

12   PRRAD, Accra, CSO 11/14/25, Motor Cycles, Medical Department, 1933–1935.

Furthermore, the TOMOS motorcycle was ideal for the geographic terrain in the north since it was a robust motorcycle suitable for gravel roads. In the 1970s, the military government of Colonel Kutu Akyeampong brought in more motorcycles and supplied them to the staff of the Ministry of Agriculture as part of his 'Operation Feed Yourself Programme', which was aimed at ensuring food security in the country.[13]

In focusing on motorcycles it is important to note that apart from those that were used for official duties, motorcycles up to the 1980s were generally used for private purposes, such as for individual mobility and domestic errands like fetching water and firewood as well as for conveying farm produce to the market. Butchers, in particular, used motorbikes to move around to buy animals for slaughter in the towns and villages. But just as with horses, motorbikes even at this stage came to serve as status symbols for the low-income earners who could afford them.

In the late 1980s and early 1990s, a particular brand of motorbike—the Yamaha Dame, popularly called 'Yamaha Down' (so-called because of its small size and its gearing system, which had all first, second, and third gears going down)—came into vogue and dominated most communities in the north. The working class and shopkeepers went in for Yamaha Dames, and for the youth it marked a coming of age. Informants indicate how it was fun to pick up girls on a Yamaha Dame and how ladies preferred it to vehicles. Ladies were more visible on the motorbike, and their 'vital statistics' could be displayed while speeding along! 'In a car, all these are concealed,' said one informant. A teacher in Tamale recounted how he would frequently pick ladies up on his Yamaha Dame, ride very quickly, and then apply the brakes, forcing the ladies to slide forward until their breasts touched his back and they grabbed hold of him in order not to fall off, an action he described as 'creating bodily momentum'. Many young men confirmed this practice among motor riders. In a way, one could argue that the motorbike aided the development of social and marital relations in the north.[14]

---

13   Information provided by Sawyer Ndamele, Accra, 12 December 2014. Sawyer worked for several years with the Agricultural Research Station in Nyankpala and also with German Agricultural programmes in northern Ghana. He is currently a senior staff member at the University of Ghana Agricultural Research station in Nungua, Accra. Both in Nyankpala and Accra, Sawyer worked with the mechanical and animal traction units.

14   Interview with Tahiru Mohammed, Tamale, 20 January 2015. Tahiru has transitioned from riding bicycles and motorcycles to an old, used motor vehicle. He professes his love for motorcycles and always goes back to using one whenever his car breaks down or he cannot afford fuel to run the car.

From what has been discussed so far, it is evident why the introduction of any form of cycle will gain some form of acceptability in the northern part of Ghana. We turn our attention now to the tricycle.

Roads to Prosperity: The Tricycle Revolution in Tamale

By definition, a tricycle is a three-wheeled cycle, commonly human-powered; and hence the tricycle motor is a three-wheeled cycle fitted with an internal combustion engine.[15] A combustion engine generates motive power by the burning of petrol, oil, or other fuel with air inside the engine, the hot gases produced being used to drive a piston or do other work as they expand.[16] There are various types of these tricycles, but the one under discussions is fitted with a carrier or trailer at the back and is popularly referred to as the Motor King.

In Ghana, the origin of tricycles fitted with a combustion engine can be credited to the John Agyekum Kufour government (2000–2008). Having won the elections in Ghana in 2000, then President Kufour set out to handle three important problems in the country: sanitation, health, and transportation. In order to deal efficiently with issues of waste in the major cities and towns in Ghana, he formed a waste management company called ZOOMLION. The company employed youths, some of whom were provided with human-powered tricycles. They moved from one house to another to help in the collection of refuse. This mode of transport was particularly ideal in the cities because of the obvious problems of mobility in the city of Accra and Kumasi. These are places where some residential and commercial neighbourhoods have narrow alleyways and are often inaccessible to larger vehicles.

As previously indicated, the collection of refuse gave much needed employment to youths at very little overhead cost, while achieving the purpose of keeping the environment clean. Later, the tricycles were motorized with small gasoline-powered engines. By 2005, motorbikes built in the form of tricycles began to be operated by ZOOMLION.

The introduction of the engine-powered tricycle for waste management had an unintended consequence and, indeed, transformed the transportation landscape in Ghana, especially in the north. In 2007, Motor King, a company dealing in all sorts of products with the same name as the brand name, set up in Tamale in northern Ghana and began to assemble tricycles from complete

---

15   S. Grava, *Urban Transportation Systems: Choices for Communities* (New York: McGraw-Hill, 2003), p. 114.

16   J.-B. Gewald, 'People, Mines and Cars', p. 37.

knockdown parts. These tricycles were meant to help farmers address the transportation needs of carrying their produce from farm to home and from home to market over bad roads. However, given the poverty rates in that part of the country, few farmers could personally afford to buy a tricycle just for the purpose of carrying farm produce. Invariably, it was entrepreneurs in the urban areas who, while not engaged in farming, saw an opportunity in the ownership of tricycles and began to buy them for carrying goods from markets to homes. These tricycles effectively replaced push trucks as the popular means of conveying goods from home to market and from market to homes. Using tricycles is also considerably cheaper than taxis, and they can carry more goods than a taxi.[17] The tricycles operated by these entrepreneurs did not go far afield but worked within the urban and peri-urban areas, carting goods, tanks of water, and sometimes sand for building sites. Initially, they were not seen as much of a threat by operators of other means of transportation. Since tricycles could not operate within the crowded and narrow confines of markets, push truck operators could still make a living carrying goods from within the markets to outside the market, where tricycles could be hired to carry both the goods and the owner to a further destination at little cost.

In December 2012, the Youth in Community Transport Services of the Ghana Youth Employment and Entrepreneurial Development Agency (GYEEDA) launched the Community Motor Tricycle Project, under which 1,000 youths were to be trained in each region on the operation of tricycles. The tricycles were to be used to provide diverse transport services in communities but were not to be used for the transportation of human beings. The following year, the Local Enterprise and Skill Development Programme (LESDEP) gave out tricycles to youths registered in the programme. In Tamale, over 200 tricycles were handed over to the regional minister. Under the programme, 120,000 youths were to be trained to operate tricycles. Politicians in the northern sector of the country also saw tricycles as a way of increasing development in their constituencies and providing the youth with a means of livelihood.

The tricycles were well suited to the conditions of the areas. Economically, they were cheaper, much cheaper than a used car or bus, and so were affordable since under the government programmes the youths were to work with them and pay their cost over time. This government intervention began a proliferation of tricycles in the three northern regions of Ghana: Northern Region, Upper East Region, and Upper West Region. Accessibility also aided in the success story of tricycles. Since many operators of taxis and mini-buses were loath to go on the bad roads that linked rural communities to towns, and there were

17   Interview with Jacob Abubakari, Tamale, 28 December 2013.

PHOTO 1   *A Motor King with passengers and goods on the Tamale–Saveligu highway*

no buses and taxis in these rural communities, the only means of transportation that could carry many people were tricycles.

Even though they were meant for carrying goods and foodstuffs, the technology was adapted to meet the needs of the people. In communities where nobody benefited from the government programmes, the community members came together to pool resources to buy a tricycle, which is given to one of the youths to operate and account for to the leaders of the community. The tricycle in the community becomes the bus that carries people to other communities for funerals, marriage ceremonies, festivals, and other engagements. The tricycles are able to negotiate the paths and poorly developed roads. It is the tricycles that carry passengers to the urban centre on market days, albeit only to the outskirts of the town, since other transport unions protested loudly against the use of tricycles in human transport within the towns.

In rural areas, the tricycles have become life savers, as they often operate as ambulances, carrying expectant mothers to the nearest maternity clinic over roads that no ambulance could move on. This is a much more comfortable option than the pregnant woman having to sit on a bicycle or motorbike for a drive of probably 20 km to a clinic. In the same way, critically ill people can be quickly rushed to hospital. Just as they act as ambulances, they are also the hearses that carry bodies from the hospitals to the rural communities, saving people from having to use bicycles and motorbikes.

Operating tricycles has become a livelihood opportunity for many. In the towns, young men who used to use push trucks have transitioned to tricycles and are making a living carrying goods and passengers on market days. It may be argued that if roads were better, these would not have been adopted and adapted to the uses to which they have been put. Some push-truck operators who have not transitioned to tricycles but have been virtually driven out of business have come up with innovative ways of using their push trucks to make a living. They have become itinerant salesmen, piling goods on the trucks and pushing them around to sell. They usually get the goods from a shop and sell for a commission. Even in this line of business, they are challenged by operators of tricycles, who can load up more and go further afield to communities that would otherwise have no access to the goods that they have to sell.

Economic and Social Mobility

Generally the operators of tricycles are driven by economic motives. The investment made by entrepreneurs and parastatal organizations such as MASLOC, GYEEDA, and LESDEP are all aimed at generating income. However, a much deeper analysis of the operations indicates that the riders themselves derive much more profit and gain social status and recognition in the process. Most of the riders interviewed claim that they make an average profit of about GHS 50 per day (about EUR 13) after deducting operational costs and paying their 'masters' (the owners of the tricycles). This has led some who were operating push trucks to move into the riding of tricycles. Taking an average working time of 25 days in a month, it means they make about GHS 1,250 a month (about EUR 325). This amount is comparable to the monthly income of a first-degree holder who works in the Ghanaian civil service. In much the same way, owners of tricycles indicate that the profits derived from daily 'sales' to the riders has made it possible for owners to acquire landed property such as houses, shops, and stores. They have also been able to buy other means of transport, such as taxis and buses, which bring in further income.

This economic empowerment has made it possible for owners and riders of tricycles to have upward social mobility. For example, from their transition as jobless urban dwellers or unhappy pushers of trucks to drivers of powered tricycles, the riders have suddenly become eligible bachelors who are a catch for young ladies looking for a responsible young man to marry. In the same way that in bygone years a young man had to prove capable of being able to look after a wife and children by being able to raise a hundred yam mounds a day, these days, having an economically viable job, such as operating a tricycle, equates to raising a hundred yam mounds.[18]

It used to be that young men operating push trucks were little regarded in terms of social standing, and there were frequent altercations between them and traders in the markets. They were often insulted as dirty, sweaty truck pushers. Apart from that, many thought of them as people who used drugs, such as 'Capital E' (ephedrine), *bunkuma* (datura), blue blue (valium), and marijuana. This negative image of young men has changed with their transition from push trucks to tricycles, with residual memories coming up only when they are involved in an accident. Those operating tricycles as passenger vehicles are more often than not seen to be better dressed and neater than their erstwhile counterparts, the push-truck operators. In these times of economic challenges and high costs of transportation, tricycles and their operators are seen as saviours of the rural people and the urban poor, in terms of providing them with a cheaper means of transportation. By this means, the operators are elevated several notches in social status above their clientele. Now on an equal footing with other transport owners and operators, the operators of tricycles can with confidence attend social gatherings such as weddings, naming ceremonies, and funerals. They are invited for family meetings and discussions, since they can equally contribute both ideas and money. Further giving them a standing in society is the strong association that they have formed for their welfare. The united front they present has given them the social power and standing to be able to stand up to the animosity and challenges from other transport operators, such as the taxi and *trotro* drivers.

In a way, one could conclude that the popularity of the tricycle in Tamale is due to the numerous advantages and opportunities that it provides. This phenomenon can be considered a logical extension of the bicycle and motorbike culture in Tamale.

So bi nya dagna? ('Is Someone Injured?'): The Bad End to Tricycles

In 2013, while conducting interviews for this study, each informant was asked to mention at least two names for the Motor King in any Ghanaian language. We asked this question knowing very well the extent to which people appropriate

---

18   For more on yams and marriage, see E. Akyeampong & S. Ntewusu (2014), 'Rum, Gin and Maize: Deities and Ritual Change in the Gold Coast During the Atlantic Era (16th Century to 1850)', *Afrique: Débats, méthodes et terrains d'histoire* 5.

technology in Africa. Appropriation is not only about the real utilization of a technological object, but also names or terms offer insights into the effects of the usage of an object in African societies. Names given for Motor King were varied and included the following: *so be nya dagna* ('is someone injured?'); *kur nirba* ('killer of people'); and *kal laa-hum-ma* (a short phrase from the Islamic prayer for the dead). We discovered the same is true for the Upper West Region of Ghana, where the people referred to the tricycle as *nyaaba lorry* ('lorry of embarrassment').

An analysis of the local names for the tricycle indicates that despite the opportunities offered by this technology, people were also mindful of its negative consequences. What then are the negative consequences associated with this mode of transport?

In the first place, the tricycle business poses a great danger to society. In spite of the bad roads and paths on which they operate, operators drive so fast that they end up spilling passengers, with many casualties and sometimes fatalities. This is behind the tricycle's name in Dagbani: *so be nya dagna*. Also, because the front end is a motorbike, vehicles and other road users compensate for the width of a motorbike and not the width of the back bucket of the tricycle. In fact, so many accidents have been recorded that in August 2012, Mr. Alban Bagbin, a Member of Parliament for Nadowli West of the Upper West Region, appealed on the floor of the Ghanaian Parliament to the police to arrest and prosecute any tricycle riders who cause accidents through carelessness.[19]

Despite this call from Mr. Bagbin, more tricycles are being acquired and operators have been virtually immune from sanctions. This is because of government involvement in the acquisition and operation of the tricycles. A conundrum has arisen. As part of the youth employment programme by the Ghana government, tricycles were given to the youth to operate and pay back the cost. On the one hand, they are not licensed by the licensing authority to operate as commercial vehicles; therefore, by law, they are private vehicles and can operate only as such. They should not carry goods as a commercial venture, nor are they permitted to carry passengers. Since they are not registered as passenger vehicles, there is no insurance coverage for any passengers who are injured in accidents.[20] On the other hand, the operators have to engage in commercial and passenger activities in order to make the money to be able to repay the government for the tricycles.

---

19   Interview with Honourable Alban Bagbin, Parliament House, Accra, 8 January 2015. Bagbin is the current majority speaker in Parliament. He trained as a lawyer and has been in Ghana's Parliament since 1992.

20   *Daily Graphic*, 'Motor-King Tricycle, a Blessing or Curse', Monday, 13 May 2013.

Besides injuries, Motor Kings are increasingly implicated in officially reported cases of deaths, in the Tamale metropolis in particular and the Northern Region in general, by the National Road Safety Commission. For example, most of the reported cases of fatal accidents in Tamale involving buses were caused by Motor Kings crossing the vehicles. Besides accidents with other mobile vehicles, Motor Kings have also crashed into people, especially at night, when their lights usually mislead pedestrians into thinking they are normal motorbikes, only for the side of the vehicle to crush the passengers to death. It is on record that every month at least ten people die from *accidents* involving tricycles.[21]

Furthermore, most of the operators in Tamale are known to commit a number of road offences, such as riding the wrong way through one-way roads or crossing when a stop sign is on. Most operators ride without the helmets and driver's license required of all motor riders. The problem of corruption among road traffic enforcement agents, who are easily induced into ignoring traffic misdemeanours when given bribes, remains a major impediment to curtailing the excesses of tricycle riders.

Finally, an impending problem so far has to do with the tensions and sometimes fights that are occurring between Motor King operators and other transport operators. Motor King operators in Tamale are at war with taxi drivers, truck pushers, and passenger transport unions, who accuse them of taking over their business and intentionally crashing into the sides or back of their vehicles with the intention of damaging their vehicles.

Conclusion

While acknowledging the fact that commercial tricycles have offered many transport advantages in the form of easy manoeuvrability in traffic, ability to travel on bad roads, high demand responsiveness, and good speed of service, it is also true that they have led to a phenomenal increase in road accidents resulting in serious injuries, deaths, and increased traffic management problems. However, their introduction and use show that the north of Ghana will leave no opportunity unexploited when it comes to cycle-based modes of transport. The locals consider cycles as roads to social and economic prosperity, since cycles fit well with their economic, cultural, and geographical setting.

---

21   *Ghana News Agency*, 'Tricycles Contribute to Road Crashes in Northern Region', Tuesday, 24 July 2012.

References

Gewald, J.-B., S. Luning & K. van Walraven (eds) (2009), *The Speed of Change: Motor Vehicles and People in Africa, 1890–2000*. Leiden: Brill.

Grava, S. (2003), *Urban Transportation Systems: Choices for Communities*. New York: McGraw-Hill.

Grieco, M.S., J. Turner & E.A. Kwakye (1994), A Tale of Two Cultures: Ethnicity and Cycling Behaviour in Urban Ghana, in: 73rd Annual Meeting of the Transportation Research Board (January). Washington DC.

MacGaffey, W. (2006–2007), A History of Tamale, 1907–1957. *Transactions of the Historical Society of Ghana*, New Series 10: 110.

Ntewusu, S.A. (2014), The Road to Development: The Construction and Use of the Great North Road in Gold Coast, Ghana. Leiden: ASC Working Paper.

Oppong, C. (1973), *Growing up in Dagbon*. Accra-Tema, Ghana Publishing Corporation.

Soeters, S. (2012), Tamale 1907–1957: Between Colonial Trade and Colonial Chieftainship. PhD Thesis, University of Leiden.

CHAPTER 13

Nigerians in Transit: The Trader and the Religious in Jerusalem House, Ghana

Akinyinka Akinyoade

Introduction

Migration of people in Africa is one of its most important demographic features. In West Africa, the cocoa farms in Ghana and Côte d'Ivoire attract large numbers of seasonal labourers, especially from Burkina Faso. Ghanaian fishermen abound in coastal areas of the sub-region; those of other vocations are found in the Sahelian areas of Mali, while some put their skills to use in the mines of Sierra Leone and Liberia. Nigerians, noted for commerce and trade, have been found as far afield as the Democratic Republic of the Congo (DRC) and Swaziland and have participated in artisanal mining of precious minerals nearby in Ghana (Peil 1974). Over a hundred years ago, a significant feature of labour on Ghana's Sekondi–Tarkwa–Kumasi railway line was the use of indentured workers. As at May 1902, 7,000 of 16,000 workers were from Lagos, and the Lagos colonial administration charged £1 for each worker recruited (Tsey 2013). The main groups comprised immigrants from Lagos, specifically the Yoruba.

Arising from these migrant workers were two types of feedback related to wealth acquisition. Firstly, they were working on a rail line that led to the place where Ghana's gold is produced, and perhaps family members who were first-hand receivers of such crucial information might have had access to gold, as descendants would later attest. Secondly, the Lagos colonial administration levy appears to have been the first official attempt at harnessing remittances from Nigerian individuals participating in rail line construction in Ghana. Even in the absence of direct access to gold, it represented an opportunity to earn some income for those who wanted to quit the agricultural sector in the increasingly urbanized Lagos area. Thus, back in Nigeria, for those that received feedback from relatives working on the rail line in Ghana, there arose an attraction to travel. Access to gold became the pull factor; shrinking opportunities for land ownership for farming in Lagos became the push factor. Many of these Yoruba were later to travel to Ghana via another route and eluded the £1 charge by the Lagos colonial administration. They entered Ghana in the northern sector and stayed and helped develop two transit villages—Banda and Chinderi— which are about 27 km apart in the northern part of the Volta, after which many moved down south to rendezvous with their relatives who were working in the rail line construction sites that led to gold.[1] On this account, we see that social factors, particularly those related to household and family structures, play a critical role in determining patterns of migration and development.

However, the traditional configurations of Nigerian migrant flows into Ghana, as well as the nature of transit points within Ghana, have changed in recent years (Adepoju 2003). By accident of geographic location of the Yoruba in Lagos, the early sets of economic migrants into Ghana from Nigeria were the Yoruba of southwest Nigeria, where the seat of colonial administration was located. Over a century later, official as well as anecdotal accounts indicate that the Ibo of southeast Nigeria are found in increasing numbers in Ghana, particularly in Accra. Also in search of wealth, the itinerant nature of the Igbo businessman presupposes different processes of settling in Ghana. For instance, when compared with what used to obtain a century ago, the mode of travelling into Ghana has changed, as have the socio-economic setting, urban settlement patterns, and government policies that preclude or encourage immigration.

This study examines transience in the route to prosperity of the latter-day arrivals in Ghana, specifically in Accra. This is done with special reference to Jerusalem House, a compound accommodating 50–100 persons at any given time (according to accounts of the landlord and tenants, respectively) and a notable transit point for Ibo immigrants in the Odorkor area of Accra. The establishment of Jerusalem House, its governance structure, and the social interactions relevant for the Ibo and their neighbours will be assessed. Relevant comparisons will be made to the hub of early Yoruba immigrants in Anagokoji, a suburb of Ho in the Volta Region.

In this study, other configurations of connectivity explored are the notion of family in Jerusalem House and how it plays an important role in the settling process of Ibo migrants. Specific arrangements examined are the ways in which human, social, and financial capital acquisition and investment are negotiated in individual and group bases, and how this has led to new definitions of the family for the migrant. In addition, this study also qualitatively examines how government policies related to the welcome afforded to, and/or the duration of stay of Nigerian migrants have evolved in the past four decades; the incentives and the constraints, and particularly how the current $300,000 business registration policy for foreigner-owned businesses stipulated by the Ghanaian government is being accepted, rejected, and circumvented (in connivance with Ghanaians) by the current crop of Nigerian migrants.

---

1   In-depth interview: Khadija, aged 28, of mixed Nigerian–Ghanaian parenthood, granddaughter of first-generation Nigerian immigrant.

Government policies vary and, of course, change over time in relation to the size and perceived characteristics of undocumented migrant populations. Governments of receiving countries adduce reasons for immigration curbs of undocumented flows, especially when there is some level of resentment on the part of the local populace to their government's management of dwindling economic fortunes. For instance, Brennan (1984) reported that during the Intergovernmental Committee on Migration (ICM) Conference (Geneva, April 1983), Nigeria's Director of Immigration Services saw a correlation between irregular migration and

> the increasing wave of armed robbery; reduction of job opportunities for Nigerians; transference of communicable diseases; sky-rocketing prices of goods; accommodation problems; inability of health facilities to cope with the teeming population; trafficking in Nigerian currency and religious disturbances.
>
> SAMBO 1983: 3

Such government policies are reactive and oftentimes inimical to the local-level integration enjoyed by the immigrant. First, official animosity to irregular immigrants runs counter to the higher degree of tolerance enjoyed by immigrants and their immediate host communities (probably due in part to cultural similarities). Second, host governments respond by sacrificing immigrants on the altar of political survival. The intervention to curb undocumented flows is based on the assumption that locals would immediately take up jobs (mostly menial) vacated by expelled immigrants, ensuring not only economic rejuvenation of families but also a safer social environment once the immigrants have gone. This expectation was not realized in Ghana after the 1970 Aliens Compliance Order; and it did not happen in Nigeria after the 1983 expulsions. Indeed, within six months of expulsion, the Ghanaians were back in Nigeria (Brydon 1985). In Ghana, Nigerians started amending their names to sound less Nigerian by adding the odd letter (e.g. changing Adebayo to Adebayor, with an added r), adopting English names such as Coker, Roland, and so on (popular in Central Region), or adopting Muslim names (as is widespread in northern Ghana).

A number of questions guided this research. What narrative is emerging from immigrants of Nigerian origin in transit at Jerusalem House? What accounts for the divergence (if any) in the main story themes? Newspaper headlines which are negative towards the average Nigerian immigrant are not few and far between, yet the Ibo traders in Jerusalem House appear to 'know their place' in Odorkor. How is this lived and negotiated? In what ways do this crop of Nigerian immigrants define the family, and how do they conveniently capture the boundary of the family in Jerusalem House? And the $300000 question: how do the Nigerian migrants cope with the institutional arrangements to curb regular as well as irregular migration flows into Ghana? Importantly, studies of migration between Ghana and Nigeria focus largely on Ghanaians in Nigeria. There are very few studies of Nigerians in Ghana; and, when found, such studies are outdated or simply current journalistic or anecdotal tales. The intention of this study is to move us into a systematic evaluation of the transit experiences of Nigerians in Ghana.

The study hereafter is divided into four sections. The first looks broadly at the movements of persons in West Africa, followed by a section on the specific connections of migration between Nigeria and Ghana. Following this are two sections that deal with the methodology of the research and the analysis of data obtained for understanding contemporary socio-economic configurations of this famous transit house.

Movements in West Africa

Large movements of people have been noted within and between the countries of West Africa (Beals et al. 1967), particularly migration for employment (Addo 1974). Receiving countries appear to be ever more diffused with migrant flows (Anarfi et al. 2003), and Nigerians play a key role in these movements (de Hass 2006). In the past century, Nigerian immigrants in Ghana were mostly of the Yoruba and Hausa ethnic stock. Assessment of social commentaries and newspaper articles in Ghana in the past decade reveals an ever-increasing arrival of the Ibo[2] group. Anecdotal evidence also indicates that while the Yoruba and Hausa seem to consider Ghana as their new home, the Ibo, now reportedly numerically superior among Nigerian immigrants, are in a constant state of flux. It is widely believed that the Ibo use Ghana as a stage in their migration process or a stepping stone to their intended final physical and/or socio-economic destination. The notion of stepwise migration, which implies a spatial relocation by steps or stages from a migrant's origin to an intended destination (invariably a more developed place), is a concept that has generated considerable empirical work and theoretical argument since Ravenstein's initial statements on migration 'laws' (Conway 1980). And, according to Beals and Menezes (1970), temporary migration is more efficient than permanent

---

2   This can be written as Ibo or Igbo.

migration. This may help to determine whether Ibo migrants perceive Ghana as an efficient stage in their migratory process.

By the second quarter of the twentieth century, Nigerians constituted the largest single group among the subjects of other British West African colonies resident in Ghana and made up a sizeable proportion of all aliens in the country. Rouch (1959) noted that in Ghana many migrants from Niger, Mali, and Nigeria were self-employed traders rather than wage labourers. Also documented was the presence of a sizeable population of emigrant traders from Nigeria, Niger, and Mali in Accra markets (Anarfi *et al.* 2000). At that time, the cocoa industry required intensive labour and provided inducements in the form of high wages (Ababio 1999). The decline in the cocoa industry in the 1970s and 1980s resulted in a dramatic fall in this kind of seasonal migration. Eades (1973) noted that large numbers of Yoruba migrants, mostly traders, had settled in Tamale during the colonial period and the early years of independence. The popular 'Lagosians', with a population of around 150,000 in 1969, were the largest group of immigrant traders in Ghana and had gained a dominant position in the country's distribution system.

Tit-for-Tat Expulsions as Foundations of Transience?

For Nigerians, the first few years after independence (1960) were a charged season of ethnic and political rivalries, *coup d'etats*, the attempted secession of Biafra, and the civil war. All these combined to push its citizens to seek greener pastures outside the country, especially in Ghana. But Busia in Ghana, elected to power in October 1969, had hinted earlier in July 1969 to embassies that foreign nationals were to be given nine months to get their papers in order or would be expelled. The July warning went unheeded; similar warnings had been issued before in West Africa but had not been acted upon.

In no time, the newly elected Busia government, on the heels of national economic misfortunes, used the popular press to label 'aliens' as scapegoats for the reversal in national progress. In November 1969, the government promulgated the Aliens Compliance Order, ordering all aliens to process their residence permits within two weeks or to leave the country. It was estimated that about 250,000 aliens that failed to comply with the order and those that could not obtain the necessary papers were expelled between December 1969 and early 1970. The majority of those affected appeared to have been Nigerian traders (Hausa and Yoruba) who had been living and working in Ghana for decades. This group had 'maintained their ethnic foci...over several generations by regular visits to and exchange of information with their home communities and by marrying members of their own ethnic groups' (Anarfi *et al.* 2000).

In the wake of deportation, affected aliens took along their capital, which destroyed a considerable part of the Ghanaian trading sector. The latter became more obvious as indigent 'Ghanaian trading aspirants lacked both the skills and the connections to be able adequately to reconstruct trade' (Anarfi *et al.* 2003). In the wider West Africa community, Ghana's Aliens Compliance Order caused considerable ill-feeling and disturbed an informal balance in relationships among states whose populations had played host to and incorporated traders and travellers for hundreds of years across the sub-region. But not all the Nigerian migrants left; many devised ways of merging into the Ghanaian socio-economic landscape. These and their subsequent generations form part of the subjects of this inquiry, as will be examined in other sections of this study.

Also, in the wake of expulsion from Ghana, some Nigerians easily relocated back to their origins, as the expulsion coincided with a time when the Nigerian civil war (1966–1970) was receding and signs of the oil boom increased the level of optimism for all and sundry. Nigeria was ushered as a wealthy country into the early 1970s with the proceeds from oil. Relative to the Ghanaian situation, petrol and machine parts were cheap and widely available in Nigeria: this, at least, was Ghanaians' perception of the situation. Therefore, it was not surprising that by the late 1970s, Ghanaians took advantage of the formal freedom to travel in West Africa, guaranteed by a charter of the Economic Community of West African States (ECOWAS) and facilitated by a relative affinity to the English-speaking country next door, and moved to look for work in Nigeria. The situation in Ghana was bad at this time, as the purchasing power of wage and salaried workers, whose incomes had been static in the public sector, was wiped out by rampant inflation (estimated at about 200% per annum). In the early 1980s, the daily minimum wage of a labourer, which was raised to 25 cedis, was hardly enough to buy a quarter of yam tuber (insufficient to prepare a meal for an adult). Ghanaians therefore thronged to Nigeria.

The arrival of Ghanaians in Nigeria was unofficially estimated at 300 migrants daily in the early 1980s. In December 1980, the Ghana High Commission in Lagos had approximately 150,000 Ghanaians duly registered. Back in Ghana, about 13% of the 163 paid-up members of the Ghana Institute of Architects had addresses in Nigeria (Asiedu 2007). Unfortunately, Nigeria's oil and economic boom waned at the end of the 1970s. A brief spurt in the early 1980s provided only a glimmer of hope, which immediately dimmed as oil prices fell further and Nigeria could not meet its balance of payments. The Nigerian public negatively received austerity measures introduced by the government; and by January 1983, the Shagari-led federal government looked towards aliens as scapegoats for Nigeria's predicament. Ghanaians constituted a very large chunk of the foreigners thus labelled. Indeed, the expulsion order of 17 January 1983 affected them in a huge way. Commentators rather saw it as a political manoeuvre on the part of Shagari to create a more favourable climate in the run-up to the national elections slated for August/September 1983.

Aliens that had official immigration papers were allowed to stay; those without papers had to leave the country by 31 January 1983. Nigeria deported about two million people in 1983, with Ghanaians constituting 45–60% of the deportees. But six months into 1983, Ghanaians had already started trickling back to Nigeria. One of the independent newspapers, *The Voice* (22–28 August edition), remarked on the return of Ghanaians, which appeared to coincide with the time after which results of Nigeria's elections had been announced. Job prospects were not bright in Ghana, both in the short and medium terms, prompting many to return to Nigeria to eke out a living. Research conducted by Brydon (1985) revealed that the kinds of work Ghanaian men reported their unskilled female counterparts engaged in included prostitution (in hotels, beer bars, and wayside uncompleted buildings), while some of the skilled women who had regular jobs still practised prostitution after the closing time of their jobs.

The 1983 expulsions of Ghanaians from Nigeria were not direct reprisals for the 1969/70 effects of the Aliens Compliance Order, which had affected hundreds of thousands of Nigerians. Brydon (*ibid.*) suggested that both acts were rather 'expressions of political and economic frustration and in the context of both Nigeria and Ghana's relations with the North'. And indeed, 'what remains to be explained is the presence of so many Ghanaians in Nigeria and, earlier, of so many Nigerians in Ghana'. Why, only a year after the 1983 decrees (and the subsequent misery of thousands on the journey home), were Ghanaians, and others, now back in Nigeria? And why, or perhaps how, had the Nigerians permitted them to come back (*ibid.*)?

Recently in Ghana, the presence of Nigerians has been estimated at 1 million,[3] about 5% of all inhabitants of Ghana. If this is to be viewed in terms of the electoral fortunes of Ghanaian politicians, this proportion counts for recognition in the political landscape. On the socio-economic front, the Governor of Nigeria's Central Bank indicated that about 71,000 Nigerian students are being schooled in Ghana, spending up to $1 billion a year. Chairman of the Committee of Pro-Chancellors of Nigerian Universities Wale Babalakin stated that Nigerian students number 75,000 in Ghana, paying about $15 million to

---

3   Information obtained from Nigeria Embassy, Accra.

Ghanaian schools.[4] Irrespective of the kinds of assessments conducted, the influx of Nigerians and the size of the Nigerian population in Ghana and their economic contributions are of no small measure. Size indeed matters; so does distribution and structure of the population.

This dynamic also accounts for why it is important to examine the socio-economic configuration of Nigerian immigrants, specifically of contemporary Ibo migrants in transit at Jerusalem House. How did Jerusalem House come about, and what accounts for its importance as a transit point for the Ibo of Nigeria? Perhaps the non-related expulsions created a mindset of short stays in the minds of latter-day migrants? This study examines how Jerusalem House is governed and why it is unique compared with the transit experience of earlier migrants from Nigeria.

Methodology

In order to achieve the objectives of this study, qualitative information was obtained from two categories of Nigerians in Ghana. On one hand are the second- and third-generation Nigerians who straddle Nigerian/Ghanaian identity; on the other hand are the Ibos, new arrivals who are generally considered as first-generation Ibo arrivals. The study relies extensively on in-depth interviews[5] of individuals who fell into these two categories, particularly the occupants of Jerusalem House in the Odorkor suburb of Accra. Near this location, a focus group discussion (FGD) was also conducted for a homogenous group of third-generation Yoruba who had earlier lived with their parents in Anagokoji-Ho in Volta Region. Secondary statistical data on the numbers and diversity of Nigerian migrants in Ghana were obtained from the Nigerian Embassy and the Ghana Statistical Service (GSS), as well as from the extant literature on the history and profile of Nigerians in Ghana.

During the individual and FGD enquiries, a number of subjective measures related to 'success' (employment, trade, acquisition of assets, and investment in children's education) were examined, along with more qualitative evaluations of 'transience'. This facilitated the assessment of how the sense of belonging, solidarity, family obligation, and protection in an uncertain and risky environment were important for different actors.

---

4   *The National Mirror*, 18 October 2012, http://www.nationalmirroronline.net/new/burgeoning
    -nigerian-student-population-in-ghana.

5   Special thanks to Mr Salim Abdul Bature (a.k.a. Alhaji); he was instrumental to the identifica-
    tion of respondents.

Brief Description of the Samples

The age range of most respondents fell between 20 and 42 years. In Jerusalem House, the respondents were essentially males, as they formed nearly 99% of all tenants living in the building. This skewed sampling has inherent biases for the interpretation of data, but this was an exploratory study and I was mainly concerned with having categories of Nigerian immigrants (of working age) represented in sufficient numbers. Males form the bulk of migrants.

There is a general perception that Ibos are more numerous than other Nigerian groups, despite their relatively recent arrival in Ghana compared with that of the Hausa and Yoruba. Despite their larger number, however, they are mainly short stayers. It appears that temporary migration is more efficient than permanent migration; hence, it becomes more increasingly difficult for the Ibo migrant to define where 'home' is. A feature of the social system of Ibo migrants in Ghana is community identity, found in associations that are formal manifestations of migrant social networks (Bosiakoh 2009). Governance of an association (whose members were interviewed for this study) is unique by virtue of the fact that the main leader for a time period is not necessarily a permanent resident of Ghana, but he maintains a business there which he comes around regularly to manage.

Results Jerusalem House

Jerusalem House is owned by Adjettey Sowah, a Ghanaian aged 74 years at the time of interview in August 2013. He proudly informed us that he is related to a famous family of reverends, musicians, and footballers. Located in Odorkor, Jerusalem House is actually a cluster of three houses, two L-shaped and one a short block of about five rooms, all huddled together to form a compound. The gaps between the houses serve as entry points. There is no main gate; perhaps the main entrance might be considered as the one near the larger dirt road. Entering through this point, immediately on the visitor's left is a room that serves as a shop, run by the wife of Adjettey Sowah. Items sold in this room may be termed modern-day petty items that are ubiquitous in the informal sector: mobile phone recharge cards, cooking condiments, sweets, etc. But business is brisk as customers with different needs troop in and out. The shop lady appears forever busy, as indeed is the entire compound. Her shop is the first room in the L-shaped building of many rooms occupied by different tenants, mostly Nigerians. To the extreme right, at the end of this long L-shape, is a shorter

L-shaped building. The first room here is a chapel, where the owner of Jerusalem House consented to be interviewed.

Mr Sowah has considerable worldwide travel experience, which he gained when he represented Ghana at the highest international level of table tennis. In the early 1970s, he used to visit Nigeria primarily to participate in table tennis competitions. He made friends there and encouraged them to visit him whenever they came to Accra. The first Nigerian to take up the invitation was an Ibo man who trades in electrical sockets, which he obtained from Japan and sold in Nigeria and Ghana. Over time, this trader became a regular visitor who also introduced other Nigerian traders to stay at Mr Sowah's house whenever they were on business trips to Accra. The proceeds he made from short-term rents were used for the construction of two other buildings, bringing the total to three—the cluster of buildings called Jerusalem House. Though he grew up as a strong Muslim, diverse religious groups he had encountered during his travel to international competitions always fascinated him. After an international game in Mexico in 1978, he devoted more time to comparative study of Islam and Christianity. He encountered the name 'old Jerusalem' and 'new Jerusalem' in the Bible and this inspired him. His conversion to Christianity took place when he prayed on 7 December 2001, in the Christian way, that the convulsions one of his sons suffered from for years would cease. He recalled that it was a powerful moment when the boy's body trembling stopped, and at that moment he urged his wife that they convert to Christianity. 'I named my residence Jerusalem House immediately.'

The positive reputation of Jerusalem House was enhanced by an event that started negatively as a police raid:

> On a tip-off, one day security agents came to my house to arrest Nigerians without reason. There were allegations they deal in bad activities, which I challenged. I had a dream of this police invasion. They searched to no avail. Apparently somebody gave them a wrong tip-off. I showed them records of the Nigerian tenants that I have—their names, days of entry, kinds of business they do. I even know some of their houses in Nigeria. Dealers of motor spare parts, including Ghanaian businessmen based in Mokola, Kaneshie all rushed to my place when they learned of the police attempt to arrest Nigerians in my house. Later I was invited to the central police headquarters, where the police explained the arrest attempt. Especially they were surprised at the type of information I had on my tenants that absolved them of the allegations of dealing in drugs. From that time, Jerusalem House had a good reputation with the police and

neighbours, such that if any Nigerian is known to be residing here, then there is no fear that he might be up to any bad activity.

Interview with ADJETTEY SOWAH, Jerusalem House

Opinions differ on the exact number of occupants of Jerusalem House. The landlord estimated 'there are about 50 tenants here'. Nigerians interviewed in Odorkor claimed there are about a hundred living there at any given time. They live in about 12 rooms, and the landlord keeps a list of all the Nigerians who have ever stayed there, including details of their passports and commercial activities. While this list is a treasure trove of archival information on Nigerian travellers, it appears that the landlord is a pseudo-official of Ghana's immigration department. Mr Sowah claimed he prefers to have a steady stream of Nigerians who are engaged in genuine businesses and use his place as transit accommodation when they visit Accra on business trips. Yet, Jerusalem House is not a hotel; some of such visitors have been staying there in the medium term. The steady stream of renters also guarantees him appreciable income. Earnings from table tennis games were used for the construction of the first building in the cluster; rents paid by tenants financed the construction of the additional two buildings when he retired from table tennis. Ibo traders who are always on the move provided steady rent; and given the media landscape that is awash with stories of 'bad Nigerians', he dealt only with the good ones and preserved the reputation of Jerusalem House with the register he tendered in the aftermath of the police raid on the premises.

The arrival of Nigerians and the steady stream in and out of Jerusalem House had been causing jitters in the neighbourhood. This is in the context of a media awash with stories of Nigerians involved in dirty business elsewhere in Ghana. Moreover, the Nigerians come from Lagos, a city with its own reputation enhanced by myths and realities of returnee Ghanaians and the fabled 'Lagosians', as Nigerians were referred to in the 1960s in Ghana. Opinion is divided as to whether the landlord of Jerusalem House is an agent of the state that wants to keep tabs on Nigerians. Why else would he document Nigerian tenants? On the other hand, despite Jerusalem House not being an annex of Ghana's immigration office, Nigerian tenants are willing to submit copies of their papers to him. For some of the traders, their regular trips from and to Nigeria mean they need an ever-ready, suitable accommodation point when they are in Accra, one that is cheaper than a hotel and where familiar faces reside. Submitting documents and being regular visitors indemnifies the migrants against the toil and hardship of looking for new accommodation in subsequent visits on business.

Jerusalem House does not harbour the prejudice or stigma migrants may suffer elsewhere. Most of these traders have no registered businesses and conduct their commercial activities in the informal sector. In fact, one of them that retails ceramic floor tiles claims to do his business by showing samples to drivers at vantage points on road junctions or pedestrian crossings. Interested buyers are encouraged to get out of their cars to inspect other designs in a nearby kiosk. He gets buyers in this way and thus continues his trade. Also, in this way, he does not pay any form of tax to the state; and since his business is not registered, he is technically exempted from paying the $300,000 refundable registration fee required by the Ghanaian government for foreign business owners to operate in Ghana.

This registration charge by the government has been generating uproar for the past two years. The government introduced the levy to dissuade foreigners from encroaching into small-scale and medium enterprises and to favour the majority Ghanaians interested in business. The Nigerians, who appear to be dominating small and medium enterprises, see the levy as acting against the spirit of ECOWAS, and protests have sprung up on a few occasions. Foreigners are required to obtain a residence permit if they wish to stay more than 90 days or to engage in economic work. The Ibo traders stay less than 90 days during business trips; many conduct trading activities or businesses that are not duly registered (thus tax-free for profits made or goods sold). Nigerians claim that they are in commercial activities that Ghanaians would not necessarily engage in. Moreover, Ghanaian customers do not pay for goods in bulk; they pay in bits and pieces, and this suits the average Ibo trader, as long as the customer is indebted to him. Thus the Ibo traders see themselves as essential to the functioning of the Ghanaian economy in Accra, and indeed meet the needs of average Ghanaians.

Examples include a 39-year old male who deals in motor spare parts imported from Nigeria. He has been doing business in Accra for nearly seven years and presently resides in Odorkor. He used to live with his older brother in Jerusalem House, but his brother has relocated to Swaziland. He is likely to move to Swaziland when his visa is ready. This trader is now less enthusiastic about doing business in Ghana:

> Ghanaians prefer to make periodic payments for goods bought, so it takes longer to accumulate profits. Also, the $300,000 business registration law has tainted the business climate; it is not clear if ECOWAS and Nigerian government has approved this requirement for Ghana to demand this from ECOWAS citizens.

Another male, aged 29 years, who hails from Enugu (southeast Nigeria), has been trading between Nigeria and Ghana for the past four months. He lives in

Jerusalem House. He does deals in shoe trading and shipping mobile phone accessories into Ghana from Nigeria.

The occupants of Jerusalem House meet daily in the chapel before going out on business.

> We are a family here; all tenants participate in morning devotion in the chapel before going out on daily activities. I initially wanted to divide this chapel location into two for my grandchildren, but the Lord told me that I should reserve the space as a house chapel for morning devotion for my family and the tenants, every weekday from 6.30 to 7.30 hours.
>
> Interview with ADJETTEY SOWAH, Jerusalem House

Mr. Sowah also records that a good proportion of the Ibo that transit through Jerusalem House do not return to Nigeria, but they move on to southern Africa: Zimbabwe, Mozambique, etc. This stepwise migration was confirmed by some of the Ibo tenants of Jerusalem House, interviewed at a popular restaurant noted for serving Nigerian food, particularly *gari* and vegetable stew, a delicacy of the Ibo. Originally from Imo State, the 42-year old lady restaurant owner has been living in Accra for 12 years because she got married to a Ghanaian man.

> On arrival in Accra, I lived first in Jerusalem House in Odorkor, which had more than a hundred tenants, mostly of Imo State origin at that time. Now, most of them have moved on to Angola, Mozambique, and South Africa. They used to bring goods [from Nigeria] to sell in Accra, but differentials in exchange rate between the cedi and naira affected their profit margins, and it made them relocate to southern Africa.
>
> Interview at restaurant, Odorkor, August 2013

The restaurant owner's husband sells building materials in partnership with the aforementioned Nigerian 36-year old trader (who retails floor tiles by showing samples to motorists held up briefly at traffic lights). According to this trader:

> The $300,000 registration fee story is true, but it can only affect those who are registered or those established in Makola market. I am not affected. I have been staying with my 'cousin', who also sells aluminium doors in Accra for the past three years. But I will stay one more year; then I will move to Swaziland.
>
> Interview at restaurant, Odorkor, August 2013

Accra is increasingly used as a stepping stone to greener pastures in other countries by the Ibo migrant traders. Jerusalem House serves as a buffer transit zone in the travel process, ranging from as little as three months' stay to as much as four years. In Jerusalem House Nigerian migrants see each other as family—brothers, cousins—irrespective of blood ties. They assemble monthly in a 'family meeting', a form of migrant association. This is similar to Yusuf's (2015: 154) findings in northern Nigeria, where it was found that one prominent development arising from the presence of migrants was the establishment of community and home town associations in the places of transit or host communities. In Accra, migrant associations were established to foster understanding and socio-economic interactions among members; they are important aspects of economic arrangements or social welfare opportunities for faster integration of the migrant. For instance, meetings are used as platforms for addressing issues of common interest and settling disputes, as well as for social interactions. This serves a dual purpose: the migrants do not lose touch with home, as they maintain contact through the association, and such associations also help new arrivals adjust to the new environment, especially when migrants share the same town or Nigerian state of origin. The associations also function as channels through which monetary remittances can be sent home to Nigeria, in cases of emergency or periodic transfers for investment in private development projects. The remittances are rarely recorded (unlike the action of the Lagos colonial administration), as they are sent through private individuals of the association. Also in Jerusalem House, the association gives members easier access to loans not accessible to them in the formal banking sector.

According to a Nigerian trader who deals in electrical fittings for houses and brings products from Nigeria, there is no long-term prospect of solidifying his business base in Ghana. This is blamed on the slow rate of profit turnover, on the back of the poor system of payment for goods purchased by Ghanaian customers and the unfavourable naira–cedi exchange rate.

> As a businessman and trader, I will go to China where I have contacts, mainly Nigerian friends. I don't need a permanent accommodation here, so I stay in Jerusalem House. We hold family meetings so that we extend help to each other in times of individual difficulties. For example, foreigners do not have access to loans from Ghanaian banks. Sometimes, whether business is good or bad, we give loans[6] to members to finance

---

6   Others interviewees added that Nigerians meet in different ethnic associations monthly— the Ibos, Yoruba, and Hausa. Essentially, these associations are led by chairmen, and the associations do not have a political orientation/agenda. They render financial help to members that are sick or have problems with the police.

business, about N100,000 (approximately $500) maximum, which attracts 5% interest, payable within four months. Bulk of the money is from monthly contributions of members. If a borrower defaults, the law guiding administration of loans, it attracts extra interest: it forces members to render account at appropriate time, which helps others to access loans. Despite poor business environment, nobody wants to return to Nigeria as failure.

The pattern of stay is different when compared with first-generation Yoruba migrants. They were petty traders who conducted their businesses in the Ghanaian hinterland, moving from one locality to another.

The Yoruba are spread in rural areas. They are petty traders in the hinterland, and they move from one locality to the other. These localities have different market days. The Yoruba traders explore this by displaying their wares at different markets on special market days for localities. Sometimes, where they make more profit, they settle there for longer period. One of such places is Anagokoji in Ho, in the Volta Region. Anago means Yoruba; koji is community, thus Anagokoji is Yoruba community.

When our great-grandfathers came, they were merchants; the Ghanaian chiefs welcomed them and gave them parcels of land in the outskirts of Ho in the Volta Region, a century ago. Such lands in the outskirts looked barren at that time, and the immigrants from Nigeria virtually got parcels for free. Gradually, over time, the immigrants put up residential buildings as they traded; others went into farming and made adjoining lands agriculturally productive where possible, and the place got a life of its own. It became a locality you could find Yoruba Nigerians. New immigrants automatically went there to start new lives; and ways of Yoruba life for weddings, child naming ceremonies, funerals, and other celebrations were conducted in the Yoruba way. There is a recognized leader of the Yoruba in Anagokodzi. The title is Asaju [leader].

ALHAJI AND SIBLINGS, interviewed at their residence in Odorkor, Accra, 31 August 2013

According to the interviewed descendants of migrants of Yoruba origin, Nigerians dominate commerce in Ghana because of Nigeria's larger population and economy. They alluded to the fact that most of the goods and commodities traded in Ghana are imported from Nigeria, though more Chinese people and goods seem to be coming from China in recent times.

If you go to Kwame Nkrumah Circle, all the mobile phone shops are occupied [owned] by Nigerians. At night, all enjoyment and entertainment
spots are full of Nigerians. Yoruba and Ibo are widely spoken in the streets
of Accra as if you are in Nigeria. In Mokola market and Tudu [the local
and international bus terminal], half of the population are Nigerians.
Now, they even speak the Ga [vernacular in Greater Accra region] more
than the Ghanaians. Those people have no reason to stay permanently in
Ghana to become Ghanaians; they go back to Nigeria every now and
then. They don't have roots here.

ALHAJI, interviewed at residence in Odorkor, Accra, 31 August 2013

There are some transit houses like Jerusalem House in Odorkor where Ibo
people stay first in before moving out to other places in Accra. Such
houses can be traced. But let us be careful; we classify all other Nigerian
who is not Yoruba or Hausa as Ibo. As things stand today, the Ibo will
outnumber any other tribe of Nigerian origin in Ghana. The unfortunate
incidence of 1969, where Busia government confiscated houses, saw many
leave Ghana. But it has not deterred Nigerians from coming to Ghana.
Even then, many of those affected used ingenious schemes to bypass the
evacuation order and stay in Ghana. Ibo people don't stay for long; they
only come here for business and leave after a short while. Maybe they fear
another evacuation order. We see now that new orders are indirect.

ALHAJI, interviewed at residence in Odorkor, Accra, 31 August 2013

Nigerian traders in Ghana have been under pressure to move out by the local
authorities at the instance of their Ghanaian counterparts. At first came the
$300,000 registration fee charged by Ghanaian authorities for all foreign busi-
ness owners (small or large), in order to allow them to operate or continue
operations in Ghana. Also, the year 2014 was one of turbulence and instability
for Nigerian traders in ten regions of Ghana, as the Ghana Ministry of Trade
and Industry threatened to implement the Ghana Investment Promotion
Centre (GIPC) Act, 2013 (Act 865), which prohibits foreign[7] traders from trading in its 48 markets across the country.[8]

---

7   Nigeria and other ECOWAS member countries are recognized by Ghana's constitution as for-
    eign, despite the existence of the ECOWAS protocol on sub-regional trade, which gives some
    leverage to nationals of member states.
8   A. Oluwapelumi, 'For Nigerian Traders in Ghana, It's Still No Respite in Sight', *Nigerian
    Tribune*, 3 November 2014, http://www.afrisonet.com/2014/11/for-nigerian-traders-in-ghana
    -its-still.html.

In September 2014, the ministry issued a 30-day ultimatum to all foreign traders to quit the local markets or else face eviction and be prosecuted in a court that will be set up to prosecute foreign retail traders. In a press release, it stated the following:

> Despite numerous interventions by the government to encourage non-Ghanaians engaged in retail trading in the market place to relocate, some non-Ghanaians have refused to comply with the directive. The non-Ghanaians who further contravene the provisions of the Act 865 in the GIPC Law 2013 shall be prosecuted.

According to the National President of the Nigeria Union of Traders Association in Ghana (NUTAG), Deacon John Ukala: 'We actually don't know what to do any longer about...the Ghanaian government.' (Oluwapelumi, 2014). He said that against the backdrop of the threat to implement GIPC Act 865, many of the members of NUTAG had returned to Nigeria. When most of them suffered huge losses during the lock-down of about 150 shops owned by Nigerians in Accra and Kumasi, which occurred between 2007 and 2014, they still had over one hundred members in Accra alone. Ukala estimated that Nigerian traders could have numbered over 10,000, though not all of them were registered with NUTAG

A section of Nigerian traders believes that market competition favoured Nigerians, and the fact that they had more customers because they did not make their goods as expensive as their Ghanaian counterparts was behind the threat to implement the GIPC Act 865. The Act is turning Ghana into an unfavourable business climate, which will not help Ibo traders stay in the country. Nigeria's Ambassador to Ghana, Mr Onafowokan, in a press conference with selected Nigerian journalists on 23 October 2014, explained that the embassy sought for the possibility of allocating land for a Nigerian market in Accra from Ghana's Deputy Minister of Trade and Industry, who in turn promised to liaise with Ghana's Minister of Trade and Industry. As the ambassador pointed out:

> The bond of friendly nations should not be dampened by irritant issues of trade, economics, culture and diplomacy, which are against the spirit of ECOWAS treaties which are in force and of which the two countries are signatories.
>
> OLUWAPELUMI 2014

He further assured the press conference: 'Ghanaian authorities will allow Nigerian traders in Ghana to continue their petty trading, pending the time

land will be allocated for Nigerian traders by the government of Ghana.'
(Nigeria Ambassador, quoted in Oluwapelumi 2014). This may eventually
develop into another zone of transit.

Ghana's Minister of Trade, Dr Ekwow Spio-Garbrah, sounded a conciliatory
note:

> [E]ven as we point out the non-Ghanaians that are infringing our laws
> and the Ghanaians who may be accommodating them, let us also be
> mindful of the potential impact from a reciprocity point of view when it
> comes to international relations. There may be Ghanaians also involved
> in all kinds of petty trading, shop-keeping activities in neighbouring
> countries. If we take that action, these countries have similar laws, and if
> they choose to enforce them, then we could have some very interesting
> situations. And that is not what we are looking for, where we have tit for
> tat type of activity in the ECOWAS region.
>
> OLUWAPELUMI 2014

Conclusion

The traditional migration configuration of Nigerians in Ghana is undergoing
rapid change in terms of Nigerian composition (Yoruba, Hausa, now Ibo) and
perception of the country as being simultaneously a place of destination and
transit for migrants of Nigerian origin. Accra remains the point of destination
for the Ibo. Although the Yoruba are also found in Accra, in mixed population
with Hausa in predominantly Muslim neighbourhoods (Nima, New Town,
Tudu), the Yoruba are more spread out to smaller towns, sometimes homogenous in those localities but politically diverse in structure.

Migration has been a well-established part of life for most Yoruba and Ibo.
Their use of Ghana as a spring board to prosperity and greener pastures
appears similar at the onset but divergent in the medium term in respect of
length of stay. For the Yoruba, the initial attraction was based on feedback
obtained from workers who left Lagos to build the rail network to the mines in
Ghana. Gold mining and trading opportunities abound was the message, and
thus other Yoruba left southwest Nigeria in search of gold over a century ago.
Trading opportunities appeal to the new migrants—the Ibo, who eventually use Ghana as a springboard for South–South migration to Angola and
Mozambique and the Far East.

Perhaps caution has been built into the minds of the Ibo traders and their
itinerant approach to trading, so as not to see Ghana as a place of destination.

This is reinforced against a backdrop of mutual deportations and the recent introduction of a $300,000 fee for business registration, a fee which has seen many relocate to Nigeria or elsewhere in Africa.

Ibo traders continue the centuries-old migration of Nigerians to Ghana and not necessarily using routes that were pioneered by Yoruba migrants. The configuration of connectivity has changed, in terms of composition of migrants and local populations, of socio-economic dynamics, and of political realities. New social realities are being created for newfound acceptance in the continuously changing faces of Nigerians in one location and their diverse economic endeavours. The faces of the cohorts of occupants are changing, but their main profile, as traders, remains the same.

Jerusalem House has multiple layers as a zone of transit. It mediates a specific zone of interaction, official and unofficial, binding people's behaviour through the conscious use of religion and a pseudo-government agency. It earned its reputation for unconnected reasons: it is a physical and economic buffer zone on the Ibo traders' route to prosperity. Perhaps the weekday morning devotions are symptomatic of the command-and-control mindset of a former athlete, who has been used to regimen for years, dating back to the time when he was on top of his game. The records compiled by Adjettey Sowah represent an archival treasure trove of profiles of Nigerians for a future study.

Economic relations have brought Ibo migrants into direct contact with locals, thus fostering social relations. This development has eroded encumbrances, dispelled myths of Nigerians as wild, and led to the integration of many Lagosians, as Nigerians were called, into the society. The first generations of Ibo immigrants were traders who did not display any intention to settle in Ghana for long periods. Despite the networks and membership of associations, many of them did not and will not assimilate totally into Ghanaian society. Their temporary stays in Ghana and relatively frequent shuttling to and from Nigeria to restock their shops have implications for quite a number of them to develop plural identities: one useful for Ghana, and the other for Nigeria (or their next stage of migration). As Falola has indicated, not every migrant wants to integrate; some prefer to be outsiders, in which their 'outsidedness' is also a source of power.[9]

---

9   T. Falola, a talk at the Black Atlantic Lecture entitled 'Historicizing Black Atlantic, Comparative, Colonialism, Transnational and Citizenship', at Vanderbilt University, 10 February 2011, cited in Yusuf (2015: 153).

References

Ababio, O. (1999), *Gold Mining in Adansi, Precolonial and Modern*. Department of History. Legon: University of Ghana.

Addo, N.O. (1974), Foreign Workers in Ghana. *International Labour Review* 109(1).

Adepoju, A. (2003), Migration in West Africa. *Development* 46(3): 37–41.

Anarfi, J.K., K. Awusabo-Asare *et al.* (2000), Push and Pull Factors of International Migration. Country Report: Ghana. Eurostat Working Papers 2000/E(10).

Anarfi, J., S. Kwankye, O.-M. Ababio & R. Tiemoko (2003), Migration from and to Ghana: A Background Paper. Working Paper C4, Development Research Centre on Migration, Globalisation and Poverty, University of Sussex.

Asiedu, Alex B. (2007), "Some developmental effects of international migration of skilled labor from Ghana", Department of Geography and Resource Development, University of Ghana, Legon. Accessed online March 2015, http://uaps2007.princeton .edu/papers/70447.

Beals, R.E., M.B. Levy & L.N. Moses (1967), Rationality and Migration in Ghana. *The Review of Economics and Statistics* 49(4): 480–486.

Beals, R.E. & R.E. Menezes (1970), Migrant Labour and Agricultural Output in Ghana. Oxford Economic Papers 22(CD): 109–127.

Bosiakoh, T.A. (2009), The Role of Migrant Associations in Adjustment, Integration and Development: The Case of Nigerian Migrant Associations in Accra, Ghana. http://www.imi.ox.ac.uk/pdfs/notes/antwi-bosiakoh.pdf. Accessed 15 July 2015.

Brennan, E.M. (1984), Irregular Migration: Policy Responses in Africa and Asia. *International Migration Review* 18(3): 409–425. (Special Issue: Irregular Migration: An International Perspective.)

Brydon, L. (1985), Ghanaian Responses to the Nigerian Expulsions of 1983. *African Affairs* 84(337): 561–585.

Conway, D. (1980), Step-wise Migration: Toward a Clarification of the Mechanism. *International Migration Review* 14(1): 3–14.

Eades, J.S. (1973), *Strangers and Traders: Yoruba Migrants, Markets and the State in Northern Ghana*. Edinburgh University Press.

Haas, H. de (2006), International Migration and National Development: Viewpoints and Policy Initiatives in Countries of Origin. The Case of Nigeria. Working papers, Migration and Development series, Report 6, December, International Migration Institute.

Oluwapelumi, A. (2014), 'For Nigerian Traders in Ghana, It's Still No Respite in Sight', http://www.afrisonet.com/2014/11/for-nigerian-traders-in-ghana-its-still.html. Accessed 15 July 2015.

Peil, M. (1974), Ghana's Aliens. *International Migration Review* 8(3): 367–381.

Rouch, J. (1959), The Study of Migration. *West Africa* 29: 417–419.

Sambo, L. (1983), 'Information Paper on Nigeria's Quit Order on Illegal Aliens'. Paper presented at Inter-governmental Committee for Migration (ICM), Seminar on Undocumented Migrants or Migrants in an Irregular Situation, Geneva, April 11–15.

Tsey, K. (2013), *From Head-Loading to the Iron Horse: Railway Building in Colonial Ghana and the Origins of Tropical Development*. Mankon, Bamenda: Langaa Research and Publishing CIG, p. 69.

Yusuf, S.T. (2015), The Socio-Economic Impact of the Railway in Northern Nigeria: A Study in Transformation of the Rural Communities Along the Rail Line Between Kano and Zaria. PhD Thesis, Institute of History, Leiden University.

CHAPTER 14

Ghanaian Migrants in the Netherlands: Germany as a Transit Zone

Amisah Zenabu Bakuri[1]

Preface

As part of my Research Master programme at the University of Groningen, I was required to do an internship; and, fortunately, I had an internship opportunity with the African Studies Centre (ASC) in Leiden. At the ASC I worked with the collaborative research group 'Roads to Prosperity'. I was required to write a research paper on 'transit' migration. As a Ghanaian and with my initial curiosity in the term *burger*—a term used in Ghana in reference to any individual who has travelled outside the country—I decided to conduct research on Ghanaians in the Netherlands who had come via Germany. This is basically because the term *burger* is contested. It is often argued to be derived from the German city Hamburg, but it means 'migrant' in general, regardless of whether the migrant in question actually settles in Hamburg or elsewhere. I wondered whether the term *burger* was indeed a reference to Hamburger, someone who lived in Hamburg, or to the Dutch *burger*, which means citizen, or to the German *burger*, which also meaning citizen—since some Ghanaian migrants have acquired citizenship status in these European states. Hence, this background informed my choice of Germany and the Netherlands to understand both transit migration and Ghanaian migrants in the Netherlands on their roads to socio-economic prosperity.

Introduction

At present, nearly all countries in the world are concurrently countries of origin, destination, and transit for international migrants. The growing complexity of migratory patterns and their influence on development have all contributed to migration becoming a priority for in-depth research. Ghanaian migrants are an example of a migrant group that maintains strong familial ties

---

[1] Special thanks to all 'Roads to Prosperity' research members, especially Rijk van Dijk, for their useful comments on this paper.

and bonds between host communities and people back in Ghana (Akyeampong 2000; Van Dijk 2001; Asiedu 2005; Arthur 2008). This paper presents the findings and analysis of a snowball sampling of 12 Ghanaian migrants (*burgers*) currently based in the Netherlands who came via Germany. For them, Germany was a place of transit.

Some *burgers* pass through (transit) several countries before reaching their final destination. There are a number of factors involved that cause migrants to go through other countries, such as distance between Ghana and destination countries, attachment to native place, difficulty in acquiring a visa or inability to get residence permits or work permits, travelling cost, maintenance of double establishments, social condemnation, migratory laws, discouragement by recipient countries, language, religion, and customs. An established misconception about migration is that it is usually seen as a simple move from one place to another (Skeldon 1997); however, migration is a very dynamic process.

This study explores the experiences of some *burgers* in the Netherlands who came through Germany. In particular, this paper answers the question of why migrants stay 'in transit' and what their experiences are in transit. Focusing on the interviews conducted, the research will also discover whether the interviewees perceived Germany as a place of transit or Germany became a place of transit over time. Questions such as why some Ghanaians move to Germany, why they continue on to the Netherlands, and what connections they maintain with their home country will be answered.

Concepts and Theories

Many concepts and theories have been used in migration studies. For the purpose of this research, transit migration, transnational migration, and chain migration will be discussed. Much emphasis will be placed on transit migration, as several studies have already explored migration concepts such as transnationalism and chain migration.[2] Broadly speaking, transnationalism refers to multiple ties and interactions linking people or institutions across several nation states, therefore spreading mobility across the globe. New technologies, particularly telecommunications, serve to connect people all over the world, making many people belong to more than one society or country at the same time (Levitt 2004; Levitt & Schiller 2004). Chain migration can be simply defined as that migration pattern where prospective migrants benefit

---

2   See Caldwell (1968); Levitt, DeWind & Vertovec (2003); Østergaard-Nielsen (2003); Fong, Cao & Chan (2010).

from their primary relationship with previous migrants on the opportunities (transportation, accommodation, employment, organizations) available at destination countries (MacDonald & MacDonald 1964).

The Concept of Transit Migration

> [...] transit is an extremely fluid concept, and therefore a tricky socio-logical object, which is difficult to define, operationalize, and capture empirically, and which is subject to several biases influenced by highly politicized discourse. Notwithstanding, as a result of this complexity, the transit phenomenon needs to be further problematized and studied [...].
>
> CASTAGNONE 2011: 3

Transit migration as a term has persisted in discussions of migration, but its nature, meaning, usefulness, and appropriateness have been undecided and can be challenged (Cassarino & Fargues 2006; Düvell 2006, 2008; Castagnone 2011). The changing aspirations and motives of migrants with time make it very difficult to explain transit migration; hence, different meanings have been given to the notion of transit migration (Papadopoulou 2009).

In between origin and destination in migration, some situations with certain factors impede the movement of a person to the actual (intended) destination, often leading to transit. Such factors are varied and diverse. These factors can be positive for some migrants, and the same factors may be negative for others and neutral for still others (Düvell 2006; Collyer, Düvell & de Haas 2012).

Transit migrants enter and reside (voluntarily or involuntarily, planned or unplanned) in a country for various amounts of time with the intention of obtaining access to a third country/countries (Pitea 2010). Migrants are often prevented or hindered from continuing their migration journey and may end up 'stranded' in what was originally thought to be their transit country. Transit zones (countries) can become (in)voluntary destinations because some migrants may choose to settle in places as a second-best option, while other migrants are forced to stay 'waiting' for their opportunity to make the next step of their journey on their road to prosperity. Migration does not definitely end when someone stays for some years in a specific destination. For many migrants, migration consists of repeated moves and temporary settlements; their plans and dreams, as well as the available migration opportunities, are rather more variable than fixed.

In summary, regardless of the intentions of migrants, their journey and/or travel plans may change over time. A final destination can actually turn out to be only one step in a much larger journey; on the other hand, a short stopover can end up as a final destination. In this paper we argue that transit migration can only be known retrospectively, which is the main reason that migrants in this study were interviewed to connect transit migration to their migration processes in general.

The whole concept of transit migration is very complex and needs to be inquired into in depth through a comprehensive and critical approach. To help understand transit migration, this study looks at some Ghanaian migrants based in the Netherlands. Transit migration in this paper is understood as part of a broader migration process; and in doing so, some of the unanswered questions in (transit) migration will be answered through interviews.

Migration History of Ghana

West African populations have had a phenomenal predisposition for mobility over a long period of time (Arthur 1991; Adepoju 2002; DFID 2004; Adepoju 2005; de Haas 2007). This is notably true in the case of Ghana, where migration enjoys a long tradition. Migration in Ghana exhibits a changing pattern of movement in response to opportunity structures at destinations as well as conditions in Ghana (Schans *et al.* 2013). It has been noted that from the end of the 1960s, however, Ghana ceased to be a receiving country for migrants and became a major sending country in Sub-Saharan Africa as a whole (Tonah 2007).

Approximately 10–15% of the total Ghanaian population are said to live abroad (Peil 1974). As there are no central statistics about Ghanaian migrants, various figures have been given for Ghanaians living abroad (Tonah 2007). For instance, Peil (1995) notes that an estimated more than 12% of the entire Ghanaian population lived abroad in 1995. Bump (2006) estimated about 10–20% of the population of Ghana lived abroad in the mid-1990s. The greater number of migrants can be located on the African continent, especially in West African cities (Anarfi *et al.* 2003). Since the end of apartheid in South Africa in the mid-1990s, countries in southern Africa have become especially attractive to Ghanaian migrants.

A considerable number of Ghanaian migrants live in the UK (the former colonizer),[3] with others distributed across the US, Canada, the Netherlands, Spain, Italy, and Germany. Consequently, sizeable Ghanaian migrant communities have emerged in European cities such as London, Hamburg, Frankfurt, Milan, Naples, and Amsterdam.

---

3 Traditionally, Ghanaian have found their way to the UK, owing to historical ties and knowledge of the English language.

Ghanaians in Germany

The Ghanaian diaspora is noted as the largest migrant group from Sub-Saharan Africa in Germany.[4] However, available statistics do not provide comprehensive figures to enhance discussion and analysis of Ghanaians in Germany. This challenge is not limited to Germany alone but occurs also in other countries, owing to 'illegal' or undocumented migrants.

In 2007, the German Federal Statistics Office estimated 20,329 Ghanaian citizens were official residents in Germany. It also noted that about 8,194 Ghanaian citizens became German citizens between 1980 and 2007 (GTZ 2009). These are the figures provided by the Federal Statistics Office, but unofficially it has been estimated that about twice this number of undocumented Ghanaian migrants live in Germany. This could be as a result of some migrants entering with a valid visa and overstaying the visa duration without a residence permit after three months have lapsed (Mazzucuto 2008a).

During the 1950s and 1960s, the main motive for Ghanaian migrants to be in Germany was to obtain higher education or training. After completing their studies, most returned to Ghana. During this period it was estimated that the economic situation of Ghana was stable until around 1967, after the first *coup d'état* that overthrew Dr. Kwame Nkrumah.[5] These educational migrants were considerably low in number; notwithstanding, they played a significant role as pioneers for other migrants, who were to go to Germany after the Ghanaian economy declined.

With further economic deterioration from the mid-1970s, more Ghanaians migrated to Germany. On the other hand, Nigeria's economy was booming as a result of its oil industry and thus attracted many Ghanaian labour migrants. The emigration of Ghanaians had accelerated by the 1980s, owing to continued economic as well as political crises, and the expulsion of Ghanaians from Nigeria in 1983 and 1985 prompted more Ghanaians to migrate to European countries (Donkor 2005). This included Ghanaians who had raised enough money from working in Nigeria and were able to afford to move to European destinations such as Germany. German residence and work permits were often obtained by applying for asylum. Asylum seeking for Ghanaians as a practice

---

4   The Ghanaian Diaspora in Germany: Its Contribution to Development in Ghana: Summary. Available at http://migrationeducation.org/52.1.html?&rid=177&cHash=3342fc52d57e0e92 focbcadf6556f45a. Accessed 11 February 2013.

5   The first president of independent Ghana, until the army and police seized power in 1966 and he found asylum in Guinea.

to stay in Germany came to a halt when Ghana was declared a 'safe country of origin' in 1993 (Eichholzer 2007).

The networks developed by Ghanaians residing in Germany and other destination countries have over the years facilitated chain migration.[6] In the 1990s, for instance, it was noted that poverty reduction and remittances transferred to families in Ghana became an important motive for young Ghanaians to travel abroad. The decision to migrate has not been up to the individual alone; sometimes these decisions are taken and supported by the (extended) family as well as friends. In return for the support given by family and friends for the migration, the migrant is therefore expected to remit funds, as well as invest in other family members or friends for a follow-up migration. Hence, some Ghanaians in Germany have also invested in other family members to join them in Germany.

The history of Ghanaians migrating to Germany is characterized by four types of migration, which played a role in various phases. There has been a shift in the emphasis of Ghanaian migration, through the following phases:

1. educational migration
2. asylum-seeking migration
3. family reunification
4. economic migrants[7]

The main areas of residence for Ghanaians in Germany are noted to be in the cities and towns such as Hamburg, Berlin, Baden-Württemberg, North Rhine Westphalia, and Hesse, as well as the Ruhr region and the Frankfurt/Main metropolitan area (GTZ 2009). More than one-fifth (22.7%) of the Ghanaian migrants live in Hamburg, meaning that the highest percentage of Ghanaians in Germany lives in this city (*ibid.*).

There is a higher presence of Ghanaian migrants in the larger cities because arguably in cities there are better job opportunities and earning potential; hence, they are more suitable for economic migrants. The geographic concentration of Ghanaians in Hamburg can be explained by a long tradition of Ghanaian migration to Hamburg, which is reinforced by the establishment of migration networks which facilitate chain migration (GTZ 2009; Nieswand 2008). Nieswand (2008) notes that in Ghana (*Ham*)*burger* is used to refer to

---

6 A chain migration is a series of migrations within a family. A chain migration begins with one family member who sends money to bring other family members to a new location. Chain migrations result in migration fields, where there are clusters of people in certain areas.

7 It must be noted that some of these phases could overlap.

migrants, suggesting that the term *burger* is derived from the long tradition of Ghanaians migrating to Hamburg and the chain migration associated with it. The unofficial Ghana web dictionary defines *burger* as a Ghanaian living abroad. It also attributes the word to an origin in the word *Hamburger*, a resident of the German city Hamburg.[8] From the interviews conducted, interviewees generally said that *burger* comes from *Hamburger* because of several Ghanaians who returned from Germany (they did not necessarily come from Hamburg) to Ghana, compared with Ghanaians in other countries who returned under the Assisted Voluntary Return program (VRP).[9] These returned migrants from Germany often lived ostentatious lifestyles that became the talk of the town.[10]

Transnational connections between Ghanaian migrants in Germany are often involved in social networks of relatives and friends. They often maintain close social relationships among each other within Germany and across several European borders, as well as across the Atlantic to the US and Canada. Reciprocal obligations and solidarity within families often connect migrants and non-migrants in Ghana. Transnational private, civil society, religious group, political party, and economic relations allow many Ghanaian migrants to live in transnational social spaces that influence their life sphere and social activities (Tonah 2007; Nieswand 2008).

Most of the Ghanaian migrants in Germany who arrived in the 1970s and 1980s arrived as 'economic' refugees, but at that time they sought asylum.[11] This was as a result of transformations in the world economy, such as economic crises, coupled with political crisis in Ghana as a result of military takeovers, bringing about major changes in migratory trends.

Asylum seeking (*aduro gye*) offered protection for some Ghanaian migrants, but it was mainly for those who were politically persecuted by their state of origin and had not found a safe haven elsewhere. In Akan, *aduro gye* literally means 'taking medication', and every asylum seeker is believed to have no peace as a result of not being settled in a host country, a state of affairs which represents sickness or infirmity. So, by seeking asylum, one is looking for a

---

8   http://www.ghanaweb.com/GhanaHomePage/dictionary/dict_b.php. Accessed 14 March 2014.

9   In 1979, at the request of the West German government, the International Organization for Migration (IOM) created the first European voluntary return programme, to assist asylum seekers in leaving Germany and returning to their country of origin, a programme from which many Ghanaians benefited. This program did not exist in many countries at the time. http://stopdeportations.wordpress.com/2012/10/01/myth-number-3-the-iom -help-migrants-who-want-to-return-home-voluntarily. Accessed 14 March 2014.

10   Interview transcript, 2013.

11   Key informants and interviewees attested to this fact.

cure. The peace every asylum seeker wants in the other country is related to a sick person looking for medication to cure his ailment, and that is how *aduro gye* has been commonly used as a term for asylum seeking. Hence, most of these migrants were temporary refugees. Even the additional laws of the Geneva Convention, which protects those whose life and health is endangered on return to their home countries even if the strict conditions of political persecution do not apply, still did not grant many Ghanaian migrants refugee status.

The recognition as a political refugee conferred a secure residence status for migrants for a considerable length of time; hence, some of the interviewees recounted how they had to make up stories to gain refugee status. This does not mean that all asylum seekers made up stories, and some presented genuine cases. Nevertheless, many had to write and tell stories to gain asylum in Germany. They were often given temporary protection, which could eventually secure them legal residence status. Falola and Afolabi (2007) note that there were a high number of Ghanaian asylum applicants in Germany, making it very difficult to reconstruct the path between entry of Ghanaians into Germany and their ability to get residence permits or even how they are able to change their legal status from being resident or asylum seekers to citizens. But in the main, seeking protection ended up either in an outright rejection, followed by absconding or return, or in a tolerated limbo status as asylum seekers[12] (Vogel & Norbert n.d.). Permits to stay in Germany could be given based on the following:[13]

1. pursuing education
2. having been granted political asylum
3. entering into marriage with a German

Many Ghanaians could not easily get legal permits based on the above criteria, and so they went through difficult times to get legal documents to work or stay in Germany. Most of these migrants had no convincing grounds other than economic reasons for the need for a legal residence permit.[14]

---

12 This is when asylum applications are accepted but have not been decided on, so the asylum seeker is permitted to reside in the host country without any status yet given to the application. These tolerated migrants have many legal limitations imposed on them, such as in relation to finding a legal job. They receive very low public welfare entitlements, and toleration in the country is not permanent.

13 Interview transcript, The Hague, 18 October 2013.

14 Interview transcript, The Hague, 18 October 2013.

Awuah (2005) noted that in the 1980s some Ghanaian migrants created a bad name for Ghanaians in general. This was because many Ghanaian businessmen and women took goods on credit from German shops. Some of these Ghanaians left for Ghana and never returned, while others shipped the goods to Ghana to maintain their *burger* status back home. Companies that had run into losses because of the attitude of some of these Ghanaians reported them to the police. In so doing, the police and immigration authorities' attention was drawn to illegal immigrants and particularly Ghanaians. The immigration authorities and the police's hunt for illegal immigrants forced 'undocumented' migrants to move to other European countries, while some went into hiding (Awuah 2005). Some of these migrants could not continue hiding and therefore moved to the Netherlands.

Ghanaians in Netherlands

The first remarkable wave of Ghanaian migration to the Netherlands took place during the 1980s (Orozco & Mohogu 2007), a period noted as the peak of unprecedented migration out of Ghana (Donkor 2005). This period was characterized by drought, famine, bush fires, political instability, and the expulsion of Ghanaians from Nigeria. This pushed people out of Ghana, and returnees from Nigeria were motivated to migrate and look for new destinations in Europe, such as the Netherlands.

The Netherlands became very attractive to Ghanaian migrants owing to its very strong policy emphasis on multiculturalism, compared with other European countries (Koopmans *et al.* 2005; Schans *et al.* 2013). Ghanaians are considered to be one of the most significant African migrant groups in the Netherlands. However, in terms of the share of all migrants, the Ghanaian population represents in comparison a minority (Mazzucato 2008b; CBS 2014).

The number of Ghanaians in the Netherlands remains uncertain despite official figures. It was estimated that over 3,000 Ghanaian migrants lived in the Netherlands unofficially in 1992 (Stadsdeel Zuidoost 1992).[15] The Centraal Bureau voor de Statistiek (CBS) in 2013 reported that 5,212 Ghanaian migrants are officially registered in the Netherlands, the majority (53%) of whom are females (Table 1).

---

15   Following a plane crash in a suburb of Amsterdam, when it was noted that many Ghanaians were either directly or indirectly victims of this disaster, the Ghanaian population in 1992 quickly became a 'hot item' in the media as well as for academic research. It was assumed that Ghanaian migrants would face several challenges (Knipscheer *et al.* 2000).

TABLE 1 *Statistics of Ghanaian migrants in the Netherlands (2013)*

Age	Male	Female	Male and female
0–20	499	578	1,077
20–65	1,956	2,163	4,119
65 and older	12	4	16
Total	2,467	2,745	5,212

SOURCE: STATISTICS NETHERLANDS, DEN HAAG/HEERLEN, 7 FEBRUARY 2014

This CBS data, however, does not include the large number of undocumented Ghanaian migrants in the Netherlands. The actual figure is likely to be much higher than suggested by official statistics.

Approximately 41% of Ghanaian migrants in the Netherlands live in the urban centre of Amsterdam, especially in the southeastern suburb (Bijlmer) (OIS 1995; Orozco & Mohogu 2007), followed by the city of The Hague (30%).

The Ghanaian migrants in the Netherlands organize themselves in associations on the basis of religious, ethnic, and occasionally political lines.[16] According to the Ghana Embassy in the Netherlands, these groups exceed 70 in number, with the majority based in Amsterdam and the remainder spread across The Hague, Rotterdam, and Utrecht.[17] These Ghanaian associations have well-developed networks and usually contain the type of networks that provide community living and other services connected to the everyday lives of these migrants in the Netherlands. Some of these migrants resort to sex work as a form of livelihood.

This study, however, focuses mainly on Ghanaians in The Hague. The focus on The Hague is as a result of it being the city with the second-largest Ghanaian migrant population in the Netherlands. Moreover, during a conversation with Rijk van Dijk,[18] he noted that many of the studies on Ghanaian migrants have focused on Amsterdam, resulting in 'respondent fatigue'.

---

16   Examples of such groups include Sikaman Foundation, Ghana Students Association Enschede, and Council of Ghanaian Chiefs in the Netherlands Foundation (CoGhaC Foundation).

17   Ghana Embassy. Accessed online, 2014.

18   Rijk van Dijk is an anthropologist and an expert on Pentecostalism, globalization, transnationalism, migration, youth, and healing.

Study Methodology

This study is exploratory and descriptive in nature. A comprehensive approach was used, including capturing the cultural, political, historical, and socio-economic status of the respondents that influenced their decision to migrate. We also looked at why they had to transit and sought to discover if their final destination was in the Netherlands or not. This is because some migrants may not have clearly defined 'paths' to migrate along. Being employed in low-paying jobs, they may also have had a hard time adjusting to a foreign cultural environment—leading, as a result, to transit. Exploration and description of their *burger*-ness was elucidated in totality. The study was aimed at collecting qualitative data through review of the extant literature, personal interviews, and key informant interviews.

Data collection began with one informant. A rapport was created as contacts were established through church gatherings in The Hague and through the key informants. A snowball method was employed, starting with a Ghanaian pastor and chief with whom rapport had been developed earlier.

I use the word 'illegal' for migrants when they do not have the proper documents to reside or work in the Netherlands. Some of these migrants acknowledge and use this term in daily conversation. However, organizations such as the International Organization of Migration (IOM) and the European Union prefer the terms 'irregular' or 'undocumented' because these terms may seem less stigmatizing than 'illegal'. I sometimes use 'illegal' not because I want to engage in the legal or judicial debate surrounding these terms but because this is the term most of my interviewees were conversant with. For many Ghanaians, it is considered impolite to ask about one's legal status, and some Ghanaians would rather lie than speak openly about it. Thus, I never brought up the topic of individual migrants' legal status unless they first referred to it. Fortunately, most interviewees mentioned their legal status when discussing why they moved from Germany to the Netherlands.

Some interviewees warned me beforehand that are many illegal Ghanaian migrants in the Netherlands and that if more research is done on them, researchers may reveal the hideouts of these illegal migrants. One interviewee said:

> Every research is about Ghanaians. I can say that I have been interviewed by several people who write on Ghanaian migrants in Netherlands. *Yabre mo mpo* ['We are even tired of you researchers'].

These Ghanaian migrants who came to the Netherlands via Germany were relatively unknown to the researcher, but once the confidence of a Ghanaian traditional leader and church leader had been won, it was much easier to find other migrants in this category. The aim was to interview in total 12 migrants based in The Hague who formerly resided in Germany.

Characteristics of Respondents

Gender and Age

According to demographic investigations, Ghanaians in the Netherlands are mostly single men and women from cities in Ghana and aged 25–40 years (Nimako 1993). The 12 people interviewed were between the ages of 46 and 56; however, these people came to the Netherlands between the ages of 17 and 30. It was during this same age span that these migrants left Germany for the Netherlands. Nine of the interviewees were raised in a city in Ghana. More men (8) than women (4) took part in this research.

Marital Status

All interviewees were either married or lived together with their partner. Seven were married to a European (from the Netherlands) before and are currently married to Ghanaians. Eight embarked on their journey to Germany when single. Nine lived with a partner and children. Furthermore, two lived with a partner alone, with one living with family members (cousins).

Education

The average education of the Ghanaians in Amsterdam is of secondary to higher level (Nimako 1993). In this study, most of the interviewees (8) followed senior secondary courses. One had completed technical school. One had primary school education, and another had junior high school education. One had also completed training college in Ghana. In almost all cases, the subjects had completed their education in Ghana, with the exception of one who was able to further his education in Germany to the tertiary level.

Employment Status

Eleven of the interviewees had a paid job but most (9) were in lower-income jobs; one is on social welfare. One is a teacher, one is self-employed with his own construction firm, and two are sales persons (one in a Ghanaian shop and the other in a supermarket). Two are drivers (company driver and taxi driver). Five were in the cleaning business (*schoonmaakster*) in factories and private homes. The woman on social welfare noted that her status is as a result of ill health making her unable to work, so the government gives her a monthly stipend.

Period

All migrants interviewed came to Germany in the 1980s, some owing to the political instability and economic depression in Ghana and the violation of human rights under the regime of J.J. Rawlings,[19] as also noted by Noordergraaf and Grunsven (1994). The participants in our study migrated to the Netherlands after an average of 1–5 years' stay in Germany. They have lived in the Netherlands for about 15–23 years. All 12 respondents reported economic reasons as the main motive for migration or staying in Europe. In addition to economic reasons, the political situation also motivated people to leave Ghana. Furthermore, one person mentioned family reunification as a reason for going to Germany, and continuing further to the Netherlands owing to economic reasons. One of the migrants came with a partner and children.

Most of these migrants thought it would be easy to find a job and earn money (Tichelman 1996), and others knew that it would not be easy but they would definitely find their way around. Hence, respondents mentioned expectations such as a good life and a better future (11), and political peace and stability (1). Four interviewees held the opinion that their expectations of coming to Europe had not come true; four others thought this was partly so, while three said that life in the Netherlands fell short of their expectations. One respondent noted that he had not fulfilled his expectations at all: the tightening up of foreigner legislation and a lack of better jobs were reasons given.

Limitations and Restrictions

Before discussing the findings of this study, there are a number of methodological limitations to mention. Anonymity and confidentiality (in some cases) present problems when discussing findings. Furthermore, a considerable methodological challenge was the location of Ghanaian migrants in Netherlands who came through Germany. In order to obtain the community cohort, snowball sampling was used. A group of people recommended potential participants for the study. Those participants then recommended additional participants, and so on. The risk exists that such a selection will have problems such as having the same circle of friends (generational cohorts) and people in one particular church or social group (all interviewees were Christians). I argue that this methodology is an adequate compromise between methodological rigidity and practical feasibility.

---

19   J.J. Rawlings was the leader of two *coup d'états*, in 1979 and 1981. He was in power from
      1981–2000, and from 1982 he was a democratically elected president.

Again, some (4) of the respondents were much more comfortable speaking in Akan (it was their primary language and easier to express themselves in); five used English but intermittently spoke Akan.[20] In such cases, data was collected in one language (Akan) and the findings are presented in another (English). A number of translation-related decisions had to be made, but the researcher tried her best to maintain the original meaning of the narratives. It must be noted that this did not pose much of a problem to the researcher, as Akan is her mother tongue.

Discussion

Reasons for Migrating

Migrants are confronted with profound changes in all life domains. In this study, we examine the lives of some Ghanaians who reside in the Netherlands who came through Germany. We try to discover reasons why these individuals left Ghana for Germany and their motivation to further continue to the Netherlands. In addition, we wanted to understand if the aims for their journey have been achieved and what connections they maintain with people back in Ghana.

The decision to migrate out of Ghana is noted to be a response to a combination of several factors, such as socio-economic and political ones. Also, these factors can be placed within the push–pull theoretical framework as put forward by Lee (1966) in his work, *A Theory of Migration*. Lee's conclusions that unfavourable conditions in one place 'push' people out, and favourable conditions in an external location 'pull' them in, and that the primary cause of migration is economic in nature, are still valid and can be observed in this study. However, this is not a case of one-theory-fits-all for the migrants interviewed. Some of the reasons given by the interviewees for setting out from Ghana are noted below:

> I wanted somewhere much better than Ghana. I first thought of Canada; but after talking to some friends and relatives, I realized it was much easier getting Germany visa compared to Canada visa. At that time getting to East Germany was a bit easier; and talking to people abroad who came home, they suggested Germany as the best way to get out of Ghana to Europe. Some people I discussed my intent with showed me

---

20   Generally, it was noticed that those who spoke in English were very formal in the discussions, while most who spoke in Akan were less formal and open to discuss issues at length.

how to get my visa and all that was needed to embark on my trip. So that is how come I went to Germany.[21]

The above interviewee mentioned that most of the Ghanaians who went to Germany in the early 1980s used East Germany (the German Democratic Republic) as a transit zone to West Germany, adding that at that time it was much easier to get to East Germany because Ghanaians did not require a visa to enter the country. Prior to 1975, Ghanaians also did not require a visa to enter West Germany. But from 1975 a visa was required, and this limited the emigration of Ghanaians to West Germany. Nevertheless, up until 1986, entering East Germany did not require a visa, and thereby Ghanaians took advantage of the opportunity to enter West Germany via East Germany (Berlin-Schönefeld). Hence, for some of these migrants, East Germany became a stepping stone or a zone of transit to West Germany, which also in turn later became a zone of transit.

One interviewee noted:

> Since I had no job on my own, things were a bit difficult. My father, who was the breadwinner of the family, also passed on and left us with a bit of hardship. So I decided to embark on this journey without knowing where exactly I was going. Getting Benelux visa was easier, so I first went to Belgium and I hustled through to Luxemburg, Netherlands, Germany, and back to Netherlands. Even though it was hard here, I found some illegal jobs to do to be able to support my mum and family, who invested in my journey to Europe.[22]

Another interviewee reported:

> I was okay in Ghana, but you have to strive on to greater heights. There are so many things I could do if I come to Europe for my family back home. Things were very difficult in the 1980s in Ghana. See the political tensions and all that. It was important to go out and look for something and bring home.[23]

A 46-year old interviewee gave his reason for migrating from Ghana to the Netherlands as follows:

---

21   Interview transcript, male, 46 years, The Hague, 10 November 2013.
22   Interview transcript, male, 52 years, The Hague, 16 October 2013.
23   Interview transcript, male, 50 years, The Hague, 3 November 2013.

I really wanted to travel out of Ghana. Anytime I saw the burgers back home I was impressed by their lifestyles—cars, clothes, and even the way they remit their families. So, that really motivated me to travel. I wanted to go to US but it proved very difficult for me to get the visa. I was lucky enough to get East Germany visa. I wanted to seek asylum in East Germany, but since it was a poor country they didn't allow me to stay. I then acquired West Germany visa and sought asylum there.[24]

Looking at the various narratives above, it can be observed that it is not so much the actual factors at the origin and destination (pull–push factors) alone that motivate individuals to migrate. Personal issues and awareness of conditions elsewhere are all evaluated by the individual. People become aware of the situations in the destination countries based on knowledge received from personal contacts or from sources of information which are not universally available. For instance, one respondent noted:

I was working with a German company in Ghana in road construction. The company finally moved to Libya, and I was transferred to Libya too. So I moved to Libya with my wife and child. I was in Libya since 1980 to 1990. During my ten years in Libya I was sometimes asked to go and work in Germany, Netherlands, Switzerland, UK, and Italy. In 1990, I came on vacation with my family in Germany and decided not to go back to Libya. This is because my dream country was in Europe (the Netherlands). I knew Germany will get me closer to my dream land than Libya would.[25]

The above narration makes it clear that some people have options to compare different places before making a decision on where to migrate to. Such information (not always exact) and the opportunity to get it are not available to everyone who intends or plans to migrate. From the interviews conducted, in reality some of the advantages and disadvantages of an area are imagined on the basis of incomplete data, while this information is better understood by living in those communities. Imagined information creates some kind of ignorance or mystery about the area of destination.

In addition, there are some individuals who welcome change, with few questions asked. For some individuals, there must be an irresistible motivation to migrate, while for others little pressure or promise is enough. The decision to migrate, therefore, is never based completely on facts or a particular reason

---

24   Interview transcript, male, 49 years, The Hague, 29 September 2013.
25   Interview transcript, male, 56 years, The Hague, 6 October 2013.

or motivation. There are times that emotions determine why people migrate, and many exceptions to generalizations about reasons why people migrate should be considered. The narratives below are clear examples:

> I came abroad because after proceeds from our joint cocoa farm, my husband travelled to France with all our money. After two years of not hearing from him, I decided to follow him abroad. I could not get France visa easily but fortunately *enough I got* Benelux visa at the time. I got to Belgium, and I was arrested after it was detected that my papers were not accurate. I found a way to run away from police custody because it will be a disgrace to go home after a fruitless journey (because I sold all my properties to embark on this journey). I then left for Germany from Belgium.[26]

A 48-year old woman in The Hague noted:

> I had no plan to travel outside, but my husband was lucky enough to get the chance to go to Germany. After he settled a while, he found some means to come for me and our children [two children].[27]

Certainly, not all persons who migrate reach this decision themselves. The narratives above indicate how children are carried along by their parents, whether they desire to migrate or not. Wives sometimes accompany their husbands. This seems to correspond with Kofman (2004) and Awumbila *et al.* (2008) in their observation that in the past, women accompanied their spouses, but in contemporary times women migrate independently.

Intervening obstacles (Lee 1966) also feature in the lives of some of these Ghanaian migrants. For the decision to migrate out of Ghana depends on the information available. Where does one get this information?

> Some friends of mine living in Germany came back home, and I gave them so much pressure to help me travel abroad after saving a considerable amount of money. Seeing lifestyles of those burgers who came and the way they are able to take care of their families living back home, I knew abrokyire beye de [there is luxury abroad]. We then sat down, got ink and cassava, looked at the visas of my friends, and nicely carved out

---

26   Interview transcript, female, 53 years, The Hague, 20 October 2013.
27   Interview transcript, female, 48 years, The Hague, 16 October 2013.

the visa shape from the cassava, and then after a considerable try, we found a better match and then stamped my passport.[28]

In answering this, it seems plausible, as a framework for understanding the sources of ideas which ultimately lead to migration, that people employ social networks. These networks provide various resources which the migrants tap into to enhance their decision to migrate out of Ghana and even stay in Germany. Potential migrants act on available information from networks of friends and relations to arrive at the decision to migrate. For some, this information is implicit, as it is evident from what they see as the benefits of migrating. This last narrative is particularly interesting, considering how people can be so innovative when it comes to certain aspirations they want to meet. How did they even think that cassava and ink could be used to make a visa stamp? This is just a small example of the extent to which people will go to embark on this *burger* journey.

In summary, several reasons caused these migrants to set out from Ghana. Some of the migrants had definite plans leaving Ghana but changed them along the way; others were not very sure of where exactly they were going. One thing that puts these migrants in the same category is that they all left Ghana through Germany to the Netherlands, but their stories in relation to reasons for migrating are very different. For some of these migrants, social networks played an important role in the decision to migrate. Indirect and direct information flows served as a pull factor for others. It was also noted that some of these migrants had to accompany their families.

One point that is clear is that one cannot find a particular pattern for all these migrants: each story is unique. In order to generalize or find a particular pattern, some important unique characteristics may be overlooked. After finding some reasons why these migrants left Ghana, it must be noted that some had to go through other transit countries, such as Libya, Belgium, Togo, Luxemburg, UK, Switzerland, Italy, and even the Netherlands (current country of residence) before finally settling in the Netherlands. Despite the fact that these migrants went through several transit countries, this paper will focus only on Germany.

Germany as Transit

Migration is not a straightforward process whereby migrants simply move from one country to another (Wahlbeck 2009). Instead, many migrants are in

---

28   Interview transcript, male, 48 years, The Hague, 27 October 2013.

transit for some period of time, sometimes years.[29] Most interviewees indicated that in Germany they maintained a high level of self-organization. Some respondents indicated that they often belonged to ethnically oriented groups or hometown associations, religious groups, political party associations, and the Ghana Union.

The churches and community groups were important central points of contact for communities living in the diaspora, and they also act as intermediaries for transnational connections. Van Dijk (1997, 2001, 2002a, 2002b) notes the role religion plays in the formation of identity among Ghanaians in foreign lands, and this was further confirmed by interviewees and evident from the visits the researcher made to some of the Ghanaian churches in The Hague (Acts Revival Church, for example). The hometown associations of migrants provide the opportunity for fund raising to support development projects such as schools or clinics in their home area, thereby helping migrants stay connected to their home countries. The respondents also indicated that despite some of the problems they faced as 'illegal' migrants, these hometown associations and religious groups helped them to feel at home, discuss job opportunities and accommodation issues, and help new Ghanaian migrants settle, as well as to embark on development projects back in Ghana.

Some of the reasons that eventually made Germany a transit rather than final destination country included getting 'papers' or documents to legitimize the migrants' stay or to permit them to work. Some of these migrants had to leave Germany so that they were not deported back to Ghana. Marriage served as another reason for these migrants to move to the Netherlands. Some of these *burgers* married Dutch women or men to enable them get 'papers'. Most interviewees indicated that they had acquired their Dutch residence permit and consequently Dutch passport through their Dutch spouses. Van Dijk (2004) notes that the settlement and growth of the Ghanaian migrant community in the Netherlands is undoubtedly based to a large extent on marriage relationships. He further explains that marriage became so important for the Ghanaian immigrant group in the Netherlands because of its civic nature and the legal documents that come along with it.

Marriage therefore became an important means for many Ghanaian migrants to enter the Netherlands. In fact, marriage or 'papers' were the main motivations or reasons for almost all interviewees to migrate to the Netherlands. Let us first look at these three narratives:

---

29   In between Ghana and the Netherlands, there existed situations that caused these migrants to reside in Germany for a considerable length of time.

The government agency in charge of refugees gave me six months to investigate into my story to find out how true that was. I was given money, clothes and chits for the six months to get basic necessities. Within five months, I didn't want to be deported due to the embarrassment attached with it and because I had not achieved the set purpose why I was abroad: to get economically stable. I looked elsewhere. I first left to Belgium; but it was quite difficult living there, so I proceeded to Netherlands, and through hustling I finally gained legal status. And my dream has been of going to Canada, and it's still a dream.[30]

As one interviewee indicated:

Living in Europe without papers[31] is difficult. You keep hiding and not free. I found a better way to acquire my papers in Netherlands, so I left Germany for the Netherlands.[32]

Again, a different reason was given by another respondent:

In my early years in Belgium, I met a German woman who was helping me with several things and who understood my situation. After five years of not hearing from my husband, I went to Germany to stay with this woman temporarily and then met some Ghanaian guys. We kept contacts. They lived in Netherlands but often come to Germany to buy things. I finally got married to one, and that is how I got to the Netherlands.[33]

It is very clear from the above narratives that pressing issues, especially centring on legal documents, made Germany a transit country. Even for some Ghanaian migrants, the Netherlands is perceived as a place of transit. Some of these migrants did not intend to make Germany a transit country, but it ended up being a transit country. Though marriage was an important way to acquire legal documents, interviewees did not feel comfortable talking about these marriages and how some ended up on the rocks, as well as the huge amounts of money they paid to get married to the spouses through whom they had their 'papers'. As noted by some of the respondents, apart from the issue of acquiring

---

30   Interview transcript, male, 46 years, The Hague, 10 November 2013.
31   'Papers' in this case refers to legal residence and working permits.
32   Interview transcript, male, 48 years, The Hague, 27 October 2013.
33   Interview transcript, female, 53 years, The Hague, 20 October 2013.

legal documents they would choose Germany over the Netherlands. As one of them said:

> There were lots of jobs for us to do than here, but it's all good. In Germany, when they do not like you, they show it; but Dutch can be smiling with you, but they don't like you (I call it Dutch hypocrisy). Their discrimination is done underground, but its implications are very severe than what the Germans do. You find a lot of things in Germany much cheaper (like food and electronics), a more comprehensive insurance, and so forth. I can give you several examples of the worse experiences some of our Ghanaian brothers went through here in Netherlands, but when we went to Germany with similar issues (if not same) it was easily solved.[34]

Another was quite neutral:

> I don't mind. Europe is Europe. Provided I get food, work, shelter, and I am able to remit my family, I am okay.[35]

Another respondent noted:

> It is very difficult to make the comparison. In Germany I was not yet settled, and unsure of what my life was going to be like. In Holland I found a very loving wife, started a living here. Now I work as a taxi chauffeur. How do I make such a comparison?[36]

Life in transit can be planned or unplanned, but it depends on what the migrant makes of it. A final destination can be much better than a transit zone; but the opposite is also true. Transit can be temporary, for a few days; but it can also take years, depending on the situation and the individual migrant.

Connections Home

Ghanaian migrants and their families live transnational lives (Mazzucato 2008a, 2008b; Schans et al. 2013). Living a transnational life has been advanced with the development in information and communication technology (mobile

---

34   Interview transcript, male, 50 years, The Hague, 3 November 2013.
35   Interview transcript, female, 48 years, The Hague, 16 October 2013
36   Interview transcript, male, 46 years, The Hague, 10 November 2013.

phones, telephones, televisions including satellite and cable networks, Internet, etc.), cheaper air travel, and infrastructural development, thereby giving impetus to increased flows of people, goods, money, and ideas, connecting them to different locations across the globe.

This research had as one of its goals to discover the contacts migrants have with people back in Ghana. Such contacts are very different in nature, ranging from receiving remittances to visits and phone calls. Furthermore, current migration theories, such as the New Economics of Labour Migration (Stark 1984, 1991), posit that migrant's decisions are not made by individual actors but by families or households. Hence, they collectively act to maximize expected interest from the investment in a migrant and to minimize risks. This is an argument put forward to explain why migrants remit funds home: to pay back the initial investment the household made in sending the migrant overseas. But the interviews conducted showed no correlations between family support or investment and remittances.

All interviewees except one often remitted funds to their family back home. This can best be explained as a result of 'feeling responsible for family survival' and the family being a source of social security for migrants (Van Dijk 2002b: 192). Also, some family members believe that a migrant is now well-to-do, and hence they pressure migrants to remit funds.

According to an analysis by Tonah (2007), Ghanaian migrants living abroad do not have any other choice but to maintain ties with friends, families, and social institutions, as well as to invest at home. In order to obtain recognition and be accepted by their society back home, some have to do this regardless of their precarious socio-economic status abroad.

In practice, the remittances of these migrants can consist of goods and not only of money. These goods range from clothes, to electrical appliances such as refrigerators and computers, to foodstuffs (transcript of interviews, 2013). The following narratives from interviews are illustrative of the connections that migrants maintain with home:

> I call often to my family. I remit almost all the time. Every small money I get, I make sure at least 25% goes to my family home. I send pictures and we try to keep in touch often. Sometimes I send a few items such as clothes, electric appliances, and anything I can send if possible.[37]

Another noted:

---

37 Interview transcript, female, 48 years, The Hague, 16 October 2013.

> Previously things were better in Europe. I have helped build a house and
> sent two cars, but now it is not like previously. But I remit my family
> always. They really invested in me, so I owe them the little I can.[38]

Although most interviewees indicated that they remit funds home regularly
and often visit Ghana, one indicated that he rarely remitted and hardly ever
visits family members:

> When I was in Libya, I used to; but things are not the same anymore. I do
> not remit anymore. For a long time I have not visited Ghana. I was in
> Ghana some time ago but not to visit. Someone employed me to go and
> furnish his house for him. In the past ten years, I have been home once
> with my wife and children. But I keep in contact with my family back
> home always, thanks to Skype, phones, and WhatsApp. The Internet has
> made it much easier for some of us.[39]

He added that remitting in times of difficulty has created the idea for most
young people in Ghana that there is a 'money tree' in Europe that people come
and pluck cash from. His advice was that people should be sincere and honest
about the fact that Europe is not as rosy as it may seem.

Research into international migration in Ghana has often emphasized
remittances because of the economic impact associated with them both at the
macro and micro levels. At the macro level, remittances to Ghana are estimated
to be equal to or more than official development assistance, and this seems to
be confirmed by the small-scale research conducted here: most interviewees,
with the exception of one, indicated that it was their responsibility to remit.
Some interviewees noted that to embark on this journey, their family had to
contribute financially towards their costs; it was an investment. Hence, there is
a responsibility to remit regularly, even in times of financial difficulties.

Is the Netherlands the Final Destination?

The original goal of most of these migrants is to find financial success in the
host country and one day settle in the country of their birth. But, as time goes
by, plans change (interviews, 2013); and after years or even decades of spending
the better part of one's life abroad, 'home' can become an unfamiliar territory
requiring very careful mind training and readjustments. The interviewees noted
that the constant power cuts, water shortages, traffic congestion, depreciation

---

38   Interview transcript, male, 52 years, The Hague, 16 October 2013.
39   Interview transcript, male, 56 years, The Hague, 6 October 2013.

of the Ghanaian currency (cedi), poor infrastructure, and many other reasons discourage them from going to settle permanently in Ghana. As one interviewee said:

> There is no room for us to return unprepared or make economic 'mistakes', because the folks back home will literally eat us alive and force us to run out of Ghana and die with sadness and misery.[40]

According to another:

> I really want to go back home, but now the problem is my wife and my kids. They don't want to go to Ghana. There is better health care, better education, better jobs for my kids here than back home. Even our political leaders come here for health care. These are the things keeping some of us here. My kids will soon give birth, and I will be glad to be here to offer them all the support needed.[41]

A third interviewee said:

> No, I have my family here, so for us we are happy here and life goes on smoothly. That's fine. I don't think I will go and settle in Ghana, but my mind can change anytime, depending on circumstances and situations.[42]

The above narratives indicate how difficult it can be for some of these migrants to go back to settle in Ghana, unprepared socially, financially, and even culturally. Some of the interviewees indicated that staying abroad has several advantages; hence, they do not want to go back to Ghana. Another reason for wanting to continue staying in Europe is because of economics factors. Some of the migrants asked rhetorically: 'What job will I do in Ghana considering my educational status?' Others made it clear that they have to save enough money for their lifetime because it will be difficult to readjust in Ghana without being economically stable.

Transit?

It would be wrong to think of these Ghanaian migrants' journey to the Netherlands and Germany as to places of permanent settlement or even final

---

40   Interview transcript, male, 50 years, The Hague, 3 November 2013.
41   Interview transcript, male, 46 years, The Hague, 10 November 2013.
42   Interview transcript, male, 56 years, The Hague, 6 October 2013.

destination. For some, their home country Ghana will not be their permanent settlement, but others believe that Ghana may be their final destination and permanent settlement place because when they die their bodies will definitely be taken back to Ghana (more specifically, their home towns) to be buried. A more accurate metaphor for these migrants' journey may be that of a baffle gate, where these Ghanaian migrants entered Germany (East/West) for a period of time and then left for other countries, including the Netherlands; and while currently living in the Netherlands, some still perceive it as a place of transit.

After exploring the stories of these migrants, the question then is this: which people are more likely to transit? Many migrants are very likely to be involved in transit migration; and in a similar way, all countries are simultaneously countries of origin, transit, and final destination for migrants. Gender, education, age, work experience, language, social network, legal status of migrant, marital status, and economic independence are all factors that can influence transit migration in one way or another.

From this research and other research conducted on Ghanaian migrants, it appears that, traditionally, some women moved along with their spouses; however, others migrated independently over time (Awumbila *et al.* 2008). Men are then more likely to be involved in transit migration than women; but considering the changing aspects of migration for women, it is very difficult to draw such a conclusion. For instance, one 52-year old interviewee indicated that he was the man and had to fight for the survival of his family, so he would be happy to have the wife settled with the children while he migrated to seek greener pastures for the family. He added that because of his spouse and children, it is difficult to keep moving even when conditions are not the best. At least his wife and children can stay in one place to avoid an interruption to the children's education, while he can move in search of better opportunities. Another interviewee discussed how it was very difficult to transit when married and more especially when you have children; when he was single, it was his sole decision to either settle in a particular place or not, but now it is a whole family's decision.

Migrant children may be differently affected by the institutional setting and support structures of the host countries' education systems as well as cultural settings and available opportunities. The social context in which these migrant children grow up is an important determinant for transit migration or otherwise. In the same way, it is likely that parental decisions about the educational attainment of their children are affected by where parents see their children's future. These factors make it very difficult to generalize about why people transit, as this involves different decisions, different people, different aspirations, and different cultural and social backgrounds of migrants.

Transit migration is also influenced by the age of the migrant. At a youthful age one is very vibrant and can keep moving or would like to explore the world, but at an older age most migrants would not want to keep moving from/to countries. Therefore, the older generation is less likely to be involved in transit migration. Some interviewees indicated that in old age it is better to go home (Ghana) because even when you die, your body will be sent to Ghana—so why should one not go to Ghana and settle permanently there when old and weak? Besides, you cannot do any meaningful work to avoid the cost and problems for your family after your death, and it is much more expensive to send a corpse home compared with an able-bodied person.

Transit migration and education are also intertwined in some ways. Education and skills acquisition can play important roles at different stages of an individual's migration process. They influence one's ability to transit or not. People with higher education are more likely to get permanent and well-paid jobs, so they may not want to transit in search of better jobs, and they are more likely to be economically secure. But people with less formal education, and hence with low-paid jobs, are very likely to transit, as they may go in search of better and more viable job opportunities.

The economic success of the migrant in the destination country to a large extent determines transit migration. An individual may have a well-paid job, or have entrepreneurial skills and have invested much in establishing a business. For instance, some Ghanaian migrants in The Hague have their own Ghanaian jobs; they sell Ghanaian foodstuffs, among other items. Some migrants have established their own salons to do hair dressing and barbering. These migrants with established businesses are more likely to stay in the Netherlands—all things being equal, especially when business is booming—than those migrants employed to clean in a supermarket on a contract basis, when at any time the contract may end or probably not be renewed. One of the interviewees, who is self-employed and has his own construction firm, noted that he does not think he is going to migrate elsewhere or go back to Ghana—unless things change for the worse, which he doubts. A 55-year old woman stated that she cannot keep doing cleaning jobs, especially when old and weak; hence, if she can find a better job elsewhere, why not migrate?

Language is a crucial factor for migrants in the host country and a determinant of transit migration. Not only is language important in its own right, but it is complementary to many social interactions with others. For instance, during my visit to my aunt in London during the Christmas 2013 vacation, she introduced me to a Ghanaian family who had once lived in the Netherlands and have Dutch citizenship but who moved to England. In an interaction with them, I asked curiously why they had moved to England. The woman said:

> We like Netherlands more than London. We even have a home there and we go on vacation every year; but we need the children to learn English.

Whether you like it or not, English is becoming the academic language and is also spoken in most countries.

Thus, while a particular language is very important as a complement to existing and future skills, language may at the same time be less transferable to other countries' labour markets and educational systems in the future. In any case, language is an important driver and determinant of transit migration.

The social networks of migrants are also a factor in transit migration. It would be easy to think that migrants with social networks in host countries are more likely not to transit; however, from this research and the interviews conducted, the Ghanaian migrants in Germany had several social networks, such as religious (churches), political party, and hometown associations; but still, whether willingly or not, Germany became a zone of transit. It appears that social networks are a less determining factor in transit migration. Interviewees noted it is not so much about the social networks, despite their great importance in many ways, but that economic and legal issues are rated higher in determining whether to transit or not. One woman acknowledged that social networks provide a source of communal living and help migrants to socialize and help each other, but one needs peace of mind (legal status and money, even to contribute to some of these groups) to enjoy such social networks.

The legal status of migrants is a very important factor that also affects transit migration. As noted from the discussions above, 'illegal' migrants are not comfortable in a host country and hence have a higher tendency to transit than legal migrants. The interviewees indicated that it is always very difficult for an 'illegal' migrant to get a job, and the lucky ones who find jobs usually find low-paying jobs. Hence, 'illegal' migrants have a tendency to move or transit through countries with the hope of gaining legal status and finding a good job in order to survive and to maintain their *burger* status by remitting funds home.

From an inter-temporal point of view, the possibility of transit and even a later migration may also affect the educational, marital, and job decisions of migrants. In this case, if a migrant plans to transit, he/she is very unlikely to make many commitments in the country of transit that may keep him/her in that country. Interviewees indicated that learning the German language, for instance, did not help them much, as they had to move within a short time. However, some of the interviewees, who had already planned not to stay in Germany, noted that they learned the basics of the language so as to be able to interact with Germans in general and specifically with their co-workers, friends, and sales personnel in shops.

In conclusion, the factors and determinants of transit migration are varied and diverse, depending on the migrant involved. Some factors are more

important to migrants in deciding to transit or not, while others just complement the main factors. For the interviewees in this study, legal status and economic factors so as to maintain their social status as *burgers* were placed
higher when it came to transit migration.

Conclusion

Migrant realities are complex, change over time, and involve back and forth
movements between different cities and countries. The most frequent motives for
migration among Ghanaian migrants (*burgers*) are prestige and socio-economic
motives in general. However, if I had to sum up what predominated among the
reasons to emigrate from Ghana to Europe, I would say it was great expectations.
The remittances and goods which migrants send home give a clear message to
others to follow suit: if you want to be more prosperous, go abroad. The frequency of remittances enhances one's *burger* status, and migrants therefore
maintained strong connections back home through visits and remittances. In
spite of the strong bond these migrants maintained with people in Ghana and
the country itself, the opportunity to return to live permanently in Ghana is not
equal for all migrants, and it depends not only on financial, political, and social
circumstances but also on the possibility to re-enter Europe.

The mobility of migrants to home countries promotes the use of their transnational social networks, and this has various advantages for migrants as well as
enhancing their contribution to their home country's development. Though
they are usually willing to do so, migrants stated that they are not financially,
physically, socially, and economically prepared to settle in Ghana permanently.

One clear observation is that some migrants planned to go through different
countries before settling. In fact, for some migrants they are always on the
move in search of better socio-economic status for their survival and that of
their families and loved ones. This necessitates more in-depth research on the
fluid migration process of different migrants and all migration trajectories.

References

Adepoju, A. (2002), Fostering Free Movement of Persons in West Africa: Achievements,
    Constraints and Prospects for Intraregional Migration. *International Migration
    Review* 40(2): 3–28.
Adepoju, A. (September 2005), Migration in West Africa. A Paper for the Policy Analysis
    and Research Programme of the Global Commission on International Migration.

Akyeampong, E. (2000), Africans in the Diaspora: The Diaspora and Africa. *African Affairs* 99(395): 183–215.

Anarfi, J., S. Kwankye, A. Ofosu-Mensah & R. Tiemoko (2003), Migration from and to Ghana: A Background Paper. Working paper C4. Issued by the Development Research Centre on Migration, Globalisation and Poverty.

Arthur, J.A. (1991), International Labor Migration Patterns in West Africa. *African Studies Review* 34(3): 65–87.

Arthur, J.A. (2008), *The African Diaspora in United States and Europe: the Ghanaian experience*. Ashgate: Aldershorst.

Asiedu, A.B. (2005), Some Benefits of Migrants' Return Visits to Ghana. *Population, Space and Place* 11(1): 1–11.

Awuah, G. (2005), *As I Journey Along: Ghanaian Perception of Life in the Diaspora*. North Carolina: Lulu.com.

Awumbila, M., T. Manuh, P. Quartey, C. Tagoe & T. Antwi Boasiakoh (2008), Migration Country Paper (Ghana), University of Ghana: Centre for Migration Studies.

Bump, M. (2006), Country Profiles—Ghana: Searching for Opportunities Abroad. Washington DC: Georgetown University.

Caldwell, J.C. (1968), Determinants of Rural–Urban Migration in Ghana. *Population Studies* 22(3): 361–377.

Cassarino, J., & P. Fargues (2006), Policy Responses in MENA Countries of Transit for Migrants: An Analytical Framework for Policy Making, in: N. Sørensen, *Mediterranean Transit*. Denmark: Danish Institute for International Studies, pp. 101–107.

Castagnone, E. (2011), Transit Migration: A Piece of the Complex Mobility Puzzle. The Case of Senegalese Migration. MAFE: Migration entre l'Afrigue et l'Europe: Cahiers de l'Urmis.

CBS (2014), Statistics Netherlands. Available at: http://statline.cbs.nl/StatWeb/publica tion/?DM=SLEN&PA=37325eng&D1=a&D2=a&D3=0&D4=0&D5=85&D6=11-17&LA =EN&VW=T. Accessed 16 January 2014.

Collyer, M., F. Düvell & H. de Haas (2012), Critical Approaches to Transit Migration. *Population, Space and Place* 18(4): 415–427.

DFID (2004), *Migration in West Africa*. Development Research Centre on Migration, Globalisation and Poverty. Sussex.

Donkor, M. (2005), Marching to the Tune: Colonization, Globalization, Immigration, and the Ghanaian Diaspora. *Africa Today* 52(1): 27–44.

Düvell, F. (2006), Questioning Conventional Migration Concepts: The Case of Transit Migration. Presented to workshop on 'In Gaps and Blind Spots of Migration Research'. Budapest: Central European University.

Düvell, F. (2008), *Crossing the Fringes of Europe: Transit Migration in the EU's Neighbourhood*. Oxford: Centre on Migration, Policy and Society.

Eichholzer, E. (2007), Ever Generous Lord, How Can I Praise You? The Ghanaian Gospel Boom in Hamburg. Available at: https://www.academia.edu/1029078/Ever_Generous _Lord_How_Can_I_Praise_You_The_Ghanaian_Gospel_Boom_in_Hamburg. Accessed 3 August 2013

Falola, T. & N. Afolabi (2007), *The Human Cost of African Migration.* New York/London: Routledge.

Fong, E., X. Cao, & E. Chan (2010), Out of Sight, Out of Mind? Patterns of Transnational Contact Among Chinese and Indian Immigrants in Toronto. *Sociological Forum* 45(3): 428–449.

GTZ (2009), *The Ghanaian Diaspora in Germany: Its Contribution to Development in Ghana.* Eschborn: Deutsche Gesellschaft für.

Haas, H. de (2007), *The Myth of Invasion: Irregular Migration from West Africa to the Maghreb and the European Union.* University of Oxford: IMI Research Report.

Knipscheer, C.P.M., M.I. Broese van Groenou, G.J.F. Leene, A.T.F. Beekman & D.J.H. Deeg (2000), The Effects of Environmental Context and Personal Resources on Depressive Symptomatology in Older Age: A Test of the Lawton Model. *Ageing & Society* 20(2): 183–202.

Kofman, E. (2004), Gendered Global Migrations. *International Feminist Journal of Politics* 6(4): 643–665.

Koopmans, R., S.M. Paul & F. Passy (2005), *Contested Citizenship: Immigration and Cultural Diversity in Europe.* Minneapolis: University of Minnesota Press.

Lee, E.S. (1966), A Theory of Migration. *Demography* 3(1): 47–57.

Levitt P. (2004), Transnational Migrants: When 'Home' Means More Than One Country. Migration Information Source, (October 1). Available at: http://www.migrationpolicy .org/article/transnational-migrants-when-home-means-more-one-country. Accessed 19 July 2015.

Levitt, P., J. DeWind & S. Vertovec (2003), International Perspectives on Transnational Migration: An Introduction. *International Migration Review* 37(3): 565–575.

Levitt, P. & N.G. Schiller (2004), Conceptualizing Simultaneity: A Transnational Social Field Perspective on Society. *International Migration Review* 38(3): 1002–1039.

MacDonald, J.S. & L.D. MacDonald (1964), Chain Migration, Ethnic Neighborhood Formation and Social Networks. *The Milbank Memorial Fund Quarterly* 42(1): 82–97.

Mazzucato, V. (2008a), Simultaneity and Networks in Transnational Migration: Lessons Learned from a Simultaneous Matched Sample Methodology, in: J. DeWind & J. Holdaway, *Migration and Development Within and Across Borders: Research and Policy Perspectives on Internal and International Migration.* Geneva: International Organization for Migration, pp. 69–100.

Mazzucato, V. (2008b), The Double Engagement: Transnationalism and Integration— Ghanaian Migrants' lives. *Journal of Ethnic and Migration Studies* 34(2): 199–216.

Nieswand, B. (2008), Ghanaian Migrants in Germany and the Social Construction of the Diaspora. Göttingen. http://www.mmg.mpg.de/fileadmin/user_upload/pdf/Nieswand%202008%20Construction%20Diaspora.pdf.

Nimako, K. (1993), *Nieuwkomers in een gevestigde samenleving. Een analyse van de Ghanese Gemeenschap in Amsterdam Zuidoost.* Amsterdam: Stadsdeel Zuidoost.

Noordergraaf, W. & M. Grunsven (1994), *Standplaats Ghana.* Amsterdam: Jan Mets.

OIS (1995), Amsterdams bureau voor Onderzoek en Statistiek. Amsterdam: Stadsdrukkerij.

Orozco, M. & M. Mohogu (November 2007), Remittances from the Netherlands: A Survey. Commissioned by Oxfam-Novib, The Netherlands.

Østergaard-Nielsen, E. (2003), The Politics of Migrants' Transnational Political Practices. *International Migration Review* 37(3): 760–786.

Papadopoulou, A. (2009), *Transit migration: The missing link between emigration and settlement.* Basingstoke: Palgrave Macmillan.

Peil, M. (1974), Ghana's Aliens. *International Migration Review* 8(3): 205–229.

Peil, M. (1995), Ghanaians Abroad. *African Affairs* 94(367): 345–367.

Pitea, R. (2010), Transit Migration: Challenges in Egypt, Iraq, Jordan and Lebanon. Carim Research Reports 2010/02.

Schans, D., V. Mazzucato, B. Schoumaker, M.-L. Flahaux (2013), Changing Patterns of Ghanaian Migration. MAFE Working Paper 20, 1–51.

Skeldon, R. (1997), *Migration and development: A global perspective.* Harlow: Longman.

Stark, O. (1984), Migration Decision Making: A Review Article. *Journal of Development Economics* 14: 251–259.

Stark, O. (1991), *The Migration of Labour.* Cambridge: Basil Blackwell.

Tichelman, P. (1996), God Has an Answer to All Your Problems. Genezingssessies binnen een Ghanese pinkstergemeente in Amsterdam Zuidoost. *Medische Antropologie* 8: 306–323.

Tonah, S. (2007), Ghanaians Abroad and Their Ties Home: Cultural and Religious Dimensions of Transnational Migration. COMCAD Working Papers, No. 25, Bielefeld.

Van Dijk, R. (1997), From Camp to Encompassment: Discourses of Transsubjectivity in the Ghanaian Pentecostal Diaspora. *Journal of Religion in Africa* 27(2): 135–159.

Van Dijk, R. (2001), Time and Transcultural Technologies of the Self in the Ghanaian Pentecostal Diaspora, in: A. Corten & R.R. Marshall-Fratani (eds) *Between Babel and Pentecost: Transnational Pentecostalism in Africa and Latin America.* Bloomington: Indiana University Press, pp. 216–234

Van Dijk, R. (2002a), Ghanaian Churches in the Netherlands Religion Mediating a Tense Relationship, in: W.M. van Kessel, *Merchants, Missionaries and Migrants: 300 years of Dutch- Ghanaian Relations.* Amsterdam: KIT/Sub-Saharan Publishers, pp. 89–97.

Van Dijk, R. (2002b), Religion, Reciprocity and Restructuring Family Responsibility in the Ghanaian Pentecostal Diaspora, in: A.U.D.F. Bryceson, *Religion, Reciprocity and*

Restructuring Family Responsibility in the Ghanaian Pentecostal Diaspora. Oxford: Berg, pp. 173–196.

Van Dijk, R. (2004), Negotiating Marriage: Questions of Morality and Legitimacy in the Ghanaian Pentecostal Diaspora. *Journal of Religion in Africa* 34(4): 438–467.

Wahlbeck, Ö. (2009), Book Review of 'Transit Migration; The Missing Link Between Emigration and Settlement' by Aspasia Papadopoulou-kourkoula (Palgrave Macmillan, 2008). *Migration Letters* 6(2): 205–206.

Stadsdeel Zuidoost (1992), Ghanezen in Zuidoost, een verkennend onderzoek. Amsterdam: Stadsdeel Zuidoost.

CHAPTER 15

Kinshasa: A City of Refugees

Meike de Goede

Introduction

In 2006 I met Moïse,[1] a crippled man who was begging on the central Boulevard de Trente Juin of Kinshasa. Over the years, I maintained good contact with him, to the extent possible considering that he does not have a phone, access to the Internet, or a fixed site where he begs—because he must constantly relocate to avoid the police. He introduced me to a world in Kinshasa that is right in front of one but remains invisible to outsiders. Owing to his physical disabilities, Moïse cannot walk and is forced to hop around on his hands and knees. Through his eyes and from his perspective, owing to his limited height, Kinshasa really does look different. The boulevard is a busy road filled with expensive SUVs, in which people that do not see or register people like Moïse are transported here and there. He explained me how the social security networks of the handicapped on the boulevard work, how people look out for each other and care for each other. When he was ill, a 'colleague' of his would quickly find me on the boulevard and tell me what was going on. To my great surprise, the money I gave for his medication and doctor visits would always reach Moïse, and he always thanked me for it when we would next see each other, often months later.

Moïse has been working on the boulevard for several decades now. Being handicapped at birth, he has never done anything other than beg for survival. Moïse's life is extremely hard. For him, life has mainly been about the survival of himself and his family, about being able to provide food, and to provide money to send his children to school. Every time when I have returned to Kinshasa, it has been a relief to see that he is still alive, considering the dangers of his profession for someone that, due to his physical disabilities, is less than a metre high, hopping around between increasingly large and elevated SUVs— which, thanks to the new and improved boulevard, drive increasingly fast. The drivers cannot possibly see Moïse, who is on his hands and knees. I have often wondered how he reflects on what he has seen—the changing of tides for Mobutu, the arrival of Mzee Kabila with his rebel army, the start of the second war and the violent responses in Kinshasa, the deteriorating security situation

---

1 The personal names used in this paper are fictionalized.

© KONINKLIJKE BRILL NV, LEIDEN, 2015 | DOI 10.1163/9789004306059_016

and conditions of life—while at the same time Kinshasa has been transformed into a hub of the international community and a place where some people get incredibly rich. He had not heard of Staff Benda Bilili, a group of handicapped Kinshasa street musicians that have become popular in Europe over recent years (in a way that reminds one of a freak show). Nor did he have any thoughts about politics. The turbulent times of Congo's recent history, however, may have had a positive side effect for somebody like Moïse: people like me tend to be more generous than Congolese, or so Moïse assured me. Moïse may be surviving, but life has not significantly changed for the better for him or for most people, and the promised benefits of peace, democracy, and economic growth have remained beyond the reach of the vast majority of Kinois.

Not surprisingly, people are utterly disappointed.[2] The day after the 50th anniversary of independence, I sent an SMS to a civil servant with whom I had worked intensively during my research. 'How was the *cinquantenaire*,' I asked him, knowing that he had the day off and intended to watch the parade. '*Cinquantenaire*, not good,' he responded in an SMS. 'We have not been paid up until now.' There is little to celebrate for the ordinary Congolese. These disappointments have of course also had a profound effect on people's vision of the future. Now that the democratic opening of 2006 has been such a disappointment for those that believed the long-anticipated elections and democracy would really mean a change for the better, many are reconsidering their options. Having lost the confidence that real change will come one day, many see a better future outside the country. The sharp contrast between Moïse's life expectations and the aspirations of the other Kinois I had met could not be more stark. Sitting on the pavement with Moïse, looking at the boulevard, where the whirlwind of development, economic growth, and modernity were passing by, I realized how few aspirations Moïse had and how static his life was—and how much everybody else was trying to find ways to get out.

This paper offers some reflections on how people I have met in the Congo are trying to find ways to get out. They are stories of people that I greatly respect. The euphoria of the peace agreement and the promises it held for real change in people's everyday lives are long gone. What most Congolese are left with is disillusionment. Not only are they disillusioned with the idea that things can change for real in the Congo; they are also left with a realization that they themselves are unable to change their own lives for the better and realize their hopes and dreams. Through personal life stories, this paper reflects on the concerns of these individuals and their responses. The stories are stories

---

2   L.M. Yoka, 'Kinshasa: Bien-être et développment? Bien-être ou développement?', in: T. Trefon (ed.) *Réformes au Congo (RDC): Attentes et Désillusions* (Paris, 2009), pp. 243–251.

of how people cope while feeling trapped in a situation they cannot change. These people have developed patterns of escapism, through which they can flee mentally and avoid reality, either through witchcraft or through escaping into religion or music or dance. Others are striving to physically leave the country, because they have lost all hope that a better future for themselves and their children is possible in the Congo. My reflections are based on personal observations and exchanges with Congolese people immediately after the 2006 post-war elections and the years following, when the initial democratic opening quickly turned sour.

Belmondo was one of the first people I met in the DRC. At the time, he worked at an NGO I visited during my first research visit in 2006. Throughout my time in the Congo, Belmondo has always been an invaluable support for me—professionally as well as personally. Despite the fact that there is little to laugh about in his daily reality, Belmondo is always cheerful, always making jokes and laughing about the ridiculousness of everyday life in Kinshasa. Combating misery with humour: a tried and tested tactic that many Congolese employ to cope. He was always very open and keen to make me understand Kinshasa and the Kinois, a place and its people that fascinated me so much, but that was at times so incomprehensible to me. We often shared a *Primus* beer and spoke endlessly about Congo's current affairs, the democratic transition, the peace process, the on-going conflict in the eastern part of the country, and the challenges of everyday life.

I also learned about Belmondo's life path. The story of his life is representative of the recent history of Congo and of how people like Belmondo had hopes and ideals, how they aimed to make a difference, and how they have struggled throughout the turbulent years from the early 1990s until now.

Belmondo grew up in Bukavu, in eastern Congo. His father worked at the Bralima brewery, and hence Belmondo's preference for *Primus* instead of its rival *Skol*. 'In those days,' he recalls, 'everything was good.' He had a happy childhood. 'The salary my father earned sufficed for the family. Life was good, things worked fine.' Now, in sharp contrast: 'Nothing works; all is chaos.' Belmondo is visibly hurt when he explains that his salary does not enable him to take care of his family in the way that he would like, unlike his father. He is concerned about the future of his children. It was the 'Zaïrianization', according to Belmondo, that destroyed everything. Launched in 1973, Zaïrianization aimed to nationalize the economy. Small and medium-sized enterprises owned by foreign nationals were confiscated and 'nationalized'.[3] In practice, they

---

3   T.M. Callaghy, *The State-Society Struggle: Zaïre in Comparative Perspective* (New York, 1984); Mobutu, *Discours, Allocutions et Messages. Tome 2, Annees 1970–1975* (Paris, 1975), pp. 425–426;

were distributed among politicians and high-level civil servants and other elites. Bralima was not immune to Zaïrianization. For the employees of Bralima, like Belmondo's father, this meant a reduction in an increasingly irregular salary, while services for employees were also rapidly deteriorating. 'It was a blow that completely knocked out the company,' says Belmondo. In the early 1980s, the company was sold to Heineken. Mobutu could not risk having the beer industry collapse. Zaïrianization ruined the economy[4] and was, according to some, 'a nearly mortal self-inflicted wound'.[5] According to Belmondo, it did much more than that: 'Since then, life became difficult.'

Belmondo is trained as an engineer. He is proud of his technical skills, which have always enabled him to find work—before, during, and after the war. Before the war he worked at SNEL, Congo's infamous electricity company. One day Belmondo met an old school friend. This friend had been involved in discussions in Tanzania with Laurent Kabila and other Congolese rebels-to-be, as well as with their foreign supporters. They had discussed the possibility of starting a rebellion to overthrow Mobutu. They asked Belmondo, as an engineer working at SNEL, to shut down the power station on a certain day and time. Belmondo decided to help his old friend and did what was asked of him. He did not know what the purpose was to be. On the day that Belmondo switched off the power station, the rebel forces launched the attack at Uvira that started the armed rebellion. From that day on, Belmondo knew he was implicated. There was no way back. He decided to join the rebellion and was sent to Uganda for training. He fought with AFDL in their march to Kinshasa. Because of his technical expertise, he was a communications and intelligence officer. In this position, Belmondo became close with the leadership of the rebellion, including the current president, Joseph Kabila. This is why Belmondo has always maintained a certain admiration for Kabila, despite everything. War makes brothers.

When the rebellion was launched, it was buzzing in the air: things were going to change for real this time. The rebel army advanced fast towards Kinshasa. They were winning; people were happy. They were changing the country. It was a time when Belmondo believed that his world, his country, his life, and that of his fellow countrymen could change. And he believed that he could contribute to this process. He believed in the rebellion of AFDL. That is

G. Nzongola-Ntalaja, *The Congo from Leopold to Kabila. A People's History* (London & New York, 2002), p. 149.

4 M.G. Schatzberg, 'The State and the Economy: The "Radicalization of the Revolution" in Mobutu's Zaïre', *Canadian Journal of African Studies* vol. 14, no. 2, (1980), pp. 239–257.

5 C. Young & T. Turner, *The Rise and Decline of the Zairian State* (Madison, 1985), p. 362.

why he decided to help his former friend by cutting the power that day in Bukavu, and that is why he joined the rebellion. 'I disliked Mobutu and his way of ruling the country. I wanted to help change it,' he says. Having experienced the seeming impossibility of change through peaceful means during the past few decades under Mobutu's rule, for Belmondo and many with him war seemed the only viable strategy to realize this long-awaited change.

The first years after the removal of Mobutu's regime were full of hope. Mzee Kabila paid his soldiers regularly and better, resulting in discipline and restored order. In a public opinion poll held in April 1998, people argued that the improvement of personal and property security was the most noticeable change since Kabila's takeover of power.[6] It is still popularly remembered as a sign of change. Kabila used big words and promised to put an end to the outside interference that had ruined the country. He renamed the country from Zaïre to Congo, the country's name at independence, and he referred to Lumumba, suggesting that the second independence had finally been achieved and Lumumba's death had been avenged.[7]

However, things soon took a turn for the worse. A new war started a year later, and Mzee Kabila had eliminated some of his previous partners in the coalition, while others were being threatened. Having been so close to the people that were now under threat, Belmondo felt threatened himself and decided to flee abroad.

When the second war had come to an end, Belmondo decided to return to his country and try again to help rebuild it, to make a better future for himself and his fellow Congolese. He joined the civil society sector, which had won so much recognition in the course of the peace process and had become a key actor in the peace-building that followed. He started working at a small NGO, whose director he had known since his childhood days in Bukavu. When I met him in 2006, his concerns and disappointments about the civil society sector were emerging. Although civil society was given an important stake in the transitional governing institutions, it became clear in the following years that many of these individuals used their (perceived) legitimacy as a jumping board to access political positions. After the transition, many did not return to their work in civil society but joined the political ruling elite. It did not take

---

6   International Crisis Group, 'How Kabila Lost His Way: The Performance of Laurent Désiré Kabila's Government', ICG Democratic Republic of Congo Report, (Brussels/New York, 1999), p. 10.

7   L.-D. Kabila, 'Déclaration de Prise de Pouvoir de l'AFDL (Lubumbashi, 17 mai 1997)', in: J.M.K. Mutamba Makombo (ed.) L'Histoire du Congo par les Textes. Tome III: 1956–2003 (Kinshasa, 2006), pp. 493–495.

Belmondo long to realize that civil society was not going to make a difference after all. Five years later, he has given up on civil society altogether. 'Civil society leaders are worse than politicians in this country,' he concludes.

Belmondo has tried his best, and he has tried to believe in his country. But he is no longer able. 'I have given everything for my country; I have tried everything. I risked my life and went to war; I tried civil society. Nothing works; nothing changes for the better.' Before leaving his job in civil society, he had been able to obtain some private assignments through people he met in his NGO network. With the little capital he earned, he started a small business in ICT support. While still working at the NGO, he worked on the side on his own business ventures, thereby adding a much-needed income to his low and irregular NGO income. And he was not the only one in the office: most of his colleagues at the time had also taken up jobs on the side. The NGO offers a network of colleagues, friends, other NGOs, and international partners, a 'cover' which provides some credibility, as well as an office and access to the Internet. As is the case for so many Congolese employees of NGOs and civil servants alike, it is first and foremost a basis from which one can work on other activities that actually do provide a decent income. With that income, Belmondo sent his wife to South Africa and India to receive the medical treatment she needed. The Kinshasa hospitals are unable to offer these treatments. He sends his children to college in South Africa in the hope of their earning a degree that may actually help them achieve something in their lives. And he hopes to settle in South Africa as well, where he can build a better life for himself and a better future for his children. 'There is nothing here for me anymore,' he said.

Belmondo made efforts to contribute to changing his country for the better. He believed that the war would overthrow Mobutu's disastrous government. He believed that the peace process that followed would bring real change, that it would bring democracy and welfare. Despite his cheerfulness and his jokes about the everyday insanity of life in Kinshasa, he is, deep inside, disappointed and disillusioned because all his efforts have been in vain.

There are many people like Belmondo in Kinshasa. So many people have ended up in Kinshasa for one reason or another: they moved to Kinshasa in the slipstream of the war, looking for safety, or for employment and a better life, or hoping to find ways to leave the country. Kinshasa has grown exponentially as a city over the last 20 years. With over 11 million inhabitants, Kinshasa is the second-largest city in Sub-Saharan Africa. Every day new immigrants from all over the country arrive in Kinshasa, hoping to get their hands on even the smallest slice of prosperity that the city promises. In reality, life in Kinshasa is dire for the majority of its inhabitants. But as a young man who was desperate to leave Boende (an impoverished, remote, and isolated town in Equateur province) for Kinshasa once said to me: 'If I stay here [in Boende], I know for sure that nothing will ever change for me.' He had a point. For him, moving to Kinshasa was taking a gamble that was worth taking. The rural areas are reduced to little more than a nostalgic place of origin. They have become the romanticized villages that everybody loves but considers backward at the same time. For the vast majority, they are not places where they would ever be able to live again.

But although there may be more opportunities in Kinshasa than in the villages, success is by no means guaranteed. People thus become incredibly entrepreneurial and creative. Most of the people I met in Kinshasa and the rest of the country had several irons in the fire. Like Belmondo, they combine multiple jobs and several small incomes: working for an NGO during the week and as a priest at the weekends; being a teacher and running a small drinks venue in the evenings; being a civil servant and working as a consultant for international organizations. Everybody needs to survive; and with salaries being notoriously low and irregular, people have learned to multiply their sources of income to make ends meet.

The Kinois are often admired for their entrepreneurialism. But because it stems from genuine insecurity and something fundamentally wrong in Congolese society, it is actually deeply sad. Mobutu told the Zairians: 'Débrouillez-vous'('Fend for yourself'). People had little other option because the state definitely did not take care of them. This effectively meant a tolerance or even legitimation of all kinds of shady and corrupt practices—not only for people to get by, but also to get rich. As a consequence, the economy became more and more informal.[8] It has become a *modus operandi* that after several decades has had a profound effect on norms. Some, like Belmondo, seek legitimate ways of increasing income, while others make the most of the tolerance for corruption. Relying on your wits and your ability to creatively make some extra money is how people respond to the financial insecurity they are faced with in their daily lives. Only the elderly can remember a time when the income of one job sufficed and when the skimming off of money was not standard practice.

This insecurity also means that people have learned that success is always temporary in this turbulent country. One day you have a job, the next day you do not; one month you receive your salary, the next month you may not. People have learned to think in the short term. With a history of looting, economic nationalization, war and pillaging, and economic hardship, the future is never

8   J. MacGaffey, *The Real Economy of Zaïre. The Contribution of Smuggling and Other Unofficial Activities to National Wealth* (London, 1991).

certain. So people bet on several horses, to reduce their risks and increase economic security. You must always have a plan B. And a plan C.

This also goes for politicians, who also know that life is uncertain. The politicians I met during my research in the DRC all had other business or NGO interests besides their political work. Some of these activities on the side do serve a purpose for their role as Members of Parliament (MPs), as they enable them to be visible and active in support of their constituencies.[9] However, they also serve as a security network for these politicians. One MP told me that there are some MPs that 'only have politics. This is a problem for democracy as it makes them insecure'.[10] Insecure means financially insecure and therefore dependent, which affects their integrity as a politician. 'Politics,' he explained, 'is an unsafe bet in the Congo.' This indeed turned out to be the case. In the second elections since the democratic transition, 90% of MPs were not re-elected.[11] They would have been out of a job and regular income if they had not developed other initiatives on the side while being MPs. They run a business in the export of wood or minerals; they run an import–export company for all kinds of commodity goods; they own a farm, continue their law practice, or invest in the ICT sector. Some have set up an NGO, which has the additional benefit of the potential opportunity to harvest funding while showing a good face and joining the international world of NGOs, in which young, trendy jetsetters whizz around the world doing good.

Elites are in this sense no different from other Congolese: practically everybody combines multiple professional activities and constantly keeps an eye on potential opportunities. But the diversity of people's professional and entrepreneurial activities goes further than simply seeking additional income or reducing risk. Many also hope that one of these activities might one day offer them an opportunity to liberate themselves from the yoke of poverty and the feeling of being stuck. To have many irons in the fire, one needs a world of opportunities, a broad and diverse network. This is what Kinshasa and other urban hubs offer.

A friend who works at a Congolese NGO has for years been trying to find an opportunity to go abroad. He is one of the many of his generation who find themselves lost and feel they are wasting their efforts in the Congo. He grew up in the 1980s and 1990s, graduated from university in the late 1990s, and has

---

9   M. de Goede, *Consuming Democracy: Local Agencies and Liberal Peace in the Democratic Republic of Congo*, (Leiden, 2015), pp. 120–123.

10   Author's interview, Kinshasa, November 2009.

11   T. Trefon, 'Uncertainty and Powerlessness in Congo 2012', *Review of African Political Economy* vol. 40, no. 135, (2013), p. 143.

since been unable to achieve anything. Having lost two girlfriends in a row to expatriates has left him demoralized and feeling unable to compete on the love market. One of his ex-girlfriends has married the expatriate and now lives in Europe. With a university degree but with no opportunity to develop a career and earn a decent living, he struggles to see glimpses of hope in his daily life, to see that things may one day be different for him. He just wants to live a life like every other young person across the globe. He has lost the hope that this will one day be possible for him in the Congo. He applied for every scholarship he came across to study abroad. These were in the most diverse range of disciplines, which more often than not were miles away from his own discipline. He applied for numerous jobs abroad as well as with international organizations in Kinshasa, hoping this might bring him one step closer to getting a chance to leave. He befriended somebody from France online and tried to visit her. The visa application was rejected multiple times. In one desperate attempt, he even proposed to marry me as a practical arrangement that might help us both. It broke my heart to see how desperate he was. He stays in close contact with a politician he knows from the days when he was more politically active. He hopes that perhaps this may bring him opportunities, should this politician one day become closer to the centre of power. He does a bit of extra work for a Belgian businessman of Congolese origin, hoping to establish contacts with the Congolese diaspora in Belgium. Last year, he married the businessman's daughter. They live in Kinshasa, but she has a Belgian passport.

What this young man's story illustrates is how people need to be versatile and constantly on the look-out for opportunities. But they must also be persistent. It is interesting to observe that Kinshasa, as well as the Congo's several other main centres with high population density, are all on or near the country's borders—Kinshasa, Lubumbashi, and the Kivu provinces with Bukavu and Goma as the two main urban centres.[12] This of course is largely a consequence of the colonial design of the state and its further development in the post-colonial era. However, it also reflects an outward-looking perspective. It is as if people, like animals in a cage, are cramped against the fence. It seems the Congolese have turned their backs *en masse* on their own hinterland, leaving it to foreign companies to exploit. From urban hubs on the border like Kinshasa, the world outside may be accessed through trade, communications, employment, connections with expatriates and their companies that also concentrate in these hubs, or the simple fact that there is an airport, a road, a bridge, and embassies for visa applications—all the infrastructure

---

12   J. Herbst, *States and Power in Africa: Comparative Lessons in Authority and Control,* (Princeton, 2000), p. 149.

that facilitates exit.[13] In addition, such urban hubs are also places where international organizations, NGOs, and businesses are based, and with them a large group of people that already live transnational lives. Besides employment opportunities, this offers opportunities for establishing potentially profitable contacts and links with the world beyond the borders.[14] Kinshasa is then not only a place to go to as it was for the man in Boende, but also a place to depart from: a zone of transport and a space of connectivity with the outside world, a jumping board from where a better world can be reached. Kinshasa's own promise of prosperity for rural Congolese is thus not the only driving factor behind growing urbanization rates in Africa. Kinshasa is also a port of access to the rest of the world.

This is easiest for the elites. They have already secured their way out, should they need it. They have money, contacts abroad, the ability to travel abroad, and sometimes property, residence permits, or even foreign passports. With those securities in hand, it is easy to feel at ease in the Congo. For those with money, life can be really good in Kinshasa. They live like expatriates, who enjoy the good life in Kinshasa for as long as it lasts, knowing that they can leave whenever they want to. Like expatriates, they take their occasional shopping trip (or 'R&R') to Europe, South Africa, the US, or China to stock up on much-loved consumer goods. They have no real stake in the country any more. It often seems as if these wealthy elites have mentally left the Congo long ago. They are as disconnected from ordinary Congolese and their Congo as expatriates are. The Congo has for the elites never ceased to be an extractive state, best exploited with one foot abroad. This applies not only to the business elite, but also to politicians and increasingly to a civil society elite, who are, as Belmondo suggested, no different than other elites. During my research on Congolese politicians, many of the politicians I encountered had business interests and/or property abroad. While for these elites the Congo is an appealing place where money can be made, for the vast majority of Congolese it really is not. For the latter, the grass really is greener on the other side of the border.

The *shege*, Kinshasa's growing army of street children, are probably at the bottom of the ladder. On a few occasions, Moïse insisted that he was not a *shege*, thereby reminding me of a social hierarchy on the streets of Kinshasa. The *shege* are an interesting and relevant group in terms of escapism. Like

---

13 W. Freund, 'The Congolese Elite and the Fragmented City: The Struggle for the Emergence of a dominant Class in Kinshasa'. Crisis States Working Papers Series No.2. (London, 2009), p. 10.

14 B. Freund, 'Kinshasa: An Urban Elite Considers City, Nation and State', *Journal of Contemporary African Studies* vol. 29, no. 1, (2011), 36.

Moïse, they have nowhere to go and little prospect of a better life. They are living in a world where they are collectively rejected: rejected or abandoned by their families; rejected by society for being witches; rejected by the wealthy Congolese and expatriates in Kinshasa for their increasingly aggressive begging strategies; and rejected by the authorities for being a threat to the apparent stability in Kinshasa. Street children are regularly rounded up in the name of crime fighting, or in general sweeps to clear the streets. The terms *shege* and *kuluna* (violent and criminal street gangs) are more and more used interchangeably, which may reflect an increase in violence used by street children, a form of revenge on society as a whole.[15] Perhaps it simply reflects a perceived criminalization of street children, which justifies more aggressive responses from the authorities. A preventive measure employed by Kinshasa authorities to 'secure' important days and events—those with much (international) media attention and high-level visitors, such as elections or the 50th anniversary of the independence of the Congo—is to round up groups of street children and send them to camps in another part of the country, or to simply imprison them until everything is back to normal.[16]

Often orphaned or thrown onto the street by their parents for being witches,[17] left to fend for themselves, constantly threatened with capture by the police, these children have seemingly lost control over their lives, lives that have become a permanent struggle against hunger, sickness, crime, and violence by the authorities.[18] Paradoxically, the street is also appealing, as De Boeck and Plissart observed:

> For Kinshasa's *Bashege*, from whom traveling to Europe is not an option, the street is viewed as an alternative Shengen territory: It is the space where food, freedom, sex, drugs and money can be freely accessed. To them, the cité [...] is a world of constraints, a backward world which belongs to the past. [...] In contrast to this, Kinshasa's street children now consider the street to be modern and exciting. The street and the night form the spatial and temporal zones in which the young generate themselves in self-invented processes and narratives of globalization.

---

15   O. Kahola Tabu, 'Ordinary Violence Towards Street Children (Chegue) in Lubumbashi (D.R.C.)', in: J. Bouju & M. De Bruijn (eds) *Ordinary Violence and Social Change in Africa*, (Leiden, 2014), p. 138.

16   Human Rights Watch, 'What Future? Street Children in the Democratic Republic of Congo', (2006), pp. 21–24.

17   *Ibid.* 43–50.

18   Kahola Tabu, 'Ordinary Violence'.

Simultaneously, their material horizon, the singularity of their space, and the social geography of their live, often only extend to the corner of the street or the borderline between one neighbourhood and the next.[19]

The *shege* flee to the street and embrace life there as a form of freedom, a way to escape from abuse and their victimhood into a world where they are (seemingly) in charge. 'Shengen' (Europe) represents this freedom. Recreating this freedom in a world they can access is a practical form of escaping for those who cannot leave the Congo physically.

But they also escape into a second world, a world in which they determine their destiny and that of others.[20] This desire for empowerment and independence is also what may drive *shege's* confirmation of accusations of witchcraft. They describe how they kill and eat people, have control over themselves and others, and have access to the things they aspire to, such as food and consumer goods. Being a witch means having the ability to escape to a different world, one that offers empowerment and agency in a world where they would otherwise have none.[21]

These *shege* are in many ways, perhaps, an extreme case. But their escapism is part of a broader trend that exists in different ways at every level of society, from *shege* to the political elite. Having different means and opportunities, in the end they seek the same thing: escape from the reality of their everyday lives. Those that do not physically go abroad often dream of and scheme about going away—to Johannesburg, Luanda, Nairobi, Accra, Lagos, or Brussels, London, New York, Paris, Beijing, Shanghai. In the meantime, they develop escapisms, just as the *shege* do. A Congolese politician once said to me that Kinshasa is a 'city of refugees'.[22] He did not mean refugees in the physical sense, but in the emotional sense. He meant that the Kinois all need escapisms, such as religion, the pleasure of beer and music, witchcraft, or violence, in order to cope, because nobody is really at ease. In a perverse way, the simultaneous love for their country and the urge to get away from it is one of the few things that Congolese truly have in common.

Kinshasa is a city full of life, of *ambiance*; there is always music and always a party. The Congolese *joie de vivre* is famous, but it has a sad undertone when one realizes that this buzz is also an escape. Congolese people are in that sense

---

19   F. De Boeck & M.-F. Plissart, *Kinshasa: Tales of the Invisible City*, (Ghent and Amsterdam, 2004), p. 184.
20   *Ibid.* 158–159.
21   *Ibid.* 159–160 & 188–189.
22   Author's interview, Kinshasa, October 2009.

no different from anybody else. For music festival visitors in the UK, festivals are a way to 'cope with their increasingly dull and stressful lives'. For some, a festival offers a 'haven', where they can 'drift aimlessly' or even 'disappear'.[23] This is no different in Kinshasa, where it can safely be said that the stress of life for most people exceeds that of those in the UK. The same goes for *Primus*, Congo's number 1 beer. Beer has a mythical status in the Congo;[24] it is an essential part of daily life. Rumba and *Primus* thus function as the bread and games of modern Congo. Mobutu could not afford the beer industry to go bust. And although Kabila can afford not to provide running water to the population, he cannot afford to allow beer production to grind to a halt. And while some find solace in beer, others find solace in the church, the opium of the people.

Again others have translated their frustration into violence and aggression. Until a few years ago, violent youth gangs were an almost unknown phenomenon in Kinshasa. In recent years this phenomenon has emerged as a means through which some frustrated youths express their anger towards the rich and wealthy, towards foreigners, or just towards society and life in general. It is these youths who have known nothing else in their lives other than the promise of a better future, while in effect life has become harder and harder and the future seems to have nothing in store for them. The frustrations of living under duress, without hope that the future will be theirs, has resulted in self-loathing and in a fundamental loss of self-respect and self-esteem. They resort to drugs, alcohol, and violence.

Of course, not all people flee abroad, into rumba and beer, or into violence. Some become apathetic. Others are strengthened in their cause, such as a Congolese journalist that has left the country for what he calls a period of reflection and preparation. This period of reflection and preparation in fact means a moment to get his breath back, to recover from enduring the stress of life as a journalist in Kinshasa, to establish new contacts and pursue new opportunities. In a way, he has fled. He cannot go back because it is too dangerous for him; in addition, he gave up everything when he left—his job, his savings, his home, his car. But he needs to hold on to a different story to cope in these insecure times. Perhaps he did not flee when he left, but he now finds himself in a situation where he cannot go back. He went abroad for a project, after which he would move to Mexico to study. He wanted to further develop himself and his ideas, so that he could go back to Congo one day with renewed

---

23   L. Tickle, 'Music Festivals: The Sound of Escapism', *The Guardian,* 18 July 2011, http://www
        .theguardian.com/education/2011/jul/18/music-festivals-research.

24   J. Miklian & P. Schouten, 'Fluid Markets: The Business of Beer Meets the Ugliness of War',
        Foreign Policy, (September/October 2013), p. 74.

strength. The project turned out not to exist, and neither did the payment. This financial setback has immobilized him and ruined his plans.

But while this journalist argues that his conviction is strong, he has a desperate urge similar to the previously mentioned young Congolese man to connect with people outside Congo, through whom he can realize his ambitions and aspirations both for himself and his country as a whole. Like so many other Congolese, he argues that what is needed is not a change of president, or a change of constitution, but change at a much more fundamental level: a societal revolution, a revolution of mentality, and a radical and total dismissal of the political class as it has existed and developed into a class since 1960. He works on setting up this revolutionary movement. The ideas are there; now he needs money. *'Je suis présidentiable,'* he says. 'I have the skills and capacities, but also the drive to make things better.' The revolutionary movement will be his political platform. To help the revolutionary movement, he is setting up an online radio and TV channel. In addition, he wants to start a PhD. He is writing a book on politics in the DRC and is training journalists. He presents himself as a jack-of-all-trades and himself as the centre of all processes in which he is or wants to be involved in. *'Je suis vedette à Kin'* ('I am a rock star in Kinshasa').

I doubt the journalist will ever become president of the DRC, nor do I foresee his movement starting a revolution. Perhaps he will embark one day on his PhD. Perhaps the book will be written. And perhaps the online radio and TV channel will re-establish him as a critical journalist with an impact in the DRC. And perhaps not. I believe in none of his dreams and claims, and I believe in all of them. He has left the Congo and is insistent that he will go back—'when the time is ripe'. In the meantime, his plans offer something to hold on to. His continuous self-affirmation defies the hopelessness of the Congo and the stress of his own situation. He needs to hold on to his identity as a professional to be able to cope with the utter insecurity of his life. But that does not mean that he is not deeply concerned, traumatized, or stressed.

This journalist is one of many that tries to find ways to cope. Finding a way out, whether mentally or physically, is an important element of the coping strategies the people whose stories were recounted in this paper have developed. Although the promise of peace and peace dividends a decade ago initially gave hope that this would finally bring real change and a better life for ordinary Congolese, developments since have quickly turned this optimism on its head. The people I met and whose stories are recounted in this paper are not searching for anything extraordinary. They just want what everybody wants in life: a decent, respectable life, a fundamental freedom from want and fear, and an opportunity to offer their children a better future. This, as many people have realized since the deception of the democratic transition, is unlikely to happen in the Congo in the near future. So they look for opportunities to realize their aspirations, while in the meantime they are being entrepreneurial and creative to make ends meet. They have developed escapisms to occasionally mentally leave the everyday struggles that they cannot leave physically. Below the famous Congolese *joie de vivre* a deeply sad and traumatized population is hidden. Congolese people are no different from their international friends: we all love the Congo, but only as long as we know we can leave at some point—for a quick R&R, or indefinitely, while claiming that 'I will go back some time.'

These escapisms reflect a response to the insecurity and powerlessness that Trefon so aptly described.[25] But they are simultaneously also a response to a (perceived) certainty, namely, that things will not change for the better in the near future. Moïse might accept this. But for Belmondo this is not enough. He thus concluded that the only possibility for change for him would mean leaving the country. How can he find the energy, the drive to persist? The journalist who finds himself stranded is very much aware of the fact that he needed to get away in order to be able to persist.

Perhaps this is the other side of the Congolese 'external locus of control', which means they deny themselves agency and consider powerful others to be in control of their destinies.[26] Escaping this victimhood and regaining control over one's life requires leaving the Congo and accessing that powerful outside world. The outside world is thus simultaneously a space of oppression and of liberation. The wealthy Congolese elite, who speak very loudly of Western neo-colonial practices, are also the ones who have most access to this Western world and have considerable control over their own lives. But the entanglement with the outside world also has another element. Perhaps these reflections on people's responses to what is, in fact, their hopelessness is essentially a critique not only of Congolese governance, but also of the development sector. How can it be that a decade and a half of intense peace keeping, humanitarian assistance, and development aid has left the population more demoralized and desperate than before? How can it be that despite the billions that have been poured into the country over the past decades, people feel abandoned and not helped at all.[27] To what extent is the rest of the world fundamentally entangled in this collective Congolese trauma?

---

25   Trefon, 'Uncertainty and Powerlessness'.

26   Meike J. de Goede, '"Mundele, It Is Because of You": History, Identity and Democracy in the Congo', *Journal of Modern African Studies* 53: 4 (forthcoming 2015).

27   Yoka, 'Kinshasa'.

Printed in the United States
By Bookmasters